CONFLICTING

VISIONS

CONFLICTING VISIONS

SPIRITUAL POSSIBILITIES OF MODERN ISRAEL

DAVID HARTMAN

SCHOCKEN BOOKS

NEW YORK

Grateful acknowledgment is made to Yeshayahu Leibowitz for permission to reprint an English translation of "A Critique" by Yeshayahu
Leibowitz which originally appeared in *Petahim*, April 1979. Reprinted
by permission.

"The Challenge of Modern Israel to Traditional Judaism" originally appeared in *Modern Judaism*, October 1987, vol. 7, no. 3. Copyright © by
David Hartman.

"Maimonides' Response to the Challenge of Modernity" and "Soloveitchik's Response to Modernity" were adapted from essays that originally appeared in *Joy and Responsibility: Israel, Modernity, and the Renewal of
Judaism*, by David Hartman (Jerusalem: Posner, 1978).

Library of Congress Cataloging-in-Publication Data

Hartman, David.
   Conflicting visions : spiritual possibilities of modern Israel /
David Hartman.
      p.   cm.
   ISBN 0-8052-4060-8
   1. Judaism—20th century. 2. Judaism—Israel. 3. Judaism—
Essence, genius, nature. 4. Israel—Religion—20th century.
I. Title.
BM565.H27   1990
296'.09'049—dc20   89-43305

Book design by M 'N O Production Services, Inc.
Manufactured in the United States of America

First Edition

In memory of my beloved mother, Pesil Batya, whose love for Torah, courage in the face of adversity, and determination not to succumb to suffering enabled the love of Torah to take root in the lives of her children, grandchildren, and great-grandchildren.

The tablets and the broken fragments
of the tablets were deposited in the Ark.

Talmud, Berakhot 8b

CONTENTS

Acknowledgments

These essays reflect the spiritual search that life in the State of Israel has generated in my soul over the past twenty years. For the reflections that they contain, and for my conviction that the rebirth of Israel has far-reaching significance for the future of Jewish spirituality, I am indebted to more people than I could ever name.

To all who have built this country, all who believe that God commands Jews to live our Torah in full visibility before the nations of the world, and all who are not afraid to translate the dream of generations into reality, my gratitude is unbounded. It requires spiritual courage to test one's prayers by reality.

I would like as well to express my gratitude to the executive leadership, Boards of Directors, Friends, and Fellows of the Shalom Hartman Institute, whose continued support and firm belief in the importance of fostering new spiritual resources in Israel have sustained and encouraged all my work. It has been a privilege to address the future of Judaism and Israel in the intellectual and spiritual environment that has developed at the Institute. Intellectual honesty, boldness of concept, and serious commitment to enhancing the quality of Jewish life are the aspirations guiding all the efforts of our Advanced Institute, high school, Shiluv, Beit Hamidrash, and educational outreach programs. It is a great good fortune to belong to a community who believe that "great is learning if it can make a difference in practice." Their criticism, support, and encouragement have been greatly appreciated.

The many philosophers and scholars who have attended our conferences in Jerusalem also provided invaluable stimulation. Nor could these essays have reached their final form without Malcolm Lowe and David Weiner, who devoted themselves so energetically to editing and preparing them for publication, and Ruth Sherer, who never flinched from typing and retyping manuscripts.

Finally, my love and gratitude go to Bobby, my wife, and our children and grandchildren, who have supported me through every agonizing reappraisal and whose warmth and mental vigor have made my thinking about Israel an urgent, complex, and rewarding adventure.

CONFLICTING VISIONS

Introduction

Israel Reborn and Contemporary Judaism

This volume reflects the concerns and changes in emphasis in my thinking over the past twenty years. The first essay summarizes views expressed in my earlier book *Joy and Responsibility*,[1] which was published in 1978. As the title indicates, the essays in that volume were infused by the celebration of Israel and the enormous exuberance I felt at the new opportunities that Israel created for the Jewish people's spiritual renewal. The Judaism of Israel was going to be found not only in the Sabbath and the festivals, in celebrating the holy, but also in the daily life of the community. In Israel the six days of the week, *hol*, would also give expression to the moral and spiritual power of Judaism.

"When the Lord brought back the captives of Zion, we were as dreamers" (Ps. 126:1). Indeed, I walked as a dreamer when I came on *aliyah*, to live in Israel. I felt that in this land I had been given the opportunity of setting the Lord before me constantly. From Zion a new spirit of Torah would go forth to the entire Jewish world.

In my own religious life, my father taught me how to sing the "song of the Sabbath" that reverberated in the lives of our family for generations. My mother's piety and love of Torah and *mitzvot*, divine commandments, inspired her children to devote their lives to the study and teaching of Torah. Although very poor, my parents never lost the capacity for joyful celebration of their Judaism, which they had acquired from their own families in Jerusalem and Safed. From my family, I learned early in life that it was not suffering and persecution that kept Jews loyal to their tradition.

Accordingly, the essays in this volume are concerned neither with theodicy nor with answering the theologians who proclaimed the death of God in Auschwitz. The Holocaust is not the central organizing

3

framework for my theological reflections. The memory of Auschwitz creates within me feelings of rage, bitterness, and isolation from the world, while Israel awakens within me new feelings of hope. For me, Israel mediates the way the Jewish people seek to give expression to their yearning to trust the nations of the world.

The Halakhah, the Jewish legal tradition, taught Jews to mourn in utter silence for one day a year, the Ninth of Av, as we empathize with the tragic story of Jewish suffering. But for fifty-two weeks a year we celebrate joyfully the Sabbath, and our bodies move in a rhythm of joy each day as we study the Torah.

I could not accept the view of many secular Zionist ideologues who maintained that there was no joy in living a committed halakhic life; these thinkers argued that Jews survived in exile only because of external persecution and the messianic dream of returning to the Land of Israel. It seemed highly improbable to imagine that Jews lived with postponed gratification for two thousand years. In spite of the Zionist call for the negation of the Diaspora, *shlilat ha Golah*, I was convinced that there was untapped spiritual power in the rabbinic tradition.

In response to the prevalent image of Halakhah suggested by religious anti-Zionists, I argued that Halakhah does not cultivate passivity, resignation, and fatalism. On the contrary, I claimed that Halakhah obligates every individual Jew to fulfill the Sinaitic covenant by participating in the building of that community. Accordingly, the Zionist revolution, which energized the Jewish people to assume responsibility for their national future, was not antithetical in principle to the spirit of Halakhah, but rather, a new and exciting way of expanding the spirit of covenantal Judaism.

Reborn Israel opened new possibilities for serving God with joy as it widened the Jewish people's sense of covenantal responsibility and provided the dignity of building a Jewish society. In Israel, the Jewish people are given the opportunity to move from an identity grounded in helpless suffering to one inspired by power and creativity, from being a victimized people to becoming a normative forward-moving community.

Nationalism or New Religious Spirit?

Before I arrived in Israel, my own teacher, Rabbi Joseph Soloveitchik, had cautioned me against the enthusiasm that I felt after the Six-Day War. He tried to cool my passion by reminding me that the rabbis waited a full year following the dramatic victory over the Seleucids before they instituted the holiday of Hanukkah. For Soloveitchik, one does not change the direction of Jewish spirituality just because of an overwhelming experience. One must build from sobriety, from careful appreciation of complexity, and not allow oneself to be swept along by the enthusiasm of events.

While Soloveitchik did not respond enthusiastically to the Six-Day War, this was the catalyst that awakened me and my family to the centrality of Israel for our future life as Jews. The Six-Day War reminded us of our shared destiny. I was convinced that a Jewish civilization could not be built in the Diaspora independent of the State of Israel. Israel is not just one Jewish community among many. It organizes and gives expression to the way the Jewish nation appears in history. Israel energizes Jewish activism throughout the world on behalf of the survival of the Jewish people. Israel has permanently destroyed the Marrano-like posture of being a Jew at home and a human being in the public spheres of life.

Upon arriving in Israel, I met Professor Yeshayahu Leibowitz, who was among the first thinkers to take issue with my interpretation of the Jewish State's religious significance. In his review of *Joy and Responsibility*, which appears in the present collection, he claimed that I had made a serious mistake in attaching religious significance both to the rebirth of Israel and to the Six-Day War. Judaism, he claimed, has no greater meaning in Israel than in any other place in the world. According to Leibowitz, I had fallen into the trap of writing a theology of history, of building a religious vision on the precarious events of history. For Leibowitz, God is not mediated in historical events. The Jew serves God only by observing His commandments, which are valid both in Israel and the Diaspora.

Furthermore, in radical opposition to my religious enthusiasm for the spiritual opportunities of Israeli society, Leibowitz believed that Judaism in Israel was becoming corrupted by attempts to infuse political and national life with its symbols. Judaism was being made into an instrument to enhance our nationalist aspirations. From Zion was going forth, not Torah, but a new idolatry in which nationalism and power had become the new God of the Jewish people. Leibowitz's charge and his theology of Judaism receive serious consideration in this volume.

In the essay "Will and Significance," I argue that although Leibowitz's refusal to attribute any religious significance to the national rebirth of Israel does indeed contradict the view expressed in *Joy and*

Responsibility, I did not make the strong claim he attributed to me. Indeed, I share Leibowitz's refusal to see the State of Israel as the beginning of an inevitable messianic triumph in history.

My theological reflections on the religious significance of Israel are a response to the possibilities of Israel, not a claim about how God has designed the future of Jewish history. They are an attempt to offer a religious anthropology which welcomes the self-confident, hopeful spirit that reborn Jerusalem gives to the Jewish world.

From Dreaming to Sobriety

People frequently ask me whether I still see Israel as the source of the renewal of Judaism. Does Israel set the moral and halakhic agenda of the Jewish people? As an Orthodox Jew who appreciates pluralism and recognizes the importance of freedom of conscience and human rights, would I choose a society in which many religious and newly observant Jews do not even understand these values? How can I regard Zion as the bearer of Judaism's renewal in view of the bitter struggle between religious and secular Jews or the defacing of human dignity in our perennial conflict with the Palestinians?

What is most conspicuous in Israel today is not new directions for Jewish spirituality but a re-creation of the old framework of Eastern European Jewry. The dream and the romantic celebration of the unity of the Jewish people which I felt after the Six-Day War, the enormous sense of Jewish spiritual possibilities that Israel would release, has suffered some severe shocks and blows. It is difficult to know whether I would have had the energy to uproot an entire family and begin a new life had I foreseen what Israel would become. Nevertheless, despite everything that has occurred over the last twenty-two years, I strongly believe that Israel remains the catalyst for the renewal of Judaism in the world. In spite of disappointments and tragedies, there remains more than enough cause to celebrate the joy of living in this country.

The big dreams are gone, yet I feel energized by the daily life of a people in search of its identity. It is a privilege to participate in the struggle over the future of this nation, to live in a home that brings together all the different strands that have shaped Jewish history.

The first tablets of the law, that is to say, the vision I had when I saw Israel from the perspective of my Diaspora Jewish romanticism, are broken. But I do not believe that the covenantal possibilities of Israel have been shattered. The task now is to carve out a vision of Torah that

6

is not nurtured by dramatic events, to build quietly and slowly, planting new seeds for the flowering of Jewish spiritual renewal.

The early Zionists were pioneers who reclaimed the land inch by inch, settlement by settlement. The exaggerated anticipation into which I was drawn by the drama of the Six-Day War was based upon the belief that there would be a massive renewal and radical transformation of Jewish history. The solidarity with Israel and concern for its survival felt by all Jews during and immediately after the Six-Day War did not change the Jewish people. Living in Israel taught me that dramatic events may be catalysts, but that ultimately Jewish spiritual renewal will be made possible by the way in which we conduct our daily life. It will be nurtured and enhanced by the quality of our schools, by the way the Israel Defense Force builds discipline without injuring the dignity of the individual soldier, by the bold initiatives of the business community in creating dignified job opportunities, and by the way justice and equality are reflected in our treatment of minorities. There is no shortcut to making these things happen. This is why Judaism insisted that the dramatic revelatory event of Sinai established the normative foundations for daily life. Revelation must become Halakhah if we are to educate the community.

In response to the widespread depression felt by so many Jews after the Yom Kippur War, one leading political spokesman told me that he was not concerned. "Just let them have one more military victory and the psychology of the Six-Day War will come back again." That kind of thinking is destructive to a healthy society. The psyche of a nation and its citizens does not develop as a result of grand episodes any more than does the psyche of a family. We are a people who hunger for the dramatic. We love miracle stories. But in point of fact, Jewish civilization was built by those who had a sober appreciation of historical events and who understood that one builds a community only through a normative, disciplined life.

The Exodus from Egypt did not by itself change Jewish history. The Torah translated that event into daily rituals and standards of behavior, such as the norm of not enslaving ourselves to one another because we were once slaves in Egypt. We have not yet learned how to translate the dramatic events of our recent history into the concerns of daily life.

The Moral and Halakhic Agenda

The birth of the third Jewish commonwealth has generated many new challenges to Halakhah and Jewish theology. Israel has brought us out of the ghetto, out of a sectarian mentality. It has created a visible political reality that involves all Jews in a common destiny. In an important sense, all Jews live in Israel. The way in which we define our lives as Jews in the Diaspora is significantly influenced by the type of Jewish society we build in Israel. We have returned to Israel to continue Jewish history, but we face intense disagreements over which aspects of Jewish history should guide us in building the future.

Are we a normal people or must we strive to be a holy people? Is the covenant with God constitutive of our identity, or can nationalism replace the traditional text-centered form of life? Does the religious tradition enable us to live with dignified and self-confident secular Jews?

Halakhah traditionally classified nonobservant Jews with "children who were taken captive by the Gentiles."

> But their children and grandchildren, who, misguided by their parents, were raised among the Karaites and trained in their views, are like a child taken captive by them and raised in their religion, whose status is that of an *anus* (one who abjures the Jewish religion under duress), who, although he later learns that he is a Jew, meets Jews, observes them practice their religion, is nevertheless to be regarded as an *anus*, since he was reared in the erroneous ways of his fathers. Thus it is with those who adhere to the practices of their Karaite parents. Therefore efforts should be made to bring them back in repentance, to draw them near by friendly relations, so that they may return to the strength-giving source, i.e., the Torah.[2]

Maimonides' attitude to the descendants of the Karaites is totally out of place when cited today to justify the religious community's relationship to the secular Jews in Israel. One cannot look upon the secular Zionists who built this state as misguided children who are deprived by the environment of their culture or by their upbringing. There are proud secular Jews in Israel who have built an economy, an army, and a nation, who are passionately committed to Jewish history and to Jewish survival, but who do not regard the world of Torah and *mitzvot* as regulative of their daily life.

Many nonobservant Israelis do not feel themselves to be spiritually lost individuals seeking guidance on how to return to Torah, but rather people who believe that they have built a significant alternative to that which defined Jewish living in the past (i.e., Halakhah).

In building a nation-state, nonobservant Jews in Israel have found a rich and satisfying Jewish life. It is distasteful and vulgar to approach them from a paternalistic, authoritarian perspective. Traditional halakhic Jews cannot enter into a serious dialogue with the majority of Israelis if we infantilize and trivialize the Jewish society they have created.

The creation of the State of Israel poses yet another problem for Jews committed to Halakhah. In Israel, Jews must assume full responsibility seven days a week for the functioning of a modern nation, yet religious Jews must also live with the demand that, on the Sabbath, we reflect upon our covenantal commitment and proclaim God as the Lord of Creation. Who assumes responsibility for foreign relations and security during the Sabbath? Should halakhic Jews rely upon Jews who do not feel the commitment to and passion of Torah? Is Torah life to be parasitical on nonhalakhic Jews, who lay their bodies on the line for the security and well-being of the society? Are the daughters of nonobservant Jewish families to expose themselves to the difficult conditions of army life, while observant religious families keep their daughters at home under their protective wing?

We must not forget that God did not give the Torah to an elect Orthodox sectarian group, but to an entire people! Only one who joins the community in the liberation struggle from Egypt can participate in the convenantal listening to the divine commandments from Sinai. How can observant Jews live a life of Torah in Jerusalem if their very commitment to Torah requires that the majority of Jews not hear this spiritual message? How does Halakhah guide Jews who are responsible for a total society seven days a week?

Together with many other religious Zionists in Israel, I do not seek to build a spiritual life parasitical upon the nonobservance of the majority of Jews. We cannot demand that others do the dirty work of survival so that an elite remnant can be the bearer of the spiritual dreams of Moses.

"Come down, Moses, from the mountain," the greatest prophet in our history was told, when the Jewish people were dancing around the golden calf (Ex. 32:7). As the Midrash comments, God was saying to Moses, "All that I have given you is only because of Israel. Now that they are sinning, what use have I of you, as a single individual?" Spiritual life must be found within the community, irrespective of its level of observance; to separate oneself from the living community is to leave the covenantal framework of Judaism.

The majority of the Jews in Israel who mediate the future drama of Jewish history do not define their daily life by the authoritative foundations of Halakhah. I do not accept the non-Zionist position that the love of God and Torah requires us to build a spiritual ghetto and to act as if nothing new and significant is demanded in light of the creation of Israel. I renew the covenant in the midst of a community, the majority of which does not hear the demand of *mitzvah*. By declaring my solidarity with all the Jews of Israel, I affirm that the commandment

9

"Love your neighbor as yourself" applies not only to the neighbor who shares in the covenantal appreciation of Jewish identity but to all Jews. The brother with whom you live in Israel is not only the brother who accepts the obligation to live by Torah and *mitzvot*.

Religious Pluralism

The guiding categories of Jewish tradition were based upon a shared appreciation of the authoritative foundations of Halakhah. Since the era of Emancipation, however, there is no longer a unified perception of Jewish history guiding the entire Jewish community. Western civilization opened up new possibilities for personal meaning and significance. Different attempts were made to integrate loyalty to the tradition with the possibilities of living in an open society. To act as if nothing has happened in Jewish history since the Emancipation, to measure the authenticity of another Jew's belief systems from one's own value perspective, is to invite disaster for the third Jewish commonwealth.

Judaism in Israel, however, is under the exclusive control of the Orthodox establishment. Reform and Conservative rabbis cannot perform weddings, since their approaches to Judaism are totally delegitimized by the rabbinic authorities. How can we speak of Israel as the home of the Jewish people and yet live in a society that stands always on the brink of passing "Who is a Jew" legislation which would disenfranchise and delegitimize the religious leaders of the majority of Jews in the Diaspora?

The issue of "Who is a Jew?" does not only refer to the handful of converts who wish to be recognized as Jews by the State of Israel. Rather, the question is whether or not rabbis belonging to Reform and Conservative synagogues deserve respect as Judaic teachers, or whether the Orthodox halakhic orientation is the only legitimate mediator of how a Jew may connect himself or herself to the covenantal drama of Jewish history. One cannot embrace Zionism and the Law of Return, which welcomes Jews from all over the world to make Israel their home irrespective of their ideological belief systems, yet delegitimize Reform and Conservative rabbinic groups throughout the world. One cannot say, "All are welcome because we share a common destiny," and then deny them freedom and dignity because of their nontraditional belief systems. One cannot marshal the energies of the Jewish world for Operation Moses to rescue the Ethiopian Jews and then cast doubt on the Jewishness of these Ethiopians because they never knew the authoritative framework of the Talmud. For two thousand years this Jewish community said no to paganism in Africa. Yet when it finally came home to Israel its members were told that their Jewishness could not be fully accepted by the rabbinic halakhic tradition.

I know that it is not easy for traditional halakhists to accept Jews whose religious life was or is not guided by the rabbinic tradition. However, if the ingathering of the exiles made possible by Israel is not to lead to a sectarian and polarized society, it is urgent that we discover ways in which the tradition can offer guidelines for living with religious diversity.

Israel forces us to confront these agonizing and profoundly complex issues. The question of religious pluralism does not have the same urgency in the Diaspora, because there the public space of Jewish life is not defined by Jewish tradition. One can join three synagogues, behaving differently in each, without conflict, because the streets between them are not governed by a sovereign Jewish community. The New York police and the laws of the United States determine how Jews of different persuasions live with one another. But who determines the public space of Jerusalem? Who defines what memories and values should enter into our public framework, how the streets appear on the Sabbath, what should be eaten in restaurants, what is legitimate theater? How do Jews who have such different perceptions of what it means to be in a holy land talk to each other?

A person coming home after a long absence often thinks the whole family will look as he or she remembered them. In Israel, each group believes that the total society should mirror its own particular memories. How do we come home and yet make spiritual, psychological, and political room for those who disagree with us? Pluralism is not a luxury but an urgent necessity if Israel is to be a viable home for a people in disagreement about the meaning and significance of Jewish life. Only then will it be "good and pleasant that brethren should dwell together" (Ps. 133:1).

Civility and respectful debate must enter into Israeli society. We must learn that disagreement among Jews is healthy, creative, and impossible to avoid. We must recapture the spirit of the old rabbinic phrase "an argument for the sake of heaven must survive."[3] No one group must be given the monopoly on authenticity.

11

Living with Other Faiths

The issue of coexistence in our society, however, does not only relate to how Jews behave toward each other. How can Jewish faith and the Jewish nation reassert themselves in Israel and yet allow room for Christians and Muslims? We cannot ignore the yearnings of the entire Palestinian community for political dignity. How does the Jewish faith respond to the music and vitality of other faith experiences in its own home? We pleaded for tolerance when we were weak and powerless in the Diaspora. What shall we do now that we are the majority culture and have the political and military power to define freedom of conscience and freedom of expression?

As we walk to the Western Wall to pray, we hear the bells of Christian churches and the Muslim call to prayer. How do we sing our own song in our own home without feeling threatened by the vital spiritual experiences of different belief systems?

As a people, we have suffered at the hands of those who believed that they had the exclusive keys to God's kingdom. We have always been victims of those who wanted to bring all of humanity under one truth system, be it through the holy wars of Christianity and Islam or the secular Marxist totalitarianism of the twentieth century. We have been the constant obstacle to universalist triumphalism in history: the permanent "other," the permanent strangers who refused to compromise their own particularity when pressed to conform to universalist standards binding on all people. We were the "scandal of particularity" in history. We always defied totalitarian, religious, or cultural universalism. What do we do now with this memory of our history when we return to power in Jerusalem? How do we learn from our own historical experience as the stranger in order to respond with love and respect to the presence of the "stranger" in our midst? Did we plead for the legitimacy of our own way of life because we morally believed that universalism, cultural totalitarianism, and the importance of one truth is a destructive idea for human history? Or did we plead for tolerance merely in our own self-interest, while fundamentally believing that there is only one truth and one way that must guide all of humanity?

The "scandal of particularity" has returned to Jerusalem. As we build the third Jewish commonwealth we face the issue of how much room exists for differences in our soul. We must not repeat the sins of our oppressors. We must not slip into the tragic historical pattern of the weak acquiring power, internalizing the values of their oppressive masters, and in turn oppressing those under their rule. Rather, we must learn from the Torah that tells us, "And you shall love the stranger

12

because you were strangers in the Land of Egypt" (Deut. 10:19). We must not fall into the trap of doing unto others what others have done unto us. Our suffering will have been in vain if it does not create within our people a moral sensitivity to the rights of minorities and those who are different in our midst.

The soul of our nation is being put to the test. Our testimony to the moral integrity of Jewish history will be determined by the way we deal with the issue of the Palestinians. Of course, we must be certain that our survival in our own country is not threatened. Our security needs and our sense of being at home should never be undermined. We can be totally uncompromising in our demands for security and at the same time cognizant of the Palestinians' quest for political, economic, and cultural dignity. While we must cherish the sacredness of our own human life, our urgent need for security does not require that we deny the political and cultural renaissance of the Palestinian people. Both can live and flourish together. Most Israelis believe that there can be more than one dignified people in this land. There are resources within our tradition which may guide us as to how to affirm the dignity of our own particularity while cherishing the universal Jewish idea "Beloved is the human being created in the image of God."[4]

My God and the God of My Fathers

This collection of essays embraces the themes that I have just outlined. Part 1 reveals the passion of a dreamer who thought that the great events in recent Jewish history would bring about a radical transformation of the Jewish people's spiritual sensibility. The dream has not disappeared, but I have come to perceive more deeply the obstacles that make its realization so slow in coming. The discussion with Leibowitz in Part 2 shows how this process of rethinking was set in motion. The Messiah has not come. The Jews have not suddenly discovered unfathomed potential for love and tolerance. I had to learn how far we are from mutual appreciation and understanding. The inclination to adopt a ghetto mentality is still strong in many Jewish souls.

The essays in Part 3 provide a sympathetic account of the passion of the text-centered culture of the ghetto. At the same time, the essays suggest how Jews who are committed to the centrality of Torah can be receptive to the new challenges and possibilities posed by modernity.

The concluding essays show that the celebration of particularity need not lead to triumphalist messianism or to the idea that we are the exclusive mediators of authenticity and truth. These essays reflect the urgent need to show that the election of Israel and loyalty to the covenantal principles do not imply that only one people is the carrier of God's redemptive longing for human history. I have learned how to celebrate our Jewish particularity without feeling that the joy of the "stranger" undermines my own vitality. I have learned how to say yes to our tradition without making that affirmation dependent upon the fear and rejection of other faith communities.

We have been given two commandments in the Torah: "Love your neighbor as yourself" and "Love the stranger, because you were strangers in the land of Egypt" (Lev. 19:34). The neighbor or "other" extends our sense of communal consciousness, reminding us that there is significance in other frames of reference that we encounter. We must learn to live with both *mitzvot*. We can affirm the love for family, for nation, and for our particular historical traditions, yet know that we reflect only a fragment of God's infinite richness. No community's historical memories and tradition exhaust the full range of human spiritual possibility.

Maimonides and Soloveitchik are very important for my discussion with tradition-bound, text-centered religious communities. Maimonides opened the Jewish religious tradition to the best of human thought, while Soloveitchik exemplifies the person who passionately loves Talmud but never demands of his students intellectual compromise and timidity. He has taught us how to face the world with dignity, courage, and intellectual honesty. Both bear witness to the passion of rational sobriety. Both show a way to maintain the covenantal identity of the people without making exaggerated claims about Jewish history and without isolating the halakhic experience from the rest of humanity.

Despite the deficiencies of Israeli society, I am grateful to be able to celebrate the opportunity of living within a Jewish reality that allows me honestly to see what is painful and yet hopeful. The broken tablets, says the Midrash, were placed in the Ark together with the new tablets inscribed by Moses. The powerful dreams and exaggerated expectations that propelled me to Israel after the Six-Day War have been shattered. Yet important elements of those dreams continue to live in my soul. I believe that Israel gives the Jewish world its greatest opportunity to renew its covenantal identity.

There is a great deal of spiritual energy present in a people that has not yet arrived at a single definition of its identity. Instead of slogans about Jewish unity, Israel provides one with an intensive Jewish reality that brings into sharper focus the important disagreements in the Jewish world today. My theological reflections in these essays do not aim to provide a common denominator for all Jews or to gloss over the significance of our disagreements. Rather, I seek to shed light on the importance of disagreements conducted "for the sake of heaven" and to suggest ways in which they may be conducted in the talmudic spirit of "these and these are the words of the living God."[5]

I do not write in the spirit of Ecclesiastes, "Vanity of vanities, all is vanity" (Eccles. 1:1), but rather with a sense of urgency and hope. I do not believe that there is "nothing new under the sun." Israel vibrates with potentialities that can move us in many different directions, both positive and negative. I realize now as never before that the spiritual life is not an easy achievement. To be part of the covenantal community is to be obligated by the prophetic vision that Israel should constantly strive to bring about a just and holy society.

In reestablishing political national independence in the biblical land of the covenant, one is confronted by the past at every turn. America was built upon the belief that one can create a future without the burden of historical memory. In Israel, however, the bulldozer that clears the foundations for a new house uncovers layers of ancient civilizations. In the city of Jerusalem and throughout this country, the innovative forces of technology cannot ignore the voice of historical memory and traditions. To touch the earth of Jerusalem is to enter into a three-thousand-year-old dialogue.

We cannot avoid the question "Who is a Jew?" Properly understood, this question is all-important, and should not degenerate into squabbles over conversion and delegitimization. The question that this old-new people is really asking is, "Who are we? Where do we want to go? How are we to interpret our history? Were we born in 1948? Is it best to forget the memory of the past? Can we build our new society in the same way that American civilization was built?"

According to Professor Judith Sklare, America's greatness was that it was not burdened by too much memory. Nietzsche likewise understood that the past can inhibit new vitality, and that one can be imprisoned by loyalty to tradition and memories. All revolutionaries ask us to look forward, to overthrow and discard the past. But the State of Israel can never take this route. In terms of traditional Jewish conceptions, Israel is a revolutionary society, but it is a revolution in an ancient land that connects us with a history of three thousand years.

We cannot build a new future in Israel, therefore, unless we reinterpret our past. This is why the issue that divides the country is really, Who mediates the authenticity of our past? Without knowing where we came from, without receiving direction from our sources and understanding how to interpret the significance of Israel as a promised land, we will be in a constant state of war. Instead of celebrating the

15

new creative possibilities of love and gentleness, we shall be a society of victims terrified by memories of the past, angry because of what was done to our ancestors, and constantly seeking to compensate for the nightmarish memories of antisemitic persecutions and the Holocaust.

As I look back upon Jewish history, I know that I can never redeem my grandfather's suffering. All our renewed power cannot bring him back to life. Therefore, I must also not be paralyzed by the world that he experienced. To be open to Christianity and Islam, to rethink the new possibilities of pluralism, does not imply that we do not feel the pain of what Christian and Islamic teachings have done to the Jewish people in the past. We mourn many anniversaries of our people's suffering on the Ninth of Av, but Jewish identity must not be defined by tragedy and mourning. The talmudic tradition taught us how to light a candle in what often appeared as a dark, ugly world and how to say the Grace after Meals even if we did not have a full meal. It taught us how to celebrate the partial and the incomplete and to know that there is wisdom and strength in compromise.

The Jewish people have lived with loyalty to the experiences and aspirations of the past and with openness to the innovative possibilities offered by the present and future for the spiritual life. Loyalty to the God of our fathers did not lead us to deny the fullness and rich possibilities of our own reality. "This is *my God* and I will adore him, the *God of my fathers,* and I will exalt Him" (Ex. 15:2); both aspects have always been present in the Jewish spiritual experience.

These essays reflect my effort to listen with reverence to the past while maintaining the determination to move in new directions. I am convinced that love of Torah and God will only grow in a culture that accepts values and spiritual insights springing from the experiences of the present. With all our continuing commitment to the God of our fathers, it is only if we discern and respond to the new spiritual possibilities of the present that we can truthfully say as well, "This is my God and I will adore Him."

PART ONE

"We Were as Dreamers"

THE CELEBRATION OF STATEHOOD

Joy and Responsibility

T he talmudic halakhic tradition is not known or properly understood in the West. Impressions of Judaism are often compounded of elements of medieval Jewish scholasticism, Buber's I and Thou, and mysticism. The religious outlook of the Talmud and Halakhah is either ignored or caricatured as "pharisaism" or legalism.

The rebirth of the Jewish people in its homeland challenges us to articulate a sober and responsible halakhic anthropology capable of energizing Jews to assume responsibility for a total Jewish society. In order to appreciate better the significance of Israel for contemporary Jewish spirituality, it is important to discuss briefly three distinct outlooks reflected in different periods of Jewish history: biblical immediacy, talmudic postponement of gratification, and the modern resurgence of immediacy.

The biblical period may be categorized, for the purpose of the present analysis, as signifying immediacy; history and nature compose an organic unity. Morality and natural phenomena form a continuous whole; human moral failures have natural, organic consequences. The blood of the slain Abel cries out from the earth and Cain is sentenced to a lifetime of wandering. The earth vomits forth its inhabitants in consequence of moral corruption. Heaven and earth bear witness to Israel's covenantal agreement with God. The biblical blessings and curses illustrate how nature and history mirror Israel's covenantal relationship with God.

The biblical world promises immediate gratification for compliance with the covenant. If you observe the commandments, the rains will fall in season. The rains must fall, nature must respond, for the God of nature and the Lord of history are one. Maimonides, in his *Treatise on Resurrection*, argues that the doctrine of the resurrection of the dead was not mentioned in the Bible because it signifies a blessing whose realization is not immediate and visible. The ability to accept postponed gratification is foreign to the early biblical outlook.

The harmony between moral, historical, and natural conditions

19

stems from a world view dominated by an omnipotent, beneficent deity. Job's problem with evil was not psychological (i.e., how to cope with suffering and deprivation), but rather, ontological: How can the universe tolerate a split between God as the source of being (nature) and God as the source of morality (history)? The problem of evil for Job upset the unity and the order of the universe; Job's problem emerged from the matrix of the biblical outlook.

Biblical rewards and punishments were not regarded only as extraneous incentives for good behavior. Biblical man considered many descendants, abundant crops, and victories over enemies to be perfectly natural consequences of observing God's law.

In the talmudic period, however, biblical immediacy no longer dominated Jewish consciousness. Rabbinic Judaism was predominantly the product of historic defeat and exile. Biblical organic consciousness began to break under the weight of harsh historical conditions. In contrast to biblical promises of immediate gratification, a talmudic teacher, Rabbi Tarfon, said:

> The day is short and the work is great, and the laborers are sluggish and the wages are high and the householder is urgent. . . . The work is not upon thee to finish, nor art thou free to desist from it. . . . And know that the giving of the reward to the righteous is in the time to come.

The Talmud relates the story of a child who obeyed his father's instruction, to send away the mother bird before removing the young birds from their nest, and who subsequently fell from the tree to his death. Both in obeying his parent and in sending away the mother bird, the child was fulfilling norms for which the Bible promised long life (Ex. 20:12; Deut. 22:6–7). After verifying the precise nature of this case and concluding that such a case does, in fact, conflict with biblical promises, a talmudic teacher asserts: "There is no reward for commandments in this world."

Elsewhere in the Talmud, the rabbis are presented with a series of questions meant to reveal the indifference of reality to violations of God's commandments: "If God hates idolatry, why does He not destroy the objects of idolatry? If someone stole grain and planted it in the earth, why does it grow?" In response to such questions the pronouncement is made: *Olam ke-minhago noheg* (the world conforms to its natural course). Although the Talmud concedes that by right *(din hu)* stolen grain should not grow, nevertheless, "the world conforms to its natural course." This approach is not an Epicurean negation of the unity of the God of nature and the Lord of history, for it affirms belief

20

in a future state of harmony where one will be compelled to account for one's conduct. The crucial point of this talmudic text is the admission that natural forces and events do not mirror the moral quality of the relationship between human beings and God.

One result of the separation of nature and morality is the development of a religious personality able to tolerate delayed gratification. Biblical Jews met God in history. Momentous events, like the crossing of the Red Sea, were occasions for intense religious devotion. "And when Israel saw the wondrous power which the Lord had wielded against the Egyptians, the people feared the Lord: they had faith in the Lord and in His servant Moses" (Ex. 14:31). When God's power ceased to be apparent in history, as during the talmudic period, a new spiritual orientation began to emerge which felt divine presence and love for God in the act of fulfilling His normative message. Indicative of this orientation was a network of concepts, such as *li-shemah* (performing a norm for its own sake), *ahavah* (acting out of love rather than in order to receive a reward or to escape punishment), and *simhah shel mitzvah* (the joy of performing commandments), which centered religious attention on fulfilling the Law. In the absence of external divine confirmation and response, a talmudic teacher could assert: "The reward for performing a *mitzvah* is the performance of the *mitzvah* itself."

Alongside this historical sobriety, the talmudic tradition retained the passion for biblical immediacy, albeit in a restrained form. It was not easy to restrict the passion for God's living presence to the realm of historical memories or eschatological hopes. The biblical portrayal of God's involvement in the daily life and needs of the community could not easily be set aside. This was the source of a great tension between the religious sensibility emerging from Halakhah and the passion for biblical immediacy which focused on God's visible power in nature and history. False messiahs represented the eruption of biblical passion despite rabbinic attempts at containment. The vulnerability of Jewish history to messianic pretenders was an outgrowth, in part, of the presence of biblical consciousness alongside halakhic sobriety. Biblical memories served as a source of anarchy. The powerful dialectic at the heart of talmudic Judaism consisted in the tension between the anarchic passion of biblical memory and the disciplined religiosity of Halakhah.

In the talmudic tradition, the locus of divine presence in history is a memory that is confined to particular moments of time, such as festivals and moments of prayer. The God of history was encountered in a dramatic story with many episodes, stretching over the entire biblical period and beyond it. In prayer and in structured moments of time, the halakhic Jew reentered the biblical world of immediacy. Symbolic time kept historical immediacy alive in the midst of halakhic realism.

There are, then, two dimensions of time for the talmudic Jew: (1) empirical history, in which God's "face" remains hidden; and (2) symbolic, holy time, in which God acts as the Lord of history. In the Passover Haggadah, the ten plagues of the Bible are described in such a way that their number far exceeds ten; one teacher proves that there were sixty plagues, another, that there were three hundred. Also, after enumerating the wonders God performed for the people of Israel in the Bible, Jews read aloud *dayenu* ("enough!"), as if divine blessings in history are overabundant. In short, the Haggadah is the product of a people hungry for God's presence in history, yet compelled to focus this hunger not on their own experiences but on the vivid memory of past biblical events.

For many years I served as a rabbi in Jewish communities in the United States and Canada. God's presence in history was alive to me on Passover, Shavuot, and Sukkot, the three historical festivals. On Rosh Hashanah and Yom Kippur, the imagery of the moral judge of history calling each and every human being to judgment evoked feelings of accountability and renewed commitment. History was not problematical; however meaningful and compelling its dramatic message, it was, in the end, a symbolic history.

My theological problems were essentially outside the dramatic events of history. Kierkegaard, Freud, and existentialism were some of the foci of my intellectual and religious concerns.

Then, suddenly, I was confronted with the frightening events preceding the Six-Day War. The community of Jews in Israel was not the protagonist in a dramatic account of symbolic history but, rather, a real community of Jews facing the possibility of another Holocaust. And I was impotent to intervene. The reality of a living community in the very midst of the stormy currents of history suddenly invaded my consciousness. I was paralyzed with anxiety and dread; if anything catastrophic were to happen to this community, I felt my Judaism would be strangled. Questions of theology and theodicy were beside the point; continuing to participate in the drama of Jewish history seemed unimaginable in the event of another Holocaust. How long could we be witnesses to the silent God of history?

Then, in the aftermath of the victory of the Six-Day War, I felt compelled to come to Israel to find a way of appropriating the reality of the Jewish State. After returning from Israel, when I entered my synagogue on the Ninth of Av, a fast day commemorating the destruction of the Temple, I was struck by the incongruity of Diaspora Jews sitting downcast on the floor, reading and mourning for Jerusalem. In the Jerusalem from which I had just returned, Jews were rejoicing in the streets with dance and song. The contrast was astounding and spiritually maddening. Before the service began, I announced to the "mourners for Jerusalem": "The Jews in Jerusalem are presently jubilant." Whether this meant that symbolically identifying with Jewish defeat was at this moment pointless and that fast days such as the Ninth of Av should be abolished, I was not certain. All I knew was that my task was to tell my congregation of a reality that invaded the confines of the Story of Jewish history.

Fearing that the Jews would lose the powerful significance of the war, I went enthusiastically to my *rebbe* (teacher), Rabbi Joseph B. Soloveitchik, with the request: "Proclaim a religious festival; proclaim God's revelatory presence in history! Must God be revealed only in stories? Can we not celebrate the living God of our directly felt redemption?"

Soloveitchik responded by referring to a talmudic passage which says that the festival of Hanukkah, which celebrates the Maccabean victory and the miracle of lights, was not proclaimed immediately after the wondrous events, but rather, only a year later. Pointing out the significance of "a year later," Soloveitchik counseled me to wait and not to react in the heat of excitement.

His sobriety and restraint were out of tune with the enthusiasm and passion I felt as a result of the experience of liberation. I passionately wished to respond religiously to events, whereas he chose to be satisfied with history mediated by Halakhah.

Shortly afterwards, I left my pulpit and, with my family, went to settle in Israel. And after living in Israel a number of years, I rediscovered the age-old message of Jewish history: the uncertainty, loneliness, and isolation, and the concern for survival. In contrast to the triumphant experience of redemption following the Six-Day War, after the Yom Kippur War I rediscovered the tragic dimension of Jewish history. I felt like writing to Soloveitchik, saying, "Perhaps you were right. We must wait for the coming year before giving a religious response to events in history."

This haunting thought continues to influence my approach to Judaism. On the one hand, the living God of Judaism is revealed in Halakhah (Jewish jurisprudence), in the disciplined religiosity of the legalist and in the confined framework of the story of our ancient past. On the other hand, the reality of present-day Jewish history mediates the liv-

23

ing God of Israel and places the Jews within the context of a living community, instead of a community acting in a symbolic domain. Choosing either option exclusively is dangerous. To focus attention solely on a living God whom you believe is acting in history leads to a manic-depressive syndrome: one day He is your liberator; the next day He is your enemy. On the other hand, choosing the safety of a traditional halakhic orientation which perceives God in the ancient story results in emptying Israel of religious significance. Is the Jewish presence in Israel similar to the Jewish presence in the United States or Canada, or does the Jewish presence in Israel somehow mediate the God of the covenant for contemporary Jews?

My approach to contemporary images of the halakhic Jew moves between these two poles. In choosing to make the reality of Israel revelatory and to seek God in the vicissitudes of the history of a living community, I gave up the security of the story. Nevertheless, I did not adopt a messianic posture or abandon the realism of the halakhic, legal mind. I do not seek a return to biblical immediacy nor to mystic notions of ultimate unity. I live in Israel as a rabbinic Jew open to indications of God's presence in the events involving the fate of the living community of Israel. In participating in the building of a people as a nation, I do not feel compelled to announce imminent redemption; my conception of God's relationship to history allows Jews to return to history bearing in mind the dialectical relationship between the aspirations of the story and reality.

Three responses to the rebirth of Israel stand in contrast to the outlook I am advocating:

1. There are those in the Orthodox Jewish community who regard Israel as a spiritual danger, insofar as the living experience of God in history threatens to invade the sacred borders of the God of the story. According to this point of view, history (i.e., symbolic history) must be safeguarded, and we must forever live in anticipation of God's decision to have mercy on His people and to recreate heaven and earth. Present history, according to this view, is opaque and insignificant. The universe we inhabit is bounded by the four cubits of Halakhah. History is none of our business; the Lord, when He sees fit, will invite us to reenter history (albeit a new history).

The practical consequences of this viewpoint include barricading one's subcommunity off from the broader community, including those Orthodox Jews who view Israel positively. Television, newspapers, secular education, universities, not to mention interaction with other points of view and cultural traditions, are dangerous foreign influences to be shunned. The walls of separation extend higher and higher. The task is to safeguard the *purity* of Judaism. Nothing must change. You pray and dress in Jerusalem in the Middle East as Jews did two hundred years ago in the wintry climate of Eastern Europe. Nothing must change.

2. Another response to Israel is based on a particular interpretation of the course of history. It stems especially from Rabbi Abraham Isaac Kook, the first Ashkenazic Chief Rabbi during the British Mandate in Palestine. For those who think like him, the secularism of the Zionists who established the state simply reveals the cunning of the divine mind in furthering the plan of history. Israel is the beginning of the end. Israel and the eschatological realization of the dreams of countless generations are but two stages of the same process. Those who believe in the wisdom of *Realpolitik* and are concerned about how the nations of the world react to Israeli policies are not unlike the fool in biblical literature—they fail to detect God's providential presence. The world of the Bible is the touchstone of reality, according to this outlook. You consult the Bible to determine Israel's borders and prepare the biblical home for God who is about to reenter history. In the end, humankind is simply a pawn in the divine game-plan; the great destiny of the Jewish people is about to be revealed and no power on earth can change this in any way.

3. The third response, characteristic of ultrasecularists, celebrates the "normalization" of Jewish society in Israel, including the abolition of a Jewish covenantal consciousness. "To be like all the nations" becomes a motto for an indiscriminate acceptance of anything Israeli. Pointing to prostitution and juvenile delinquency as signs of normalcy, and then expressing pride in the Jews' becoming normal reflects the danger of embracing contemporary history totally, divorced from a past or an ideology in which the glorification of normalization has sometimes led to the paganization and brutalization of the Jewish spirit.

The outlook I am proposing does not celebrate normalcy and assimilation, nor does it announce the imminent eschatological triumph of Judaism. Rather, it seeks to be in history and to accept the responsibility of building a total society, while retaining the sobriety of the halakhic religious sensibility. In other words, this approach is rabbinic, without the mystical or biblical organic (mythic) consciousness and without the eschatological dimension. My picture of a genuinely religious person is one who is not averse to getting hands dirty; one who does not await divine intervention but who experiences God's presence in efforts to discharge the responsibility he or she feels for the total community. No aspect of social involvement is beyond the domain of service of God: "In all your ways, know Him." In extending the notion of service of God into countless areas of social behavior, we are, so to speak, breaking open the story to the flow of reality. We allow the rhythms of modern history to enter into our relationship with God.

The exposure of a total people and its tradition to modernity is filled with great opportunities as well as risks. The reality of Israel has created the opportunity to educate and to open Jews to Judaism as a way of life. Failure to inspire those who seek a Jewish content for their communal existence would reveal the weakness and the intellectual bankruptcy of contemporary religious leadership. Secular Zionism has created the social and political conditions for the entire Jewish people to renew its ancient covenant at Sinai.

One aspect of the significance of Zionism for the modern Jew lies in its enabling us to rediscover the vitality of Torah as a way of life. The religious value of events in history is not measured solely in terms of their relationship to a future messianic age, but by how they expand the area of responsibility for the implementation of Halakhah. Unlike the Diaspora, Israel contains a public domain for which Jews *qua* Jews are responsible. In Israel, Jews have the opportunity to witness the sanctifying power of Torah in the mundane marketplaces of life.

I do not subscribe to the belief in linear progress in history. What the tradition asks of Jews is that in each generation they renew the covenantal moment of Sinai. Though I am ignorant of how contemporary Israel is related to the end of history, I do know how Israel is related to the beginnings of covenantal history.

Israel provides a framework for recapturing the spirit of the fundamental organizing principles of Jewish spirituality: Creation, Exodus, *mitzvot*, and the Promised Land. The concern with using past models to interpret present conditions grows out of the belief that Israel offers Jews an unprecedented opportunity to regenerate the primary roots of Judaism. As a traditional Jew, I am grateful to Zionism and to Israel for renewing the significance of the beginning and not necessarily for bringing about the end.

My search for a way to renew the Sinai covenant leads first of all to "Egypt," in other words, to solidarity with a suffering people seeking liberation. Solitary, lonely individuals with no sense of community cannot appropriate the spiritual way of life that emanates from Sinai. Judaism is unique in that, rather than beginning with a leap of faith, it demands a leap of identification with a people and its history.

The internalization of "We were slaves to Pharaoh in Egypt" leads,

26

in our generation, to identification both with the tragic dimensions of the Holocaust and with the struggle for the peace and security of the State of Israel. This sense of solidarity with peoplehood implies that love and concern for all Jews must be independent of faith commitments and levels of *mitzvah* observance.

According to the Midrash, the Jewish slave in Egypt had abandoned the covenantal faith of Abraham. Participation in the suffering and the yearnings for security of the Jewish people imbues the solitary individual with a deep sense of collectivity. The "I" is transformed into a "we" through participation in the historic destiny of the Jewish people.

Religious Jews who are deeply concerned about the fate of all Jews must not only share the burdens of survival but must also strive to build spiritual bridges among Jews. The sense of community that precedes *mitzvah* must also influence one's approach to the observance of the commandments. Halakhah is not addressed to the singular individual but primarily to the individual rooted in the historical destiny of a community.

The quest for community ought not to be expressed solely in terms of survival. Religious educators who stress the centrality of Jewish peoplehood must strive to formulate an approach to *mitzvot* that would enable their students to share a common spiritual language with the rest of the Jewish people. The need to formulate a shared spiritual language is most evident in the State of Israel, where the common struggle for survival loses much of its meaning in the absence of belief in the significance of Jewish communal existence.

Providing spiritual understanding for Jews in the modern world is not an easy task. Whereas in the past we shared a common framework of religious authority, today the daily lives of most Jews are not organized by the principles of Halakhah. How, then, shall we teach Talmud, *mitzvot*, and Halakhah to a community that does not acknowledge the basic presuppositions of normative Halakhah? How can a believer talk to a so-called nonbeliever?

My years in the rabbinate taught me to seek ways of talking about Judaism which would be meaningful to Jews of various backgrounds. Although I had been an Orthodox rabbi in the Bronx and in Montreal for seventeen years, my congregations were made up of people of many different backgrounds and levels of observance and belief.During my rabbinic training at Yeshiva University, I was taught to answer halakhic questions. The details of the laws of *kashrut* and similar *mitzvot* were studied with rigor and devotion. Upon entering the rabbinate, I was anxious to answer the great halakhic questions of the Jewish community. I waited with anticipation, but, to my dismay, there were no questioners. Finally I realized that the role of the rabbi was not so much to provide answers as to create questions.

I found that people were not engaged with Judaism; it did not demand their serious attention. It was not, in William James's words, a live option. I realized then that my task was to fight indifference and to convince Jews to confront the Judaic tradition as an option that could not be easily dismissed.

My years in the rabbinate also taught me that a teacher must begin where his students are; the task of the teacher is to listen before speaking, to hear, and to share in the deep estrangement of Jews from their tradition, to enter that alienation and try to understand its roots. I had to postpone my answers in order to hear the new questions.

Maimonides' approach to Torah as expressed in *The Guide of the Perplexed* has been a permanent source of inspiration and guidance for me. In Maimonides, I beheld a master halakhist, whose authoritative halakhic works have guided Jews for generations, who was prepared to understand many *mitzvot* of the Torah in the light of the particular human conditions of the community of slaves that left Egypt. God, says Maimonides, speaks in the language of human beings; He takes into account the lived reality of people when formulating norms and directives. God listens carefully and sympathetically before He speaks.

In addressing a generation that is estranged from and indifferent to traditional frameworks of Jewish spirituality, one must not begin by teaching theology. To a generation that has lost an appreciation of the human significance of *mitzvot*, one should not emphasize a theocentric orientation to Halakhah. Rather than articulating the dogmatic foundations of Judaism, I focus on how the practices and conceptual frameworks of Halakhah can influence a person's character and perspective on life. I am not concerned with proving that God created the universe in six days, but rather, with understanding the human implications of accepting the doctrine of a creational universe. Belief in Creation leads one to reject passivity and to adopt an active, self-reliant attitude to history. According to Soloveitchik, the idea of God the Creator serves as a model for the Jew to imitate. One must imitate God not only by internalizing His moral attributes but also by becoming an active and responsible agent seeking to perfect an imperfect reality.

I try to correct the mistaken notion that halakhic Jews are naive, arrogant, and spiritually complacent. The demand that individuals assume responsibility for community cannot be met if they are afraid to fail. One who cannot tolerate the thought of failure, but requires constant success in order to confirm one's dignity and worth, cannot live with the innumerable demands of Halakhah. One who seeks absolute certainty will not find comfort in a spiritual tradition whose response to the disagreements between the schools of Hillel and Shammai was that both schools of thought were the words of the living God.

Rabbinic Judaism was fully aware of the various risks that Jewish communal spirituality entails. When one strives to build one's spiritual life within a living community, one must give up viewing religion in terms of salvation of the soul; one must be spiritually prepared to take great risks and make compromises. If one is not, one cannot build a relationship to God within the framework of community. In Judaism, love for God must lead to a love for real people. One who can only love an idealized community of the elect remains the victim of messianic abstractions, unable to embrace the community of real Jews in this imperfect world.

The joy of Torah emerges from feelings of adequacy, responsibility, and solidarity with community. The description of the community of Israel in the Bible is for some theologians a shocking account of rebellion and sin; for me, it is an inspiring testimony to the fact that God gave the Torah to human beings and not to angels. The continuous renewal of divine demands, despite repeated human failures, indicates that God did not operate with an idealized concept of the covenantal Jew. The giving of the Torah to a people who were prepared to return to slavery in Egypt the first time they were thirsty fills me with feelings of deep joy—fragile human beings are deemed capable of becoming responsible and mature. The giving of the Torah reflects God's belief in the human capacity to obey the Law. Rabbinic Judaism's expansion and elaboration of Halakhah further illustrate the belief in the community's ability to realize the historic task of becoming a holy people. The joy of *mitzvah* stems from recognizing that God is prepared to give limited, imperfect human beings a great covenantal task. The election of Israel testified to the willingness of the Teacher of Torah to take a stiff-necked, rebellious people and educate them, step by step, toward the ideal of becoming a nation of priests and a holy people. The continuous demand of Torah confirms God's love of and patience with His people.

The shift in emphasis from dogmatic theology, leaps of faith, and eschatological pronouncements to an analysis of the significance of religious concepts will hopefully provide the ground for a shared spiritual language for a society seeking to understand the covenantal foundations of Judaism.

Modern Jewish history has created strong existential bonds among Jews. Standing before the *kotel*, the Western Wall, one hears the echoes of Jewish hopes resounding throughout history: "Next year in Jerusalem!" When one walks through the streets of Jerusalem today, one is accompanied by all those Jews throughout history who yearned for and believed that one day Jews would return to Jerusalem. Israel is home for all Jews, of both the present and the past. The urgent question is whether, in coming home, "children," "parents," and "grandparents" can share a common spiritual language so that Judaism can once again become a live and compelling option.

The Challenge of
Modern Israel
to Traditional Judaism

T here are many today, both in Israel and abroad, who believe that the fundamental purpose of the establishment of the State of Israel was to solve the problems of Jewish suffering by providing a national home where Jews will be accepted and welcomed on the basis of the inalienable right that arises from their being members of the Jewish people.

I believe that treating Israel as a haven against persecution is an incomplete and inadequate perspective, both for making sense of the complex aspirations that led to the rebirth of Israel and for viewing contemporary life in Israeli society. Although persecution and suffering provided an essential impetus in stimulating the desire for renewed Jewish political independence, there were also deep utopian and spiritual longings that infused the Zionist revolution.[1]

Many dreamed of a new Jew, a transformation and correction of what were seen as character distortions present in exilic Jewish society. The return to the land was seen by many as a means of healing the harm inflicted upon the Jewish psyche by the situation of oppression and wandering. Even for religious thinkers such as Rabbi Abraham Isaac Kook, the first Ashkenazic Chief Rabbi appointed under the British Mandate in Palestine, the Zionist revolution was destined to release spiritual energies that had been repressed due to the unnatural existence in exile. Kook saw in the atheistic socialist revolution the seeds of a liberating religious experience. He also looked forward to a new Jewish anthropology emerging from the Zionist rebuilding of the country.[2]

Jerusalem has always been the vehicle through which Jewish hopes and dreams were expressed. Israel invites ideological passions, since it connects one to the larger historic memories of Jewish experience. Living and working in Israeli society, one cannot avoid meeting the social vision of Isaiah and the passion of Rabbi Akiva who spoke of the Song

31

of Songs as the holy of holies. Forward-looking technological con-sciousness can never fully define Jewish society in Israel, since the very geography of the country brings the forward-moving thrust into a pro-found confrontation with the historical aspirations and memories of the Jewish people.

It is thus understandable that the urgent practical questions of secu-rity and the economy do not exhaust what preoccupies Israelis. They get excited about spiritual and religious issues that seem strange to the outsider who sees Israel as a besieged country fighting for its survival. Governments fall in Israel over questions of religious principle such as alleged violation of the Sabbath and who is a Jew. The disturbing ques-tions that perplex Israel society touch upon the need for clarifying the way one applies the Jewish tradition to a modern society.

In Israel, in contrast to the Diaspora, the synagogue and Jewish fam-ily life cannot sufficiently generate the sense of religious vitality needed in order to make Judaism a viable option for the modern Israeli. It is not accidental that the national literature of the country is the Bible. This does not mean, however, that at present a biblical religious pathos infuses the country, but only that the parameters for Judaic spirituality in Israel mirror in significant ways the larger historical and political con-ditions present in the biblical outlook. There is a profound identifica-tion with the biblical anthropological outlook and an affinity with prophetic moral and messianic aspirations, even though there is a lack of understanding for the theological foundations that infuse the biblical world view.

This essay will argue that our return to the land has recreated the broader biblical, covenantal foundations of Judaism. An analysis of the various aspects of the biblical covenant will make it possible to define those features of exilic Judaism that developed in the talmudic and posttalmudic eras. While those features enabled Judaism to survive, it will be argued that they allowed mistaken perceptions of the scope of covenantal religious consciousness to arise. The achievements of mod-ern Israel, however, can stimulate us to correct those distortions. The normalization of Jewish consciousness and the acceptance of political responsibility for Jewish national existence can be understood as car-rying a stage further the reinterpretation of divine power found in the rabbinic tradition.

Creation and Covenant

The creation story in Genesis provides the theological and anthropological framework for understanding the covenantal election of Israel. The world and human beings are other than God. The gap between them provides a space within which a relationship between God and humans is possible.

It would appear that, according to the first chapters of Genesis, God initially believed that humans would reflect divinity through His own powers as Creator. Man and woman were made in God's image. Precisely this act, however, contains the seeds of alienation and rebellion against God. Because human beings are endowed with freedom of choice, mirroring God's own freedom, their freedom becomes a constituent principle separating them from God. Mirroring divinity in other respects, then, has to be a decision made by the human being and not only by the will of God. God's will meets no opposition through the creation of nature. It meets the opposition through the creation of humans. This is the fundamental significance of the story of the Garden of Eden, Cain and Abel, and the sequel up to the destruction wrought by the Flood. The Flood expresses the divine rage when God's will is frustrated. Immediately afterwards, however, we notice a complete change in Genesis when God promises not to destroy the world again because of human weakness and failure.[3]

> Then Noah built an altar to the Lord and, taking of every clean animal and of every clean bird, he offered burnt offerings on the altar. The Lord smelled the pleasing odor, and the Lord said to Himself: "Never again will I doom the earth because of man, since the devisings of man's mind are evil from his youth; nor will I ever again destroy every living being, as I have done. As long as the earth endures, seedtime and harvest, cold and heat, summer and winter, day and night shall not cease." (Gen. 8:20–22)

This is to be contrasted with the earlier chapters of Genesis, where the Lord, who sees "all that He made and behold it was very good" (Gen. 1:31), reacts to human failure with angry disappointment.

> The Lord saw how great was man's wickedness on earth, and how every plan devised by his mind was nothing but evil all the time. And the Lord regretted that He had made man on earth, and His heart was saddened. And the Lord said: "I will destroy man . . . both man and beast. . . ." (Gen. 6:5–7)

In the Creation story, man and woman are the culmination of the Creation drama and its highest fulfillment. If they fail, all of Creation

33

loses its significance for God. In the covenant with Noah, however, what God promises is to separate His ongoing activity as the Creator of nature from the behavior of human beings. Nature is now endowed with intrinsic significance as a creation of God independent of human behavior. God will no longer destroy nature because of humanity. He distances His activity as Creator of the universe from the extent to which human beings fulfill His hope that their behavior will mirror their being created in the image of God. God moves from Creator to covenant maker when He accepts that divine will alone does not ensure that the human world will mirror His hope and concern for history.

The covenant is the alternative that results from the all-powerful God of Creation's decision to become the limited Lord of history. The covenant with Abraham creates greater space between God and humankind.[4] Abraham stands at Sodom as God's responsible and dignified other. The rabbis noted this in contrasting the behavior of Abraham and Noah. When God told Noah that He was about to destroy the world, Noah accepted the news passively. But when God told Abraham that He was about to destroy merely two evil cities, Abraham pleaded at length on behalf of the innocent who might be destroyed with the guilty (Gen. 18:23–33). In the case of Abraham, indeed, God felt obliged to consult His covenantal partner before implementing His plan.

> Shall I hide from Abraham what I am about to do, since Abraham is to become a great and populous nation and all the nations of the earth are to bless themselves by him? For I have singled him out, that he may instruct his children and his posterity to keep the way of the Lord by doing what is just and right, in order that the Lord may bring about for Abraham what He has promised him. (Gen. 18:17–19)

The development toward covenantal responsibility reaches its paradigmatic expression in the moment of Sinai, when a whole nation is commissioned to implement in its total way of life the will of God as expressed in the *mitzvot*.[5] The covenant mediated by the *mitzvot* continues the shift of the frame of reference from a theocentric drama in which God seeks to maintain total control (the creation story) to a covenantal drama (history) in which a human community is charged with the responsibility of rebuilding a society that will reveal the presence of God in human life. "And I shall be sanctified in the midst of the community of Israel" (Lev. 22:32).

34

Intimacy and Action

Within the collective framework established on the basis of the Sinaitic revelation, one can distinguish a variety of modes of expression of the covenantal life of the community. Since a covenant brings those who participate in it closer together, many of those modes express forms of relational intimacy deriving from the covenant.

One very powerful symbol of intimacy between God and His people is the Temple: "Let them make Me a sanctuary that I may dwell among them" (Ex. 25:8). The Temple sacrifices had two purposes: they expressed the ongoing relationship of intimacy between God and Israel, and they sought to restore that intimacy whenever it was disrupted by the failings of human beings. There were therefore both offerings of thanksgiving and sin offerings, and also both offerings on behalf of the community as a whole and individual offerings.

The sin offerings were not concerned with redemption of the community or with salvation of the individual. The key concept is not redemption or salvation, but an atonement that restores the intimacy with God after it has been disrupted by sin or defilement. Daily sacrifices were offered on behalf of the community. Individual sacrifices were offered by anyone who had suffered defilement and had gone "outside the camp" until he or she was purified; they marked reentry into the community of the covenant. Thus even the individual sacrifices had a collective significance in that they maintained and restored the coherence of the community chosen at Sinai.

A second mode of intimacy with God, as developed by the tradition, was provided by the three great pilgrimage festivals of Pesah (Passover), Shavuot (Weeks), and Sukkot (Tabernacles). These expressed the historical consciousness of the community. The community met God in specific moments of the year to recall its great past encounters with God during the series of events by which He had brought His people out of Egyptian servitude, revealed His Torah at Sinai, and lovingly guided them through the sojourn in the desert. Whereas the intimacy that grows from sacrifice and prayer expresses the feeling that God is daily involved in one's individual personal life, the intimacy that grows from the festivals expresses the profound sense of solidarity with the whole historical community of Israel (*knesset Yisrael*)—it expresses oneness with all the generations of Jewish history. The Exodus, the receiving of the Torah, and the sojourn in the desert are not historical moments of the past which occurred to one specific generation, but a felt, personal, immediate experience of every generation. The coven-

35

antal consciousness bridges generations in history and makes those historical events into an immediate experience.

No matter in which historical conditions Jews may live, Halakhah has taught them to transcend the time of everyday experience (*hol*) and enter into the symbolic covenantal time of biblical history (*kedushat zeman*), so that they feel they are loved, protected, and liberated by God. The covenantal consciousness that grows from participating in symbolic sacred time (the festivals) enables the Jew to pray with the certainty that longing for God's redemptive love is not a vain aspiration.[6] The reality of symbolic time makes ordinary, everyday time bearable and fills it with hope.

A further very powerful mode of intimacy which mediated the covenantal identity of Israel was the weekly observance of the Sabbath. The Sabbath reminds Jews of the liberation from Egypt, of the Genesis drama of Creation, and of the intimate covenantal relationship of God with Israel. Jews bear witness, through abstaining from particular forbidden weekday work activities, that the world they live in is a creation. The holiness of the Sabbath is expressed not primarily through prayers in the synagogue but by the way one celebrates the total day. As Heschel beautifully understood, the Sabbath is a total day that envelops the community with the direct sense of God's presence.[7]

So far, covenantal Judaism has been described in terms of the modes of direct relational intimacy deriving from it. But there is another aspect of the covenant, which is also integral to it despite having been overshadowed by the experiential modes of intimacy during the centuries of exile. Besides the *covenant of intimacy* there is also the *covenant of social and political action*. In the Bible, God did not just give us the commandments forming the basis of intimacy; He also commanded that we build a kingdom, a social, economic, and political structure that mirrors the sanctifying activity of His presence in the world. On one day a week we are commanded to set the world aside, but otherwise we are commanded to be involved in it. The covenantal drama is not limited only to moments of participation in symbolic time, but also extends to the days of *hol*, of life in the secular world.[8]

In Leviticus 19, the concept of a holy community takes into account a whole range of activities that are not only related to symbolic time and ritual. "You shall be holy" (Lev. 19:2) implies not merely observing the Sabbath, abhorring idolatry, and eating sacrificial food within two days (19:3–8), but also making provision for the poor, outlawing theft and fraud, and maintaining justice (19:9–15), among many other demands, both ritual and social. The religious impulse that infuses this

36

whole variety of domains of life expresses the fact that God wants to be present in the totality of human experience.

Leviticus 19 acts as a corrective to any attempt at identifying holiness with separation from the everyday rhythms of reality. The election of Israel implies that the unity of experience, not one isolated fragment of experience, is to mediate covenantal religious consciousness. Holiness has to be embodied in the political framework of the community.[9] It is not an invitation for single individuals to withdraw in monastic silence.

The aspiration to make God present in some important way in all realms of life thus underlies the spirit behind those commandments that lead to a different social, economic, and political regime. The covenantal experience can be divided between moments when the reality of divinity is felt in a direct, personal way (moments of holy time, prayer) and times when the focus of consciousness is on interpersonal, social, and political behavior, when the God-awareness recedes into the background and is felt as an organizing framework, but lacks the intensity of those *mitzvot* which expresses relational intimacy.[10]

Learning and Prayer

When the last king of Judah and the leaders of the people are exiled to Babylon, Jeremiah prophesies a return within seventy years. There is indeed a return, but not of the kind envisaged by Jeremiah and Ezekiel.[11] The contrast with the triumphal entry of Joshua is even more evident. There are no conquering armies, no collapsing walls of Jericho. Instead of twelve tribes, only a small band of individuals returns to Jerusalem. A new Temple is built, but it is a modest structure instead of the grand building described in detail with its institutions by Ezekiel. Zerubbabel did not become the expected messianic king; he was appointed by the Great King of Persia to be governor of the Jerusalem area, a minor regional official who faded out of Jewish history.

Faced with repeatedly disappointed or only partially fulfilled expectations, the covenantal community could have reacted in various ways. It could have lost faith in the plausibility and effectiveness of the covenantal promises. Or it could have postponed all its expectations to some "great day of the Lord" when God would intervene to set the whole world to rights, though He was withdrawn from active involvement in history in the meantime. This was the way of Jewish apocalyptic writers, whose proclamations of the approaching terrible acts of God were implicit confessions of their own feelings of impotence. The way

37

chosen by Ezra and Nehemiah, however, was to seize the limited opportunities offered by an imperial ruler friendly to his Jewish subjects (compare Nehemiah 2 and Ezra 7).

Rabbinic Judaism continued this spirit developed in difficult exilic conditions when it gave the community new forms for expressing its solidarity and covenantal identity. The rabbinic period saw an expansion of community experiences, such as prayer and the public reading of the Torah, which served to reinforce covenantal consciousness. Through liturgical celebration, Jews reminded one another that their memories were not illusions. The synagogue and communal prayer became a framework for sensing the presence of God within the community. After the Temple was destroyed and the sacrifices ceased, any ten Jews who gathered together in prayer nonetheless bore witness to the ever-present love of God in their midst.

The community, wherever it found itself, now became the active carrier of God's presence in history. God, as it were, became portable through having become embodied in the halakhic life of the community. Sanctification of God was manifested not only by the grand historical drama of Ezekiel or by heroic acts of martyrdom, but also by the personal lives of pious Jews whose actions made God beloved of their fellows.[12]

Yet it would be a fundamental error to regard this development as a tendency in Judaism toward neutralizing the significance of the land.[13] The same forms of prayer that enabled Jewish communities to feel the constant presence of God were also designed to remind them of their connection with Jerusalem and the Temple. Wherever Jews lived in the Diaspora, they prayed facing toward Jerusalem. The hours of their prayers were determined in reference to the times of the daily Temple sacrifices. Daily petitional prayer included reference to the national consciousness and the hope of return.[14] Although prophets had ceased to arise and proclaim afresh the covenantal promises, the prophetic voice lived on through being absorbed into the language of prayer.

As the Mishnah, the Talmud, and the subsequent halakhic literature emerged, the Jews became increasingly a community of learning as well as a community of prayer. God was present not only when the community engaged in prayer but equally when it was engaged in Torah study.[15]

Consciousness of the importance of learning expressed itself in many ways. The Mishnah asserts, "A bastard who is a *talmid hakham* takes precedence over a high priest who is ignorant" (Horayot 3:7). The Talmud recounts how the Jews were following the high priest after the service until they caught sight of two scholars who were converts to

Judaism; they left the high priest and followed the scholars (Yoma 71b). Learning reversed the traditional social distinctions: "Be careful of the children of the poor, for from them shall go forth Torah" (Nedarim 71a). Almost as soon as a child could speak, it was told: "Moses commanded us a Torah, the inheritance of the congregation of Jacob" (Deut. 33:4). The Yiddish folksong asks, "What is the most precious commodity? That Yankele should learn Torah." It was an honor to take a poor scholar into one's house, feed him, and marry him to one's daughter with a generous dowry.

The exaltation of learning, however, always contained in itself the danger that the original purpose of learning might be forgotten. The talmudic dictum insists that "great is learning when it leads to practice" (Kiddushin 40b, etc.); but once all hopes of renewed political independence had been postponed to the days of the Messiah and the larger vision of Judaism diminished, learning could become a virtue in its own right. As the centuries of Exile went by and all the sporadic messianic movements ended in complete disaster, the Jews acquired a leadership that was highly skilled at guiding them within the framework of the covenant of intimacy, but recoiled with repugnance against any attempt to turn the Jews once again into a community that mirrored the full scope of covenantal Judaism.[16]

The *talmid hakham* is highly competent in dealing with the halakhic minutiae of frameworks for expressing the passion of the covenant of intimacy. But he is often silent or reticent before the larger demands of the covenant of action. His covenantal consciousness is directed toward religious celebration within the confines of the family, the school, and the synagogue, not toward the political realm. The challenge to articulate a Judaism that will be mirrored in the total life of a nation was postponed to the messianic era. The task in an unredeemed world was to expand upon those covenantal *mitzvot* that reinforce the unique identity and separation of Israel from the surrounding nations and religions. Holiness became identified with *mitzvot* like those dealing with marital sexual relationships and dietary laws.[17]

Secular Zionism in Revolt

The conceptions developed in the preceding sections can be used to give a characterization of the rise of Zionism and the responses to Zionism in the Jewish religious community. Zionism began over a century ago as a revolt against the conception of the Jewish people as a community of prayer and learning that had resolved to restrict the covenant

39

of political action in history until the days of the Messiah. However, the early Zionists by no means rejected the Jewish heritage in its entirety. In many cases, they treated the Bible not only as the greatest literary treasure of the revived Hebrew language but also as a major source of the ethical norms that would guide the Jews in rebuilding their ancient homeland. Although their exaltation of the Bible and disparagement of rabbinic literature may have been influenced by the attitudes of Christian theologians, just as their Jewish nationalism obviously drew inspiration from other nineteenth-century national movements, it may be asked to what extent the suppressed political activism of Judaism also played a role. Those who came from traditional families had been brought up on texts that contained echoes of the larger covenantal vision, despite the restraints on response to those echoes. The example of other national movements encouraged the casting aside of the restraints, allowing the suppressed activism to reassert itself and mingle with those elements of Zionism that were borrowed from European political ideologies of the period.

Zionism found it difficult to harmonize these ideas drawn from diverse sources. While agreed on the need to recreate an independent Jewish polity, the early Zionists went in all imaginable directions in the theological domain. Some were avowed atheists, others wanted to restore a biblical faith untrammeled by the rabbinic tradition, others were devotees of land mysticism or a religion of labor. Many were agreed, for example, on the necessity of devising new formats in which to celebrate the traditional Jewish festivals, but no agreement could be reached on what formats to adopt. In Israel today, there are still kibbutzim that celebrate Passover according to their own Haggadah as a "spring festival"; but nonreligious families typically hold a traditional Passover meal with all the usual customs, yet without halakhic commitment to what they are reciting and doing. This is not, however, perceived by most Zionists as a serious problem. If one strips away the external trappings of traditional sentimentality found in many Zionists' appreciation of Jewish customs, one discovers at the heart and vitality of their Jewish commitment the belief that concern for the survival of the Jewish people and commitment to the State of Israel are the new substitutes for traditional Judaism.[18]

The mainstream of Zionist thought rejected the traditional view that the covenant with God at Sinai was constitutive of Jewish self-understanding. For many Zionists, identification with the historical destiny of the nation was not only necessary for being a Jew; it was also sufficient. Judaism, they would say, formerly had instrumental value in preserving this nation from disintegration in exile, but Zionism, through

40

the state, has now provided a more effective instrument with which to make possible the continued existence of the Jewish people in history.

Religious Anti-Zionism

The reaction of traditional religious circles to early Zionism was intensely hostile. The fact that various European nations were regaining their independence had no significance for them. In their expectations, the third Jewish commonwealth could not arise out of political developments in the secular world, but would represent a sharp break in the succession of normal political events.[19] Nothing had happened to suggest the imminent fulfillment of the prophecies of Isaiah and Jeremiah. What they were waiting for was not handfuls of pioneers draining swamps, but a Jewish restoration having the assurance and finality promised by the following statement in the Jerusalem Talmud (Kiddushin 2:1): "Although your fathers were redeemed, they returned to being subjugated; but when you are redeemed, you shall never again be subjugated."

In an attenuated form, the same skepticism about Zionism is maintained today by Agudat Israel. The Agudah rationalizes its representation in Israel's parliament and its participation in government coalitions by pointing out how many of its own educational institutions benefit from government support. In Israel as elsewhere, it cooperates with the secular powers that be, but this must not be taken to imply any legitimization of Zionism or to ascribe any religious significance to the present Jewish state. The Agudah's academies of learning do not celebrate Israel's Independence Day. No prayers of thanksgiving are uttered for the reestablishment of Jewish national autonomy, although prayers may be offered for the safety of those fighting in Israel's defense forces.

Religious anti-Zionists certainly believe in the importance of *ahavat Yisrael* (love of Israel). No one committed to traditional Judaism can ignore the importance in Judaism of the *mitzvah* of love for one's fellow Jew.[20] In the tradition, however, commitment to the well-being of the nation was never seen as a substitute for the Torah and God. The commitment to the perpetuation of the Jewish people results from the belief that Israel is the bearer of God's message in history. Separate the message from the people and all meaning in being Jewish is destroyed. When Jewish nationhood is severed from its covenantal roots and becomes the ultimate, absolute value for the Jewish people, then what is an important *mitzvah* in Judaism becomes a new form of idolatry which must be rejected by one who is loyal to the Torah and God. What is

41

interesting about modern Judaism is the fact that this was not the only religious response to secular Zionism.

Messianic Religious Zionism

As the return to the Land of Israel gathered pace, religious elements also began to join the secular Zionist revolution. They could not resist the attraction of the early Zionist achievements and of the promised Jewish national home. When some sought to justify their participation in the Jewish march toward political independence, they found themselves obliged to claim that Zionism was in some sense a prelude to the coming of the Messiah.[21] For centuries, the only political category in traditional Jewish circles had been the messianic kingdom. Consequently, any attempt to abolish the situation of exile had to be justified within the framework of realizing the messianic promise. The best-known attempt of this kind was provided by the philosophy of Rabbi Kook, mentioned earlier. Kook offered an argument similar to Hegel's "cunning of reason": the socialist Zionists trying to build a secular utopia were God's instrument for achieving Jewish redemption. They thought that their efforts would lead to a socialistic Jewish state in which the Jewish religion would be an anachronism; but God would divert the course of events so as to turn the Jews into "a kingdom of priests and a holy nation" (Ex. 19:6). Who is to judge how the Lord of history chooses to bring about His ultimate design for the world? With this argument, Kook justified the decision of observant Jews to join forces with a secular political movement that purported to supersede Halakhah and Jewish covenantal consciousness.

Theological presuppositions of this kind enabled religious elements to forge a partnership with socialist Zionists during both the British Mandate and the early decades of the State of Israel. The political implications of such presuppositions, however, became apparent after the Six-Day War, which unleashed the potential force of these messianic longings among a substantial number of militant religious nationalists. The expansion of the territory under Israeli control to encompass most of the Promised Land was seen as confirmation that the establishment of the messianic kingdom was in the process of realization. There was a rush to set up rudimentary settlements in large numbers of places, on the assumption that Israel would shortly be swamped by the Ingathering of Exiles. As with all previous messianic expectations, reality proved otherwise. The succeeding years saw the reverses of the Yom

42

Kippur War, a drying up of Jewish immigration, and the disillusionment accompanying the final stages of the withdrawal from Sinai.

In spite of the progressive deterioration of the ecstatic mood of the Six-Day War, the dominant religious ideological perspective of religious Zionism today is still Kook's messianic theology. The vitality of the religious youth movements is still nurtured by teachings that come out of the Kook tradition. Given the predominance of this religious messianism and its accompanying concern that all of the biblical Promised Land remain under Jewish sovereignty, how the religious community will respond to a peace process that may eventually demand territorial compromise is an acute political issue whose outcome many are afraid to predict. For many supporters of Gush Emunim, a messianic movement consisting of observant Jews who insist on settling in the area occupied by Israel in 1967, loyalty to the political authority of the government cannot be at the expense of the messianic redemptive destiny of Israel. Any political compromise regarding the biblical map of Israel would undermine the very legitimacy of the Zionist enterprise. It is politically and spiritually urgent, therefore, that we find new channels for a religious appreciation of Israel's rebirth which do not link the significance of our return to political nationhood with the prophetic aspiration of messianic redemption.

A Covenantal Perspective on Zionism

Religious Zionism does not need to treat the rise of Israel as a divine ruse on the way toward realizing the messianic kingdom. There is an alternative perspective from which one can religiously embrace the secular Zionist invitation to return to the land, namely, the observation that Israel expands the possible range of halakhic involvement in human affairs beyond the circumscribed borders of home and synagogue to the public domain. Jews in Israel are given the opportunity to bring economic, social, and political issues into the center of their religious consciousness. The moral quality of the army, social and economic disparities and deprivations, the exercise of power moderated by moral sensitivities, attitudes toward minorities and the stranger, tolerance and freedom of conscience—all these are realms that may engage our sense of covenantal responsibility.[22] The existence of the State of Israel, from this perspective, prevents Judaism from being defined exclusively as a culture of learning and prayer. The realm of symbolic holy time is no longer the exclusive defining framework of Jewish identity.[23] In returning to the land, we have created the conditions through which everyday life can mediate the biblical foundations for our covenantal identity.

At first blush, the claim that the Zionist revolution has brought the demands of the covenant of action back to Jewish spiritual conscious-ness seems totally unrelated to the living conditions of Israeli society. Religious intensity in Israel is found chiefly in two camps: either the traditional ghettolike spirituality that characterized Judaism for the last centuries, or the messianic religious passion that is mediated by Gush Emunim and adherents of Rabbi Kook's theology of history.

The halakhic tendencies in the former camp reflect a conscious re-pudiation of modernity. There is not an atmosphere of celebration of the new religious opportunities that statehood has made possible, but rather plain disregard of them. The bulk of halakhic *responsa* still deal with the same halakhic questions that occupied religious leaders in our long exilic history, such as *kashrut* and marriage. Even the sabbatical and Jubilee years, which seem to touch on the social and economic vision of Judaism, have been reduced to questions of what type of food one is permitted to eat in the sabbatical year.

Furthermore, the establishment of the State of Israel has not in any way affected religious practices in the community. It has not created a hunger, be it among the observant or the secular, for a new spiritual appreciation of Jewish history. It would not be far-fetched to say that Israel is the last haven in the world for a secular Jew to feel comfortable and integrated into his or her social environment. In contrast to the Diaspora, there is a much sharper repudiation of traditional Judaism in Israeli Jewish society than in any other Jewish community around the world. If anything, moreover, antireligious feeling has been growing in response to the self-assertion of certain groups of observant Jews.

As for the second camp, those who claim that Israel is part of a nec-essary messianic drama need not be disturbed by the prevalence of secularism in Israel. On the contrary, Kook's theology of history enables them to regard the secular revolution as merely a temporary phase in God's scheme for bringing about the eventual establishment of His messianic kingdom in history. The belief in the inevitability of the mes-sianic redemptive process enables many religious Zionists to minimize the importance of the widespread lack of serious religious observance and sensitivity in the country. One can dance with Ariel Sharon on religious festivals with the same enthusiasm as *yeshivah* students dance with their Torah teachers. Army generals who lead us to victory serve the messianic process. What makes an act religious is not necessarily the motivation of the agent but the consequences that result from this act. Many atheists or religiously indifferent persons both in the army and in political life are perceived as pawns in the hands of the Lord of history, Who has seen fit to utilize the military and political power of a secular Zionist state to bring about the triumph of His messianic scheme.

How, then, can I legitimately give some plausibility to my own perspective in spite of what seems to be such countervailing evidence to the contrary? My answer will have two parts. The first will offer a positive appreciation of secular Zionism as enriching the covenantal consciousness of Judaism. The second will deal with what attitude toward Halakhah is needed in order to stimulate the Jewish religious community to respond boldly to the new opportunities and challenges that our national political existence makes possible.

The Covenant and Human Responsibility

Above I have argued that a religious person can embrace the State of Israel because it widens the range of halakhic concerns to encompass all aspects of life. From a talmudic perception in which God is mediated in halakhic action, it would be legitimate to claim that any event that challenges us to widen the application of the normative halakhic system intensifies in an important way the sense of God's presence in daily life. I wish, however, to make the stronger claim that the rejection of the traditional posture of waiting for messianic redemption can *itself* be seen as a further elaboration and intensification of the spirit of covenantal responsibility found in the biblical and, above all, in the rabbinic tradition. I am not claiming that this is what the founders of Zionism intended, but rather, that rebuilding the community's national life carries forward in many ways the rabbinic tradition's understanding of the role assigned to human beings in the covenant.

One central theological concern in the rabbinic period was to rethink the notion of divine power. The Exodus drama, the total defeat of Pharaoh, the triumphal victory of Israel over its enemies could not serve as a paradigm for understanding its later exilic powerlessness. The new Pharaoh is not defeated. Titus and his Roman army are victorious. God does not demonstrate Himself to be a "man of war" who defeats His enemies in order that He become known in history. There is a marked distance between the sage Johanan ben Zakkai who meets a Roman general and pleads for the right to build a new religious center in Yavneh and the prophet Moses who meets Pharaoh.[24] Gone is the visible sign of God's triumphal power in history.

To make sense of a living God and to give some plausible explanation to their belief that Israel was still the elect people of God, that the covenant had not been broken, that Israel was not an abandoned community in history, God's power had to be understood in ways which could explain the role of a powerless and vulnerable and often exploited people in history. "Who is as mighty as God?" (Ex. 15:11), sung when Israel crossed the sea, is now midrashically understood to mean "Who is as silent as God?"

> Vespasian sent Titus, who said: "Where is their God, the rock in whom they trusted?" (Deut. 32:37). This was the wicked Titus who blasphemed and insulted heaven. What did he do? He took a harlot by the hand and entered the holy of holies and spread out a scroll of the law and committed a sin on it. He then took out a sword and slashed the curtain. Miraculously, blood spurted out, and he thought that he had slain himself. . . . Abba Hanan said: "Who is a mighty one like Thee, O Jah? (Ps. 89:9)—Who is like Thee, mighty in self-restraint, that Thou didst hear the blaspheming insults of the wicked man and keep silent?" In the school of Rabbi Ishmael, it was taught: "Who is like Thee among the gods (elim)? (Ex. 15:11)—Who is like Thee among the dumb ones (illemim)?" (Gittin 56b)

This new-felt silence and distancing on the part of God does not appear in the rabbinic tradition to lead to insuperable religious despair and feelings of guilt and unworthiness. On the contrary, the sense of God's love is intensified. What mediates for the community God's passionate love for Israel is the Torah.

> Thou hast loved the house of Israel with everlasting love; Thou hast taught us Torah and commandments, statutes and ordinances. Therefore, Lord our God, when we lie down and when we rise up we will speak of Thy statutes, and rejoice in the words of Thy Torah and in Thy commandments forever. (Daily Prayer Book)

A religious consciousness nurtured exclusively by a sense of total dependency upon God would wait for supernatural grace to redeem one from one's wretched human condition. An overwhelming sense of sin, guilt, and unworthiness crushes the spontaneous powers of love within a human being. The suffering condition of Exile, however, did not call into question the love relationship between God and Israel. The absence of God's triumphant power in history was instead met with a profound sense of human awakening, a new unfolding of human intellectual power. The distancing posture on the part of divinity was perceived by the rabbis as an invitation for God's covenantal partner to surface and become a mature human being capable of assuming responsibility for the direction of Torah in human life.

46

They (the scribes and the prophets) are two like agents whom a king sent to a province. With regard to one, he wrote: "If he shows you my signature and seal, trust him, but otherwise do not trust him." With regard to the other, he wrote: "Even if he does not show you my signature and seal, trust him." So of the words of prophecy, it is written: "If there arises in the midst of you a prophet . . . and he gives you a sign" (Deut. 13:2); but of the words of the scribes it is written: "According to the law which they shall teach you" (Deut. 17:11). (Song of Songs Rabbah 1:2)

The scribe, whose leadership grows from his own intellectual competence, is given greater weight than the prophet, whose credentials depend upon the miraculous actions of God. The absence of miracles in the life of Israel's history does not imply divine anger or rejection of Israel. Covenantal history from the rabbinic period onward is built upon a leadership nurtured by a new covenantal appreciation of the role of the community.

In the Bible, the community is called upon to choose between "life and death," between "good and evil" (Deut. 30:15). The revelation of Torah provides a way, a direction for the community, but ultimately the responsibility for its successful implementation is in the hands of the community itself.

In the rabbinic tradition, covenantal consciousness takes on new dimensions. Israel is not only called upon to implement the covenantal norms, but equally to define and expand their content. No longer is God an active interpreter of His own law as in the biblical tradition.[25] Now he is prepared to accept the verdict of the scholars of the rabbinic academy that Torah is "not in heaven" (Deut. 30:12) and that revelation will not define the way Torah is to be applied in new situations.

The covenantal community thus takes upon itself responsibility for how the word of God is to be understood. It responds to the visible weakening of God's triumphant power in history with a new internalization of the word of Revelation through study and an expansion of the powers of love in covenantal religious consciousness. Learning becomes a new central religious passion. Rabbi Akiva, who was one of the forerunners and creative forces in establishing the wide-ranging freedom of the interpretative tradition of the Talmud, reflects in his own life total commitment and love for God, and boldly claims that the paradigmatic book for understanding Israel and God is the Song of Songs. "All the books of the Bible are holy; the Song of Songs is the holy of holies" (Yadayim 3:5). In the rabbinic period, God as Teacher and Lover became central metaphors in making sense of the covenantal relationship with the God of Israel.

Although to make sense of the Torah we neutralized the need for the prophet, we did not neutralize the need for divine, miraculous interference for the reestablishment of our national political existence. Exilic spirituality was characterized by a prayerful longing for a messianic eruption in history in order to solve the problem of Jewish exile and wandering. Jewish political liberation, returning to our covenantal national home, was often modeled upon the paradigm of supernatural grace found in the Exodus from Egypt.[26] Religious Jews were taught to wait with the same patience as the slave community waited for redemption from Egypt.

> Blessed art Thou, O Lord our God, King of the universe, Who has redeemed us and our fathers from Egypt and has brought us to this night on which we eat *matzah* and bitter herbs. O Lord our God and God of our fathers, may we live to celebrate in peace other feasts and holy seasons, joyful in the building of Thy city and happy in Thy service. And there may we eat of the sacrifices and paschal offerings whose blood shall be acceptably sprinkled on the side of Thine altar; then shall we sing unto Thee a new song for our redemption and for the deliverance of our souls. Blessed art Thou, O Lord, who has redeemed Israel! (The Haggadah)

We waited for the "appointed time" for redemption to come. We waited for a messianic figure who would structure once again the full religious significance of our community's political religious aspirations. Liberation would come from forces outside human initiative.

Traditional Jewish hope was nurtured by the belief that the future restoration would not share the vulnerabilities of the previous attempts to build a Jewish society in the Holy Land. The third Jewish commonwealth would last forever. It would be free of all the tragic features of human history. It would usher in a historical period in which humanity would be liberated from sin and suffering would be abolished from human life. In that time, the community would no longer be burdened by the haunting and problematical features of freedom, contingency, and the human propensity for evil.

Secular Zionism created the conditions under which individuals committed to a covenantal perception of Judaism are capable of restoring to Jewish life a national existence not grounded in the need for supernatural grace. The Zionist revolution thus opened up new domains of life to the rabbinic spirit of human initiative by liberating the community from the dominant mood of helpless dependency upon the Lord of history. The drama of the State of Israel is not a messianic unfolding of the final stages in Jewish religious eschatology, but a process that began at Sinai in which Israel was prepared to build its religious life on God's self-limiting love in human history. The lack of God's vis-

48

ible, triumphant victory in history was met in the rabbinic tradition with a new enlivened sense of covenantal intellectual responsibility. The felt distance and silence of God in the modern period of Jewish history can equally be met by assuming a new appreciation of our political responsibility to make the covenant of *mitzvah* find its widest possible application to life.[27]

The political renewal of the Jewish people enables us to set the Lord before us continually. The Lover model of the Song of Songs is now given a political arena, for those who understand that without divine self-limitation there can be no mature, responsible historical role for Israel in the covenantal relationship with God.

One can summarize the different stages of the covenant under the following three headings. The Bible liberated the will of the community to act with responsibility. The Talmud liberated the intellect to define the contents of Torah. Zionism liberated the will of the nation to become politically responsible and to promote the Ingathering of the Exiles without the need for miraculous grace as the condition for reestablishing Israel as a covenantal nation in history.

Tradition and Change

In order to cope effectively with the new challenges to Judaism that surface in Israeli society, it is important to rethink the relationship between Halakhah and the revelatory framework of *mitzvah* and, above all, how one combines respect for the classical Jewish traditions with the need for radical innovation. Halakhah is the ensemble of religious rules and practices defining the Jewish way of life as it has developed over the centuries. Prior to Halakhah is the revelatory category of *mitzvah*. Halakhah is the material concentration of the *mitzvah* framework by the community and its leadership at a specific time and within a specific situation.[28] Halakhah takes the eternal commandments heard in revelation and gives them a particular form suited to the current situation encountered by the listener.

Although the distinction between *mitzvah* and Halakhah is clear in principle, it is not clear where the line is to be drawn in the literary heritage of the Jewish people. Is the Bible *mitzvah* and the Talmud Halakhah? Or are only the Ten Commandments *mitzvah* and already the rest of the Bible Halakhah?[29]

Furthermore, when we listen in today's situation, what do we listen to? Just to the original commandments or also to the records of earlier listening? There have been over two thousand years of listening since

49

the completion of the Bible. And given that we listen to many listeners, to which of them do we have to justify ourselves? To the rabbis of Yavneh or the academies of Babylonia? To the Jews of twelfth-century Andalusia or seventeenth-century Amsterdam or nineteenth-century Lithuania? Or to the halakhic teachers of our generation?[30]

Traditional halakhic thinking is often conservative on account of its fundamental need to demonstrate its essential continuity with the past. Precedent and reinterpretation are the forms through which new legal decisions are normally introduced into the community. The continuity of the interpretative tradition is essential for legal continuity. What happens, however, when there are ruptures in the sense of continuity? What do we do when we meet new situations that cannot in good conscience be covered and justified within the framework of precedent?

The confused reaction of the Israeli rabbinate to the influx of Ethiopian Jews is a conspicuous example of radical new situations that emerge in Israeli society, situations that cannot be dealt with on the basis of the classical principles of the halakhic tradition. The Ethiopian Jewish community was totally cut off from the ongoing interpretative discussion of the Law for as long as two millennia. How can they be made welcome in a framework bound completely by the teachings of halakhic thinkers of the last three centuries?

Here is a Jewish community that defined its religious self-awareness by the covenantal categories of the Bible, a community that had a lively sense of *mitzvah*, as shown by their strict observance of the laws of family purity. Here is a community that stood valiantly in opposition to all forms of idolatry and proudly proclaimed before a hostile world the unity of the imageless God of history. What weight should a halakhic jurist give to their rejection of idolatry in considering their status as contemporary Jews? Is their unconditional and heroic commitment to biblical frameworks sufficient to qualify the Ethiopian Jews for immediate entry into a rabbinically trained religious community with its own uncompromising halakhic consciousness? Is the total commitment to covenantal *mitzvah* a sufficient basis, or must we have agreement on the elaborate concretization of the notion of *mitzvah* in the various halakhic forms that were elaborated during the history of rabbinic Judaism?

Yeshayahu Leibowitz has claimed that one of the sources of the failure to respond adequately and boldly to the new situations lies in the fact that the halakhic community has been confined too strictly by legal precedents and exilic traditions in its thinking about contemporary Halakhah. In the early 1950s, he called for a new way of doing Halakhah, one which is not necessarily bound by notions of precedent and reinterpretation.[31] He did not believe that the existing religious judges were capable of moving the Halakhah in new directions. He therefore appealed to the community to act, thereby creating new Halakhah through the living practice of the community independent of the accepted patterns of halakhic decision-making.

Leibowitz understood that Zionism and the establishment of the State of Israel must create new patterns of thought for the way we develop Halakhah. His work is an important example of how a serious halakhic thinker struggles to make sense of the profound commitment to serve God through *mitzvah,* together with the decision to create a qualitatively new Jewish political reality.

When one enters a totally new frame of reference, no adequate solutions for the development of Halakhah can be found without in some way regaining awareness of the wide range of values that inspired the development of the legal tradition. What may unite our own halakhic response with the practice of the covenantal community across history is not necessarily identical halakhic forms, but the seriousness with which we respond to the *mitzvot* and our commitment to continuing the covenantal identity and destiny of Israel. What we need to learn from the past is not so much how they solved particular problems, or what were the particular forms of their social, economic, and political halakhic frameworks, but rather the underlying spirit and tendency that infused their Halakhah.

In the modern world, for instance, we cannot go back to the agrarian framework of biblical society. The Bible reflects the connection of family and tribe to fixed geographical areas, the lack of a money economy, and other conditions incompatible with modern modes of economic organization. If, therefore, we want to treat the State of Israel as an opportunity to reinstitute the laws of the sabbatical and Jubilee years, we must seek to uncover the spirit of those laws. We must consider how the concern with egalitarianism, with preventing permanent economic dependence of one social group on another, and with counteracting any sense of total domination over the land or over other human beings, can find expression in contemporary economic and political thought. The biblical warning that exile comes because of the lack of observance of those laws can stimulate us to seek ways of avoiding long-term debts for housing for our children, alienation of workers from creativity, manipulation by concentrations of economic power.

The sabbatical year can have little significance for us if—as happens now—our religious communities are concerned merely with such questions as whether we are permitted to eat the crops of Jewish farmers or only those of non-Jewish ones during that year. We need instead to see the significance of the sabbatical year as an insistence that Sabbath consciousness should not be restricted to notions of intimacy in the life of Jews in their homes, but should also give direction to economic growth in a Jewish society. Similarly, if we conceived of the Jubilee year as concerned only with such requirements as giving slaves their freedom, it can mean nothing to us today, given that the biblical form of slavery does not exist in our society. Yet the demand to liberate "one who must sell himself because of economic deprivation" can have a deep meaning if we relate it to the modern tendency to invest most of human initiative and self-worth in achieving a secure economic place in society. A society that sees human dignity only in terms of economic status is implicitly undermining the covenantal understanding of the God of Creation, inasmuch as "beloved is man created in the image of God" (Avot 3:14) can be seen as demanding that our society enhance the individual uniqueness of each of its members.

Again, the traditional Halakhah includes a considerable amount of legislation concerning the king and the hereditary monarchy. There is a great gap between those laws and modern parliamentary democratic sensibilities. Yet one can learn a great deal from the spirit of those laws as it expresses itself in the discussions of the Talmud and of the *Mishneh Torah* of Maimonides. The notion underlying many laws of the king is that awareness of the temptations and corruptions of power should be built into the framework in which the king acts. In modern terms, this would imply that those who hold positions of authority and responsibility in society must be imbued with a higher normative and moral consciousness.[32]

The issues facing the future of Judaism are momentous. Never before in Jewish history has there been a concentration in one political framework of such intense yet diverse ideological positions regarding the meaning of Jewish history and Jewish identity. In a situation of such ambiguity and complexity, it is understandable why we are witnessing the tendency toward such extreme polarity between the religious and secular communities. The profound repudiation of the quest for normalcy and dialogue with the world by the majority of the religiously observant community in Israel is symptomatic of the unease that this community feels at the totally new spiritual challenges that Israel invites one to confront. The level of intolerance and anxiety found in religious discussions is an important indication of how threatening and uncertain is the challenge of modernity to Judaism.

For Judaism to flourish in a modern liberal, democratic state, we must strive for a change in religious sensibility, a moving away from the self-enclosed ghetto mentality in which Judaism nurtured its perception of God and the community out of the fixed parameters of traditional texts and insisted that God has in His world "only the four cubits of the Halakhah."

> Ben Bag-Bag said: "Study the Torah again and again, for everything is contained in it; constantly examine it, grow old and gray over it, and swerve not from it, for there is nothing more excellent than it." (Avot 5:25)

Modern Israel challenges the traditional posture which defined all of Jewish experience through the framework of Halakhah and Torah. The shifting frameworks of historical events, the different values of human cultures, have entered into the daily functioning of a self-conscious Jewish community. The radical change from a ghetto halakhic, religious sensibility to one that welcomes the new possibilities of discussion with the world is the underlying challenge that the modern Jewish quest for normalcy presents to traditional Judaism. How we respond to this challenge will define the future direction of both Judaism and the Jewish people.

This essay has been an attempt to offer an initial framework for the way in which one committed to traditional Judaism can embrace the rebirth of Jewish nationhood with a sense of joy and dignity. The rabbinic tradition responded with creative intellectual boldness to the new spiritual needs that the destruction of the Temple and exile brought for Jewish history. Rabbinic Judaism succeeded in perpetuating the halakhic community in an alien and often hostile world. Modern Judaism must learn from the innovative spirit of the talmudic tradition, even as it moves completely away from the self-sufficient, insular framework of rabbinic Judaism. Our covenantal conscience must not be nurtured by a vision of Halakhah which thrives on its repudiation of that which is other than Judaism. The rabbinic tradition taught us how to develop a spiritual culture in isolation from the world. Our task is to develop a sense of covenantal holiness while feeling integrated and part of the larger framework of different human cultures.

"And You Shall Love the Lord Your God"

Two Perspectives on the Religious Significance of Israel

The Religious Struggle of
Yeshayahu Leibowitz

T he Jewish world is familiar with Martin Buber, Franz Rosenzweig, Mordecai Kaplan, Abraham Heschel, and Joseph Soloveitchik; they are regarded as leading intellectual figures who have shaped modern religious thought. By contrast, Yeshayahu Leibowitz is little known outside Israel. Yet if one were to conduct a survey within Israel to determine which Jewish philosopher and religious thinker is most talked about and argued with, undoubtedly Leibowitz's name would appear at or near the top of the list.

Leibowitz's thinking is deeply anchored in the Israeli context. He does not address himself to the problems of religion in modern society in general, but conducts an ongoing critique of Israeli society in the light of Judaism and a critique of Judaism itself in the light of the Jewish revolution constituted by the creation of Israel. Given that his critical thrust goes in both directions—from Judaism to Israel and vice versa— one need not be surprised by the apparent paradoxes in his writings. On the one hand, Leibowitz is a Jewish patriot who, from his youth onward, rejected the Jewish people's subservience to alien political rule. On the other hand, one could scarcely find a harsher critic of chauvinistic manifestations within the Israeli establishment. When he denounces trends in Israel, therefore, it is not with the moral pathos of an alienated Jewish universalist intellectual, but with the conviction of an unwavering Zionist who fought in Israel's War of Independence and is proud of his numerous grandchildren, all living in the land. He never speaks in a tone of hopeful prayer about the future of the Jewish people because his concern is with the Jewish people as it is living today.

Another paradox is that Leibowitz is a strictly observant Jew who has not greatly influenced the majority of the religious community, but who awakens notable interest among secular circles that would otherwise be very averse to hearing moral lessons delivered by anyone wearing a *kippah* (skullcap). Despite his age, his energy matches the endless demands upon him as a public speaker, not only before his academic colleagues but at every level of society. From Dan to Beersheba, Leibowitz is invited to speak to all kinds of audiences on all sorts of occasions. He will be found addressing teachers in the north and farmers in the south. No audience is beyond his concern. Although the polemical tone of his statements and ripostes can be biting, he maintains an underlying respect for every group, be it academics, professionals, or laborers, Jewish or Arab. He will address an audience of thousands or of five people. If invited to participate in a symposium in some remote area, he will still be answering questions at three in the morning when fellow speakers half his age have gone home to bed.

In his academic pursuits, too, Leibowitz displays a versatility that many would envy. The university knows him for his serious scientific research and as a teacher of the philosophy of science. Thousands listen to his regular radio lectures on Pirkei Avot, Maimonides, and other Jewish sources. He has been deeply involved in adult education and served for years as the editor of the *Hebrew Encyclopedia*.

Every complexity and ambivalence of Israel, be it the moral and religious problematics of the country, the struggle to write a new chapter in Jewish history, the conflicts between messianists and antimessianists, religious and secularists, territorial maximalists and minimalists, the whole dynamism and confusion of Israeli intellectual and spiritual life—all these are reflected in the thought of Yeshayahu Leibowitz.

The Challenge to Judaism

Leibowitz is not alone in seeing the creation of Israel as a fundamental challenge to Judaism. In order to understand how he approaches the problem, however, his basic views on the nature of Judaism must be outlined.

According to Leibowitz, Judaism is fundamentally a communal frame of reference. Its prime concern is not with saving the soul of the individual but with providing a way of life whereby a community can express its commitment to serve God. The religious impulse motivating Judaism is the decision of a people to bear witness to the presence of God in the world through its worship and its way of life. Halakhah gives expression to the way that this community lives out its existence and defines its place in the world.

For long periods, the Jewish people was viewed by others and saw itself as a nation constituted by the rule of Torah. To Leibowitz, however, what made Jews different from other nations was not their theology; other religions share basic assumptions of Jewish monotheism, eschatology, and the like. Nor did their Bible distinguish them, for it has also been adopted by the Christians. What made the Jews unique was the Halakhah that governed their way of life. The laws governing what Jews could eat, which days they were allowed to work, when sexual relations were permitted, as well as the laws on the liturgical forms for daily and festive worship—all these structured and institutionalized the Jewish community and provided its distinct character.

The essential point for Leibowitz is that the primacy of Halakhah in Judaism is not a theological judgment but an empirical description of what in fact occurred in history. He points out that the Jewish community could tolerate hostile theological tendencies in its midst. Maimonides, for example, could regard the theology of many of his fellow Jews as mythological and even pagan, while the critics of Maimonides claimed that his theology had been corrupted by ideas taken from Greek philosophy. However, there would be no comparable toleration of conflicting halakhic practice. Those who held minority halakhic views were allowed to state them, but in their practice they were required to conform to the established majority outlook. What made the Jews a distinct communal entity in history was their commitment to serve God through a shared form of disciplined life, irrespective of their competing and contradictory conceptions of God.

Such was the character of the Jewish community until the beginning of Jewish emancipation at the end of the eighteenth century. From then on, the Jewish community's self-understanding began to break down, giving rise to what Leibowitz sees as one of the crucial questions for Judaism in the modern world. Emancipation, when it afforded the Jew the opportunity of merging completely into the surrounding non-Jewish culture, provided competition with the Jew's traditional self-understanding. One attempt to meet that challenge was the emergence of trends within Judaism that sought to amend or even abandon much of Halakhah, while preserving the synagogue as a place of worship. Secular Zionism constituted an even more powerful form of competition, since it was an ideology that aimed to redefine the Jewish people in wholly nonreligious terms as a national political community.

As I see it, the challenge to Judaism in Israel is therefore very different from the challenge in the Western Diaspora. In the latter, the assimilatory framework with which Judaism is competing is one that threatens to dissolve the Jewish ethnic group, to absorb the Jews in such a way that they are no longer identifiable as Jews. In Israel, there are two competing Jewish frameworks, both of which claim to be Jewish. One asserts that it continues Jewish history through a radical transformation of Jewish society and self-definition. The other maintains

59

that the Jewish community is doomed if it abandons its religious roots. However, Leibowitz himself does not see any essential difference between the situation in Israel and the Diaspora because he does not see any specific Jewish content in Zionism.

In the Diaspora, Jews can argue that Judaism is the necessary instrument for maintaining their identity as a particular community. That argument loses its force in the Israeli context, where there is another Jewish frame of reference, a total social, political framework that gives its members an identity as Jews. Hanging on to religion merely as an instrument for perpetuating Jewish identity makes no sense in a society whose total national political framework already gives Jews an anchorage for their identity. This fact will be very important when we discuss Leibowitz's theology, in which he argues strongly against making Judaism an instrumental value serving the perpetuation of the Jewish people.

In Israel, the religious framework is obliged to be self-justifying, not merely instrumental. It must have intrinsic significance if it is to claim Israelis within their society. Therefore, it is often impossible for Diaspora communities to understand why in Israel Judaism is talked about so much in terms of faith and religious commitment and so rarely in terms of the sociological identity frameworks about which one often hears in the Diaspora.

Leibowitz's constant argument against the secular option for defining the continuity of Jewish history is that it is a distortion of the historical framework of the Jewish people. His argument not only springs from the framework of faith but is also a purely empirical one. To claim continuity with the historical Jewish people and yet abandon Halakhah, to abandon worship of God as the essential framework of Jewish identity, is a falsification of what in fact existed in history.

To Leibowitz, the halakhic way of life is a historical fact. Halakhah is primary for understanding the visible presence and action of this community in history. Leibowitz consequently disagrees both with the religious Zionists who have joined the revolution to build political statehood and with the secular Zionists who claim to continue Jewish history although abandoning the halakhic framework. The next sections will deal with Leibowitz's criticisms of both these groups within Israeli society.

The Critique of the Religious Zionist Community

As was indicated, Judaism is for Leibowitz a way of life for a community to demonstrate in its actions and intentions its willingness to worship God in an unredeemed world (in a world that pursues its natural course). The essential subject of Judaism is not the individual but a community. Judaism is not meant to offer a way in which the individual can overcome the problems of finitude, sin, and death and find eternal salvation; it is a historical phenomenon through which a community expresses its commitment to worship God. This is axiomatic for Leibowitz and has enormous implications for his approach to the religious Zionist community and the religious opportunities that reborn Jewish statehood may afford. Hence, although he does not agree, Leibowitz understands that sector of the religious community which sees the Zionist decision for national renewal and political independence as an act of Satan, a deviation from the religious value system of the Jewish people. To the anti-Zionist ultra-Orthodox religious community, autonomous political life will be legitimate for the Jewish people only in a future eschatological messianic reality. The laws of Judaism, as they see them, require Jews to live under the rulership of alien powers. Political subjugation, alienation, lack of responsibility for the social, economic, and political conditions of society are part of the burden that the Jew must carry as long as the era of exile is not replaced by the era of the Messiah. The idea that Judaism should encompass all the social, political, and economic frameworks of society, in order to make possible total responsible citizenship, it is a messianic category. Therefore, one must be loyal to Halakhah as it developed within the conditions of exile, with its subjugation to the powers of the world. This is the religious imperative according to the ultra-Orthodox. To this community, therefore, Israel evokes no religious response, religious gratitude, or religious celebration. On the contrary, the radical fringe of this community offers prayers of mourning on Israel's Independence Day; on that day, less extreme groups, such as Agudat Israel, simply study in their *yeshivot*, their rabbinic seminaries, as usual. Nothing religiously important has happened in history, nothing that should in any way affect the ordinary patterns of Jewish life forged over the last five hundred years.

Unlike the religious conservatives, Leibowitz was one of the religious Jews who joined the political revolution to reestablish an autonomous, self-governing Jewish community. He believes that no event in the last fifteen hundred years is comparable in scope with this bold move on the part of Jews to alter their political fate in history. In the darkest period of world history, the twentieth century, when diabolical

61

evil triumphed in the world, when many Jews nearly lost all hope of any form of survival, when despair was fed both by the forces of genocide and by the forces of internal rot and assimilation, a group of people brought to completion the earlier Zionist revolution. They heroically defied the processes of disintegration and proclaimed with great vigor the Jewish people's renewed independent political existence.

Leibowitz is fully aware that this move was not motivated by a religious impulse. He claims that the Jews who participated in this great political revolution did not intend their act to be an expression of worship of God. They did not found the state in order to establish the rule of the Torah in their lives. It was, he believes, a purely natural decision of a national community to abandon the condition of alienation and subservience to foreign political powers. This nationalist impulse is a legitimate and healthy impulse within a nation. It had no religious significance because it did not grow from the intention of realizing a religious ideal. The observant Jews who participated in the creation of Israel did so out of the same natural impulse of patriotism that was present within the larger secular sector of the Jewish community in the land.

Yet this is not how most of the religious Zionist community sees things. It celebrates Israel's Independence Day and the liberation of Jerusalem in a religious way. It is willing to claim that there is a redemptive process working itself out in the reborn Jewish state. In other words, it is prepared to participate in this secular revolution because it can give it a religious meaning. To those who embraced statehood from a perspective that gives expression to their religious value system, Leibowitz poses the following questions: Can you in good conscience accept this new historical reality and yet maintain a perspective on Judaism which is fundamentally shaped by different parameters and categories? Can you participate religiously in statehood and give allegiance to a Halakhah that in no way authorized or prepared the religious community to assume the role of responsibility for the maintenance and well-being of a total political community?

What religious perspective is needed in order to give integrity to the decision of the religious community to embrace political statehood? Far too many members of the religious establishment, Leibowitz claims, refuse to realize the dishonesty of transferring to Israel the Diaspora practice of relying on nonmembers of the observant Jewish community to provide essential services. They consequently accept that the ordering of the state, its military and local needs, the police force, the fire department, the foreign service—all the structures necessary for maintaining a political order—will be run by Jews who are not loyal to Judaism. According to the laws of the Sabbath as they crystallized in the context of exile, it is impossible for observant Jews to maintain a police force in the modern world, impossible for them to run a foreign service that is available for responding to crisis situations that may occur on the Sabbath. In order for Sabbath observers to participate in the Israeli community, they must implicitly hope that there will always exist within the Jewish state a sufficient number of Jews who will violate the laws of Judaism.

This perspective is seen by Leibowitz as a distortion of the whole intention of Judaism. If, in order to maintain their Judaism, the religious community must become a sect parasitical upon a majority of the Jews disloyal to Judaism, then Judaism has lost all its religious integrity. Judaism does not merely require individual loyalty to the Sabbath and individual worship through a disciplined life. The individual's commitment to Judaism also involves the desire that the whole Jewish community remain faithful to Judaism. Judaism obligates the total community. The individual is obligated to maintain Judaism only because the total community is thus obligated.

Therefore, Leibowitz finds it obscene when the religious community celebrates political statehood as an important religious event, yet has not found the courage and the initiative needed to give this religious decision any authentic meaning. Absolute loyalty to the forms of Judaism of the past, the refusal to recognize that a total, new courageous legislative thrust is needed in order to make Judaism possible in a modern state—these attitudes express a failure to appreciate in depth what it means for an observant Jew to be committed to the renewal of Jewish political statehood. Consequently, Leibowitz ceaselessly and tirelessly argues against all attempts at making the religious community merely a pressure group that guards the interests of its own particular sector. He argues against attempts to exempt *yeshivah* students and religious girls from military service. He argues against attempts to keep religious Jews out of the police force and other lifesaving institutions needed for the maintenance of a modern state.

All this is morally obscene and creates among observant and non-observant Jews alike a distorted understanding of what Judaism should be in the modern world. Leibowitz offers a Jewish categorical imperative for the religious community: Act in such a way that you could wish all Jews to act in a similar fashion. If this principle guided the religious community, then halakhic Jews might begin to recognize what is needed in the new political reality of Israel. Judaism must so modify its legislative framework as to become capable of being lived by the total community of a modern state. Any Jewish perspective that does not imply the possibility of observance by the total community is a false application of the Judaic tradition. Halakhah obligates every member of the community. Therefore, religious Jews who embrace the State of Israel have to build a Judaism that can govern the entire community. They cannot desire statehood and yet at the same time cling unyieldingly to laws of the Sabbath that were formulated under conditions in which Jews were not responsible for the total society. If they use that halakhic framework where Jews did not assume total responsibility for society, they are in a sense still in exile and their religious affirmation of the creation of Israel is only a romantic illusion and a verbal cloak that lacks religious integrity. Leibowitz challenges the religious Zionist community to come to terms honestly with its decision to participate existentially in the rebirth of Jewish political independence. The failure to do so has been the most tragic error of the religious community to date. It does not mirror a way of life for Israel, but rather, is merely a sect whose Judaism has lost its power to claim the allegiance of the total people. To Leibowitz, the task of religious Zionism is to offer the community in Israel a total religious option for Jewish political autonomy. It must engage in the cultural battle with the secular option in its totality.

The hope in Leibowitz's early writings was that the religious community would boldly assume responsibility for developing a Judaism capable of functioning in a society wholly controlled by Jews. One cannot but feel the depth of his anger over the timidity of the official rabbinate and the hypocrisy and failure of nerve of the religious Zionist community, as manifested in the pseudosolutions offered for serious religious problems. He is appalled by the fact that the religious term "Rock of Israel" was furtively inserted into Israel's Declaration of Independence as a compromise solution, because the religious Zionists wanted it to contain a word denoting God, while the secularists could pretend that the term referred to the Israeli army. He is theologically disturbed by the prayers of the Chief Rabbinate, which announce that Israel is the beginning of redemption. He is embarrassed that the rabbinate has adopted prayers that celebrate Israeli independence while refusing to alter the references in the prayer book to the Jewish people as a powerless community in exile. He constantly exposes the failure to recognize that something radically new and exciting has occurred in Jewish history. The past institutional frameworks of the Halakhah, he insists, cannot be the exclusive guiding framework for solving the religious problems of modern Israel.

The new Israeli reality demands new legislative decisions and bold new ways of expressing worship of God in a modern Judaic state.

Leibowitz is not concerned with unswerving allegiance to traditional legal categories of change, nor with the exclusive use of old legal precedents to deal with the modern situation. He is a halakhic existentialist who feels that our decision to participate in statehood cannot find legitimization from a halakhic framework that mirrors the historical conditions of Jewish exile. There is a deeply independent spirit in Leibowitz's religious philosophy. Man has a right, if his intention is to serve God, to be bold in his halakhic decisions.

What, then, is the fundamental difference between Leibowitz's call for halakhic change and the changes in the Law made by Conservative and Reform Jews in the Diaspora? Leibowitz thinks that the tendency toward change in the Diaspora reflects a desire by Jews to accommodate themselves to a non-Jewish world, to overcome separateness by eliminating the dietary laws of *kashrut*, to minimize the laws of the Sabbath so that they can mingle socially and economically with non-Jews, to remove many of the laws that make Jews visibly different in the eyes of the Gentile community. These changes in no way express for Leibowitz an authentic religious impulse. Historically, the Jewish people were always a distinct community. Modernity and the desire for social integration have no normative weight; these are not legitimate reasons to transform Halakhah. To make life easier and more pleasant, to express oneself psychologically in a more spontaneous way, to remove the halakhic laws of sexual inhibitions and enlarge one's sexual life—all this is rejected by Leibowitz. On the level of individual discipline, Leibowitz is uncompromising in his halakhic demands. Psychological, social, and political categories belonging to the larger world of discourse are not seen by him as legitimate stimuli for the renewal and change of the halakhic framework.

On the other hand, the impulse for change that grows from the reestablishment of a Jewish national political community is indigenous to Judaism and thus can be legitimized without reference to the ethical, humanistic considerations that guided the Reform movement in the Diaspora. Given the fact that Judaism was created to guide the Jewish people, and was meant to be lived by Jews in an autonomous Jewish society, it is false and inauthentic to claim that Judaism is possible only if it is not totally responsible for the life of the community. The community's allegiance to Judaism demands that it share the burden of maintaining the physical well-being of a total Jewish society. Therefore, living under exilic political conditions is not the true expression of Judaism but a distortion, a dilution of the fullness of the halakhic challenge.

The important existential problem that Leibowitz poses for the religious community is the following: Is Judaism expected to be a way of life for the people's national political existence? If it is not, the religious Jew should join the anti-Zionist ultra-Orthodox. If one participates in the Zionist revolution and celebrates the birth of the State of Israel, then one must alter Halakhah so that Judaism can remain alive in its own autonomous political framework. This is for Leibowitz the only possible religious response to the rebirth of statehood. The most blatant manifestation of the desecration of Judaism in the modern world is the failure to show that a completely autonomous Jewish society, which is responsible for the normal secular tasks of a modern nation, can live by Halakhah. As a result, there is in his attitude to Halakhah a striking but wholly logical dichotomy. He is conservative and deeply authoritarian regarding the personal, psychological dimension of halakhic Judaism. Leibowitz does not allow personal needs to dictate the direction of Judaism. He is totally submissive to the disciplines of *kashrut* and the laws of sexual purity. At the same time, he is boldly revolutionary when it comes to those halakhic reforms needed to maintain a social, political entity called the State of Israel.

Here one sees the difference between Leibowitz and other leading Jewish religious thinkers of the present century. The difference is one of basic motivation. Rosenzweig and Hermann Cohen were seeking a way of legitimizing Judaism in a Christian society. According to Rosenzweig, Judaism bore witness to the eschatological moment in history. According to Hermann Cohen, Judaism bore witness to the messianic impulse of universality. Mordecai Kaplan tried to create a Judaism unencumbered by the problems of supernaturalism and divine election, to find a way in which Judaism is possible in a modern democratic, pluralistic society.

Soloveitchik and Heschel attempted to revive the courageous qualities of the man of faith in a secular society. Fundamentally, Soloveitchik was attempting to renew the halakhic option for the individual by showing that Judaism is a bold existential drama; Heschel sought to rehabilitate the sensibility of the individual man of faith. Their common aim was to enable the individual in a modern society to see Judaism as a serious faith option. They both sought to combat alienated, unheroic, inclinations in Jews who are in need of a father figure.

For Leibowitz, the urgent issue is not competing with Christianity or refuting secular philosophical critiques of religion, but ensuring that Judaism shall be a viable and authentic possibility for an autonomous political community. In Israel, he feels no need to convince Jews that they should not convert to Christianity; rather, he needs to convince them that they should not exchange a religious Jewish self-definition for a secular Jewish one. He has no problem with the rehabilitation of the lonely man of faith, but with the rehabilitation of a close-knit, observant Jewish community that had decided to accept political independence yet evaded the bold halakhic changes that such a decision properly entailed.

Soloveitchik and Heschel respond to the existential problems of the human condition. They demonstrate how Judaism overcomes *anomie* and provides personal dignity and uniqueness for the modern human being who is absorbed by a technological society. In the Diaspora, Judaism must solve the problems facing the individual in a mass society. In Israel, the community precedes the individual. In order for Judaism to be a serious option for the individual living in Israel, he has to be convinced that it is a viable framework for a total society. Soloveitchik and Heschel are existentialists who seek to provide authenticity for the individual Jew. Leibowitz is an existentialist who strives to provide authenticity for the community.

The Critique of Secular Zionism

Gershom Scholem rightly observed that there is a deep dialectical tension within the Zionist secular revolution. On the one hand, it casts off tradition, undermines the Jewish religious perspective, and denies the authority of Halakhah to define how Jews should live. It strives to reject the spiritual type that grew out of the exilic framework of Eastern Europe. It proclaimed a new Jew with a new spirit, capable of building and becoming responsible for a total society. The Israeli soldier, the farmer, and the kibbutznik all testify to the radical changes in national character that the Zionist revolution introduced into Jewish history. Yet, with all the anger and rejection of the past, there is a profound connection to much that shaped the identity of the Jewish people. Leibowitz disagrees with this observation of Scholem's, but I find it illuminating. In a sense, Zionism is like the young adult who rebels against his parents, cries out against their values, rejects nearly everything they stand for, and announces that he is going to leave home, never to return. He goes to the door, opens it with anger, closes it with a bang—but forgets to leave the house.

Secular Zionists rebelled against their tradition, but remained inside the national historical home of their parents. The attachment to the biblical land, to the land upon which Jewish prayers were focused throughout history, indicates that the new revolution was tied to something very old. In building their revolution within the land, Zionists both revolted against Jewish history and saw themselves as continuing it. The option of establishing a Jewish homeland in Uganda never captured the imagination of the Jewish people. It would never have succeeded, because it would have represented a complete break with the Jewish historical tradition. There is a profound traditional sentiment that accompanies the Zionist revolution. The attachment to the ancient historical past of the Jewish people goes together with the yearning for the creation of a new Jewish personality. There is, therefore, a deep need among secular Zionist ideologists to find historical legitimization for their revolution. Yet they cannot find legitimization through Halakhah, through the official religious community, or from an immediate continuity of tradition. Rather, they must step back into the earliest frameworks of Jewish history, in which the Jewish people developed and grew in their own natural society. The new must be an expression of something deep within the Jewish tradition if it is to succeed as a Jewish revolution in modern times. If Zionism were a complete break with the Jewish past, if the Israeli could not be discovered in any way in the patterns of Jewish historical memory, then in a deep sense Zionism would represent the end of Jewish history and the total assimilation of the Jewish people to the non-Jewish world.

This option could not have inspired the early Zionist ideologists. They tried to rebel, but they sought continuity as well. This explains the subtle changes that were introduced into Jewish education in Israeli society. The Talmud was viewed as a creation of exile. The legalistic minutiae of Halakhah, the classical emphasis on the study of Jewish law, the rapturous joy of the student in the talmudic academy, were rejected by the early pioneers. They found their heroic figures, not in the talmudic sages, but in the early biblical leaders such as Joshua, Gideon, and David. The books of Joshua, Judges, Samuel, and Kings became central to Jewish self-understanding. The important biblical narrative is not Exodus with its commandments and the miraculous journeying of the Jewish people in the desert, but the story of the bravery of Joshua and the judges who fought to defend Israel's national integrity. The new Israeli sees the Bible as the source not of miracle but of human courage. The biblical books that emerged from the land are a clear mirror for their own enterprise. The secular Zionist refuses to accept the Bible as it is read by the traditional religious community. He wants the Bible in its own historical context. This was the meaning of Ben-Gurion's call for a return to the Bible. Love for the biblical land, the study of biblical archaeology, walking through the country accompanied by the Bible—these became the substitute for the traditional study of the Bible and Talmud. The early Zionists sought to discover in the

Bible how their return to the land continued the earlier love of the land found there. It was the beauty of nature that inspired them. They loved the mountains, the rich pastures, the panoramic desert. The Bible was not the book in which they sought norms for daily life in the home, nor a way of understanding God's covenantal love for Israel. It was, instead, a historical document of an ancient community that was being reborn in the modern world.

This is what distinguishes the modern secular Israeli love of the Bible from love of it as Torah, as the basis of Halakhah. One cannot appreciate Leibowitz's critique of the Israeli love of the Bible without knowing how the Bible has been used by secular Zionists to legitimize their revolution against the tradition and justify themselves as continuers of ancient biblical Israel.

The Bible also served the Zionist concern to build a new society imbued with social and political justice. The biblical prophets were important figures for those Zionists seeking a deep utopian vision for the new state. Whereas Halakhah seemed to be obsessed with dietary laws and the like, Judaism for these Zionists had to be taken out of the kitchen. Citing the prophetic critique of ritual, they claimed that the essentials of Judaism had to be sought, not in Halakhah's disciplined way of life, but in the political call for justice and social equality. Judaism became identified through the prophets as a political vision for the Jewish community.

Early Zionists, therefore, used the Bible to reject the Talmud. Zionism claimed to be able to heal the diseased religious anthropology stemming from two thousand years of Diaspora. There is a deep similarity in spirit between early Zionist ideology and the critique of Judaism found in much traditional Christian theology. Students in Israeli schools know the history of the Bible. However, the majority are ignorant of the whole spiritual process that resulted from the creation of the Talmud. Anything that smacks of the centuries of exile is to be abhorred. Those centuries of Jewish history, it is implied, contained no great creative achievements. Rather, they are understood by many Israelis as no more than a series of persecutions and oppression. Nothing profoundly authentic and important could be learned from that history by the Zionist revolutionary who was creating a new kind of Jew and a new Judaic society.

During the first year after my *aliyah,* when Hanukkah came around, I was eager to see a television program that promised to deal with the significance of Hanukkah for our time. I was amazed at what I saw. It took years until I began to appreciate its significance. In the Diaspora, Hanukkah commemorates the struggle of the Maccabees to maintain their religious integrity in the Hellenistic world. Hanukkah celebrates the courage of the Jewish people to fight for Judaism and maintain its separateness from the world. The symbol of Hanukkah is the *menorah*, the Hanukkah candelabrum, which represents the power to overcome the assimilationist tendencies within Hellenism. This I knew from my education in the Diaspora. This was the mind-set with which I began to view the program. To my astonishment, no rabbi, philosopher, or teacher appeared. Instead there was a military analyst talking with a military historian who had studied the wars of Napoleon. The discussion was a comparison between the Napoleonic battles and the surprise attacks of Judah the Maccabee against the enemies of Israel. It was a lecture in comparative strategy and in the importance of surprise attack.

I was unable to explain the profound unease I felt. What had happened to the miracle of the lights, to the power of Judaism to keep the Jewish people alive and the flame of Torah burning under any conditions? What had become of the boldness of the Jews who were able to place their *menorah* throughout Jewish history on the windowsill for all to observe, to keep their light burning proudly as they faced an alien world and proclaimed their courage to remain a unique religious community? What had happened to that profound symbolic law which taught us that under conditions of persecution, when we cannot place our *menorah* on the windowsill, it must nevertheless be placed in a room where the inhabitants of the house can see the light? During times of persecution we cannot speak boldly in public, but we must at least speak to each other and strengthen the family's resolution to remain loyal to the covenant at all costs, even at the price of suffering and death.

Who among my circles in the Diaspora had thought of Judah Maccabee as a brilliant military strategist? The heroes of Hanukkah in my youth were those who had lit the *menorah* and rededicated the Temple. In the talmudic description of Hanukkah, the military aspect of the Maccabees is ignored. Even where it is mentioned in the prayer book, it is given only peripheral attention. The essential message was the courage of the Jewish people to remain loyal to their way of life.

In his writings Leibowitz constantly refers to Hanukkah in an attempt to correct what he believes is the distortion of making the Maccabees of Hanukkah a symbol of contemporary Israeli military courage. Hanukkah cannot be used as a paradigm for modern Israel. The Maccabees fought to reestablish the reign of Torah; the Israeli army fights for the reign of secular government. To Leibowitz, the Israeli army resembles the Maccabees less than the Hellenists against whom the Maccabees were fighting. Leibowitz is repelled by what he sees as the attempt of the secular Israeli to distort the tradition in order to legitimize secular nationalist aspirations. Jewish history up to the Emancipation testifies to the Jewish community's covenantal identity and loyalty to God expressed through Halakhah. To remove God and Judaism from Jewish history is to empty it of any authentic content. Similarly, to make the prophets into social revolutionaries and the Bible into a historical document legitimizing the modern secular community is to distort the seriousness with which one should take a literary document that continually proclaims its religious purpose. Leibowitz abhorred the attempt to change the prayer *Shema Yisrael* into "Hear, Israel, Israel is our people. Israel is one." The secular Zionist revolutionaries must recognize that there is nothing in pre-Emancipation history which could be used to legitimize the building of a secular Jewish society.

Religion and State

Leibowitz's major accusation against the religious Zionist establishment was that it joined the Israeli government and thus gave religious legitimacy to a secular regime. As was mentioned previously, in his early writings he urged the religious Zionist community to think in communal national terms so that religious thought and legislation should not become the monopoly of a particular interest group. Religious Jews must act as if the whole community were loyal to Torah. Their blueprint for Israeli society should demonstrate that the religious community is not a particular sectarian interest group, similar to the Druse or other minorities. This is the halakhic perspective needed by the religious community if it is to meet the challenge of reborn Israel.

The religious Zionist community, however, did not heed Leibowitz. To make things worse, they joined hands with the secular state. In response, Leibowitz took up a more difficult challenge to expose all attempts at giving Jewish religious significance to secular human institutions. In Israel, that meant giving absolute significance to the state. Leibowitz demanded that Judaism, with its concern for the worship of God, must serve as a critique of nationalism; it must expose all institutions to judgment. Judaism must make all Jews constantly vigilant against the intrinsic dangers of power.

Religious Jews therefore had two important tasks. One was to offer, in opposition to the secular vision of the Jewish state, a blueprint for a

71

total halakhic society that would be viable in the modern world. The second task was to counteract the dangers of nationalism.

Because of the centrality of peoplehood and the land within Judaism, there is an intrinsic danger in Israel that religion may be used as an instrumental value to legitimize the activities of the state and the policies of the government. For Leibowitz, it is a modern expression of idolatry to make Judaism an instrumental value to serve human purposes. When God and Halakhah are used to enhance our political aspirations, our worship has become idolatrous, if we take idolatry to be the reduction of God to a means that serves human ends. Judaism becomes paganized in legitimizing a secular government which denies that the halakhic framework constitutes the essential nature of the Jewish collectivity. To give secular Zionist institutions a religious veneer is to prostitute Judaism to the political aspirations of the Jews concerned.

Those Jews who are committed to the covenantal understanding of the Jewish people must have the courage to oppose the new secular definition of Jewishness in the modern world. There is no need to give secular nationalism a religious legitimacy in order for religious Jews to participate in Israeli society as full-fledged, loyal citizens. The Zionist revolution, which overthrew the rule of the Gentile, is a legitimate striving among Jews and embodies a healthy impulse shared with other peoples struggling for political freedom. Leibowitz does not place Jewish nationalism in a category by itself. Jewish nationalism in the modern world has nothing to do with the Maccabean revolt, since there was no specifically religious impulse behind the Zionist revolution.

Consequently, the same dangers inherent in all nationalist revolutions are present in our own national renaissance as well. If history teaches us anything, it is that patriotic sentiments can be used to justify every human folly and brutality. We Jews who have decided to embrace the political, national rebirth of the Jewish people are not immune to the corruption that affects other nations. The attempt on the part of the religious community to put a religious label on the creation of Israel by calling it the beginning of the messianic redemption is especially problematic. It creates the illusion that we are doing God's work and are therefore immune to the corruption inherent in all human activities. Let us imagine that what we do in Israel has nothing to do with the universal human hunger for power and domination, that our actions have a purity expressive of the divine imperative to redeem human history.

To Leibowitz, the major religious and moral imperative for Jews living in Israel is to keep Jewish nationalism free of all religious interpretations and legitimization. We must not endow Jewish nationalism with religious concepts such as *mitzvah, kedushah,* or *geulah* (redemption). Although Leibowitz embraced Jewish nationalism and recognized early in his life the great boon that our national renaissance may represent for Judaism, he nevertheless refused to attribute any religious significance to the decision to build a Jewish state. He did not purport to give his own nationalist aspirations a religious sanctity. Accordingly, he constantly emphasizes that Zionism has fulfilled its goals. He is not in any way disappointed. Zionism has successfully provided a framework for escaping the political rule of the Gentiles. One need go no further to explain what religious and secular Zionists have in common. Both groups have decided to use power in order to gain the advantages of being a national political entity.

The religious establishment failed to exercise the critical function demanded by Leibowitz. Instead, it sought political accommodation with the secularists. Worse still, it acquiesced in a Chief Rabbinate appointed under secular law. Religious Zionists have lost the autonomous power of the religious institutions that they possessed in the Exile. The religious community has become totally dependent upon government and therefore susceptible to its control. Leibowitz repeatedly quotes a discussion with Ben-Gurion in which the leader opposed Leibowitz's call to separate religion and state, because religion would then become too powerful. He preferred having the rabbinate within the state framework in order to control it. Religious Zionists have no dignity because they have no autonomous power. For a seat in the cabinet, they sold their soul. Leibowitz described the religious Zionists as the well-kept whore of the government. He never tires of ascribing all moral and political failures of the government to the fact that the religious Zionist community has given religious legitimacy to the state.

There is nothing wrong with the normal instinctive desire for a state, but one must know the dangers that may result from the misuse of power. Nationalism has the potential for becoming a dangerous evil impulse, *yetzer ha-ra.* As long as we know that it is potentially the *yetzer ha-ra,* we can deal with it. To subsume it under categories of redemption, to interpret our political aspirations as part of a historical process leading to a messianic society, is to fool ourselves regarding our own intrinsic human fallibility. Leibowitz sees a most revealing example of the misuse of religious categories in the service of nationalist purposes in the employment of the term *kiddush ha-Shem,* the sanctification of God's name, to describe the valor of Israeli soldiers who have fallen in battle. The talmudic term *kiddush ha-Shem* was used to describe the willingness of the Jewish people to suffer martyrdom for the sake of their loyalty to God and His Torah. How can we use this same term to de-

73

scribe the heroic fighting qualities of Israeli soldiers, however laudable those qualities may be?

As we have mentioned previously, Judaism and the Jewish people are inseparably connected. In embracing the faith of Judaism, a convert must equally pledge solidarity with all of the Jewish people. As in Ruth 1:16, "Your people shall be my people" must come before "Your God shall be my God." There is no embracing the God of Israel without also embracing the living community of Israel. The organic connection between peoplehood and faith in Judaism, however, contains the danger that the Jewish faith commitment may be turned into absolute loyalty to the Jewish people. This brings Leibowitz back to the theme of idolatry, because it is idolatry to put Jewish peoplehood in the place of God. As long as Halakhah defined the community, there was no danger of substituting loyalty to peoplehood for loyalty to God. Solidarity with Jewish peoplehood and commitment to the Torah were able to work together as long as the Jewish community saw its own existence and history as an instrument to serve God. In the modern period, however, secular Zionism aims to perpetuate Jewish existence and history, but not necessarily Judaism. Observant Jews who join this secular drama are liable to turn involvement with the needs of Israel into the new Judaism of the Jewish people. The post-Holocaust period has made this problem even more intense. The trauma of the Holocaust hangs over the hearts of modern Jewry. Saving Jewish life has become central to Jewish consciousness. If Israel is the instrument that guarantees security for Jews in the modern world, who needs to think further regarding loyalty and commitment to Israel? The post-Holocaust generation can make Jewish philanthropy the new Jewish religion.

In his less polemical moments, however, Leibowitz might admit that it is simplistic to maintain that the official rabbinate and much of the religious Zionist community in Israel were too naive to see the dangers against which he warned. Nor was it merely on account of opportunism that the religious Zionist party gave legitimacy to the state. The question of the relationship between religion and state in Israel is connected to the larger theological issue of the religious significance of historical events. Is Judaism committed to the belief in a divine blueprint in history? Does God realize His plan for history through human actions? Is the rebirth of Israel part of the redemption of the Jewish people which the prophets promised? The prayers for peace that the rabbinate instituted for the well-being of the country contain the phrase "the beginning of redemption," which clearly places the national rebirth in a messianic context. This is neither accidental nor necessarily opportunistic. For a majority of the religious community in Israel, messianic redemption is the sole category that can justify participation in the Zionist revolution. Rabbi Kook, the first Ashkenazic Chief Rabbi of Palestine under the British Mandate, sincerely argued that secular Zionism was God's instrument for preparing the way for the coming of the Messiah. It was this vision of history which enabled the religious community to make the bold move of joining forces with the revolutionary secular Zionists who were dedicated to substituting Israeli nationalism for Judaism.

The belief in the approaching redemption enabled religious Zionists to overlook the behavior of the secular Jewish community. Ideologies that promise redemption need not be bothered by the gap between what people in fact do and the ultimate significance of their actions. Communists went on believing that the Soviet Marxist revolution was leading to worldwide justice, despite the murder of thirty million people. If Israeli nationalism is a stage on the way to redemption, then religious Zionists can submit to the authority of the so-called secular state, since it is in fact to God's scheme of redemption that they are paying allegiance. In their eyes, the state is the medium through which the power of God is working itself out in history. The willingness of the official religious community to describe the heroic sacrifices of Israeli soldiers in terms of *kiddush ha-Shem*, the religious mantle that is placed on national sentiments, need not therefore be simply a rationalized form of crude personal aggrandizement and power. Instead, it can mirror a genuine religious conviction that Israel is part of a necessary process of redemption, and that the larger, historical redemptive thrust of Israel is far more significant than the lives of its individual citizens. Their lives will necessarily change as they become overwhelmingly convinced of the religious import of the events in which they are participating.

This is the religious ethos underlying Gush Emunim, which vows never to return an inch of sacred land to the rulership of non-Jews. It is not simply a nationalistic mania, but a deep religious conviction that God will return to His full redemptive splendor only if Israel is in control of the total Promised Land of the Bible. It is precisely the sincerity of their conviction that makes it all the more dangerous for the Jewish people. This perception of history, this belief in necessary redemption, this placing of secular Zionism within the framework of messianic categories, is what Leibowitz—for political as well as moral reasons—rejects and considers to be one of the most dangerous false ideologies in the modern world.

However, it would be a mistake to define Leibowitz's religious critique as a polemical response to the social and political reality of Israel.

It is, I believe, deeply rooted in his general philosophical outlook. Leibowitz has a coherent, systematic religious philosophy that goes beyond the exigencies of his political critique.

Leibowitz's Religious Philosophy

To Leibowitz, God is not to be understood in personalist, theistic terms. All attempts to describe God from the perspective of human concerns are tantamount to idolatry. In this respect, Leibowitz is religiously very close to the position articulated by Maimonides in his negative theology. Because of God's radical otherness from the human world, Maimonides claims, all descriptive language about God is either false, inadequate, or idolatrous. One cannot subsume God under any genus or species, and therefore one cannot apply to God categories used to describe human reality. Biblical religious descriptions of God are, for Maimonides, a concession to human beings who cannot think about the divine reality in noncorporeal terms. In Leibowitz's theology, one cannot talk about God; one can only act in the presence of God. Judaism does not describe the reality of God nor should one attempt to establish ways of making sense of the existence of God. Rather, religious language is prescriptive: it tries to direct man in his worship of God.

Maimonides bases himself upon logical considerations in insisting upon the transcendence of God, inasmuch as all attempts to describe God violate the uniqueness and unity of God. For example, thinking of God in corporeal terms would violate the notion of unity. In the case of Leibowitz, however, the reason for insisting upon radical divine transcendence is not logical but religious. It is not that human descriptions of God are false; rather, they are religiously inappropriate. To think of God as a way of satisfying human needs, of legitimizing ethical categories, or of enhancing and securing political structures so as to give order and coherence to human society, is to make God subservient to the needs of man.

Is man the center of value or is God the center of value? To Leibowitz, the choice is either/or. If you have chosen man as the center, you have accepted an atheistic vision. But the ethical impulse, he claims, places man at the center of value. For the religious impulse, the center of value is to act in the presence of God. Human action achieves significance only because it is willed by God and performed in His presence. Worship endows human activity with value. It is a mistake to imagine that Leibowitz does not recognize the importance of social and ethical

76

actions within a religious framework. What Leibowitz rejects is the primacy of the ethical as an autonomous category that gives the ethical its ultimate power. Religion, in Leibowitz's view, rejects and denies the significance of the ethical. In the religious framework it is not "Love thy neighbor as thyself," but rather, "Love thy neighbor, I am the Lord." Love of your neighbor takes place within the context of the worship of God. It is being in God's presence that lifts man out of his natural condition.

Man is dignified in Judaism because he is called upon to act in the presence of God, because Judaism enables him to subordinate his natural instincts and desires to the service of God. The transcendence of all that is human, the willingness to deny the given world and man's needs in it, is the ultimate essence of the religious impulse.

Leibowitz completely rejects the attempt to justify religion by arguing that it provides the basis for an ethical universe. To Leibowitz, an atheistic society can create a very serious ethical personality. Ethics is possible without faith in God. One chooses a religious world view, not to discover rules for ethics, but because one recognizes that God is the ultimate principle in reality and that the meaning of life is expressed in acts of worshipping God. For Judaism, the worship of God is expressed through the framework of Halakhah.

The centrality of *mitzvah* (divine commandment) in Judaism implies that God is a source of demand, not a guarantor of success and meaning in history. Here is where Leibowitz distinguishes Judaism from Christianity, the latter being a religion in which God redeems man and liberates him from finitude and sin. Judaism offers no promise of resolution and redemption; it does not offer solace, peace, security, meaning, or happiness to man. Whereas Christianity promises to serve man's needs, Judaism calls upon man to strive to worship God within the world that exists.

The given world, just as it is and without promises of redemption, expresses the will and wisdom of God. Nature and the condition of human behavior which create history are all willed by God in the sense that the given is the expression of divine power. All that exists is the ultimate reality of God. The principle of divine transcendence is what makes man, nature, and history intelligible and possible. This is the religious perception, according to Leibowitz. Judaism does not offer man a way of explaining the facts of the universe; it is a way of explaining what man does with those facts within the world. Judaism does not promise a transformed nature or a transformed history, but offers man direction within the world as it is. Judaism, as it is concretized in Halakhah, is, therefore, a constant effort, a constant striving to realize

77

God's commands in the world, although in essence the gap between God's demands and human action remains permanent.

The seriousness with which the Jew strives to worship God is what gives significance and purpose to reality. Leibowitz's radical negative theology grows from the religious impulse to guard the notion of worship and transcendence of God. It is an obscene violation of his sense of worship to think of God as manipulating the human world in a specific direction. To think of God as a Being who provides for my wealth, benefit, and health is to reduce Him, to use Leibowitz's metaphor, to being the superadministrator of the public health-care fund. To think of God as the corrector of the failures of man, or as a crutch that one can rely on when human efforts fail, is to make Him the grand administrator of the world. Such a view robs Judaism of its essential thrust of worship.

The essence of Leibowitz's religious philosophy is expressed in his essays on the commandments, on prayer, and on Job and Abraham. Leibowitz sees two approaches to prayer within the Jewish religious tradition. One approach treats prayer as growing from human crisis and human needs; prayer expresses the longing to have God look on my suffering and aid me in my troubles. According to the second approach to prayer, however, it is not personal need and the existential human condition that cry out for divine attentiveness, but rather the disciplined commitment to stand before God in worship irrespective of the personal conditions of man. Leibowitz rejects spontaneous prayer; he is wholly content to regard prayer as a regime and discipline that obligates man to stand before God regardless of his present psychological or social condition. The irrelevance of that condition is shown for Leibowitz by the fact that the mourner who has just buried his child and the groom who has just married his beloved are called upon to recite the same prayers.

For Leibowitz, consequently, there is no problem regarding petitional prayer in the modern world, because the essence of prayer is *not* to ask God to respond to human needs. The essence of prayer is to accept the obligation to stand in worship of God. Therefore, by tautology, all prayer is answered, because the very meaning of prayer is the willingness to accept the discipline of standing in worship of God irrespective of what the world is and irrespective of what history and human suffering present. The religious power of the man committed to the discipline of Halakhah is the ability to transcend all particular conditions of history. No matter what history subjects us to, no matter what nature reveals, no matter what we discover in the world, the ability to worship remains permanent.

78

The paradigm of the religious life for Leibowitz, the archetype of the love of God, the model of genuine worship of God, is Abraham at the *akedah*, at the moment in which he was prepared to sacrifice his son Isaac. Abraham's ability to submit to God's command, although it violated all his natural impulses of love for his child and contradicted all his dreams of building a religious community in history, created a moment in which Abraham's worship transcended all human strivings, longings, and aspirations for the world. Whatever happens to man in the world does not detract from the demand of worship, since in the worship of God the anthropocentric world is transcended completely. Abrahamic man is prepared to think in wholly theocentric categories. The triumph of the *akedah* is the triumph of theocentrism.

Leibowitz therefore has serious religious difficulty with the whole personal theistic framework found in the Judaic tradition. The source that defines his religious consciousness is not the Bible but rather the religious community that emerges out of the talmudic tradition. The living faith community of Israel mediates Leibowitz's understanding of Judaism. In the classical tradition of Judaism, the oral tradition of the Talmud defines how one is to respond to the biblical tradition. Leibowitz takes this approach to its extreme by claiming that the Bible no longer has any autonomous validity. For him, the revelatory movement of God in history, which the Bible depicts, has been replaced by the prayerful movement of man toward God found in the talmudic tradition. When in the talmudic world descriptions of revelation and miracles cease to be an essential part of the story, we notice a strengthening of the Jewish people as a religious community.

An example of this is the capacity of talmudic Judaism to combat idolatry. In the biblical world, God is described as very active and constantly interfering in human history. Yet when God acts miraculously, the community reacts by turning to idolatry. The miraculous liberation of the Jews from Egypt is followed immediately by a rebellion. The great spectacle of revelation at Sinai is followed immediately by the story of the golden calf. It would appear that the biblical narrative teaches us that miracles and direct revelation do not create a religious community. Israel remained an idolatrous community despite all the miraculous stories of God and the revelatory passion of the prophets. The Jewish people became resolutely monotheistic when the discipline of the talmudic Halakhah was internalized and institutionalized in Jewish life. When the Jews became a prayer community and adopted a life disciplined by the normative framework of Halakhah, Judaism at last succeeded in becoming a committed religious community. This living religious community shapes Leibowitz's perception of Judaism. He is

79

not interested in the theology of the Bible, but is drawn to make religious sense of Judaism as it is mediated by a living people. *Mitzvah* and its concretization in Halakhah constitute the community's way of expressing its commitment to God.

How, then, does Leibowitz deal with the biblical descriptions of God? The Exodus from Egypt and the miraculous interventions in the desert he interprets within the conceptual frameworks of the legal tradition rather than as factual historical descriptions. The sanctity of the Bible in Jewish life is not a result of revelation, but rather, of the rabbis' decision to endow the twenty-four books of the Bible with sanctity. The canon was established by the normative authority of the Talmud, not by divine intervention in history. If you regard the Bible as authoritative only in the framework of the legal authority of Jewish tradition, you are not forced to regard the Bible as a source of factual information but rather as a source of normative direction, that is, as Torah and *mitzvah*. Thus Leibowitz neutralizes the problem of the truth of the Bible's claims by his assertion that factuality is the business of science and has no intrinsic religious significance. Judaism is concerned with the way man acts before God.

The theistic vision that is found in the Bible does not need to be factual truth. Instead, it reflects a specific stage in the community's normative religious development. Before the community of Israel could truly enter a theocentric framework, it is portrayed in the Bible as having a vision of God that is anthropocentric. This is what the Talmud calls *she-lo li-shemah*, the service of God not for its own sake, since it is service of God motivated by human psychological concerns and needs. This *she-lo li-shemah* was accepted and legitimized by the Judaic tradition, but only as a stage on the road to service *li-shemah*, the service of God for its own sake. Although the authentic paradigm of Judaism is Abraham at the *akedah*, there is a great gulf separating normal human beings from the ideal archetype of Abraham. In the striving for a theocentric consciousness, Judaism accepts as a preliminary stage of man's religious life those actions which mirror an anthropocentric frame of worship. This is how Leibowitz understands the general communal approach to petitional prayer, the biblical descriptions of God, and the stories that deal with God's promises of reward and punishment. All these personalist descriptions mirror the anthropocentric focus, the *she-lo li-shemah* level of religious life. Ultimately, however, the tendency of Judaism and the essence of its religious power lie in its demand to love God unconditionally and to perform *mitzvot* motivated by pure, disinterested love of God. For philosophical reasons of this kind, Leibowitz

80

cannot use concepts drawn from biblical anthropocentrism, or from messianism and eschatology, to ascribe religious significance to the mere historical fact that Israel has been reborn as an independent polity. Reborn Israel will be significant religiously only if this community demonstrates that all of life in an autonomous Jewish society is dedicated to the worship of God.

Neither reborn Israel nor the tragic events of the twentieth century have any intrinsic religious meaning, according to Leibowitz, because all events mirror God's power just as all of nature manifests God's wisdom. No particular event can be singularly endowed with religious meaning. The particular is significant only because it participates in the totality of God's power. All events, both in nature and in history, are therefore in themselves religiously indifferent. What endows particular events with religious meaning is the free response and intention of man. The given, which cannot be altered by human beings, is not endowed with value. Value results from people's exercising their human autonomy and human intentionality in the physical and historical situation in which they exist. Leibowitz views nature and history as part of *olam ke-minhago noheg*, "the world pursues its course."[1] This *minhag*, this course of the natural world, is seen by him from a religious perspective as willed by God, the Lord of Creation. Holiness is not something intrinsic to things, either animate or inanimate. Holiness results from the actions of man in his service of God; it is a halakhic, not an ontological, category. Leibowitz therefore has nothing in common with Holocaust theologians who talk of the commanding voice of God speaking in the modern world through Auschwitz or through the military victories of the State of Israel.

Leibowitz's God is the source of all being. He is the constant in reality. God does not act particularly in behalf of any specific community. Jewish particularity grows from the Jewish community's decision to live according to the *mitzvot*. What makes Judaism unique is not God's actions in history but the unique, total way of life that constitutes the Jewish community's particular pattern of worship. Halakhah is the community's concretization of the Torah's demand to fulfill the *mitzvot*.

The halakhic concretization of the *mitzvot* can change. Indeed, Leibowitz calls for bold, innovative halakhic changes in Israel. If these changes come, if the religious community demonstrates its power to build a society dedicated to the service of God, if it demonstrates how the halakhic theocentric passion can have vital significance in the modern world, then Judaism has a future. If, however, the religious community cannot offer that vision, or if it fails to persuade the larger

81

community to shift its focus from a secular, humanistic framework to a halakhic perspective, Leibowitz does not see much hope for the continued existence of Judaism.

Leibowitz offers no theological promise that guarantees the eternity of Judaism. He knows only of a living community in the past which, because of its effort, commitment, and courage, developed and sustained Judaism under all conditions in history. Judaism's strength and continuity depend on the way the community lives. History is filled with uncertainty. The future is open-ended. Leibowitz, as a profound realist, does not underestimate the forces of assimilation and the disintegration of the religious community following Jewish emancipation. He is greatly concerned at the tendency in the Jewish people to religious and communal disintegration in the modern world. He cries out bitterly against the distorted image of Judaism found in many religious circles in Israel, whereby God is made an instrument serving the political, nationalist hungers of groups like Gush Emunim. To view God as an instrument and guarantor of the success of our political, nationalist aspirations is the height of idolatry. Will Israel change its course? Will we uproot the incipient idolatry in our midst? Will we have the courage to build a society that mirrors the new spirit needed for the renewal of Halakhah? Will the community awaken to the internal dangers of assimilation and spiritual decadence? Is there hope?

Leibowitz would reply that we know only the present task. We are shaped by what we do in the present. What we do as a community defines who we are. Neither memory nor anticipation counts, only present action. The past and the future are beyond the control of man or God and are therefore insignificant from a religious perspective. A community that lives only off its memories or its messianic anticipations is a community that has in fact sown the seeds of its own spiritual destruction. Judaism deals with the way man acts. If there is to be a future, it will only grow from what we do in the present.

Leibowitz offers us no hope, no promise, and no prayer. He offers only the voice of an honest, critical thinker who lives daily in Israel with great trepidation regarding the future, but nevertheless continues constantly, with great passion and sincerity, to march across the country with the dedication of a young man, speaking to all who are willing to listen and learn.

A Critique by
Yeshayahu Leibowitz

<hr />

This collection of David Hartman's essays, entitled *Joy and Responsibility*, is subtitled *Israel, Modernity, and the Renewal of Judaism*. The book's two titles reflect its dual significance.

The author is a rabbi, educator, and philosopher whose main purpose is to lead the hearts of contemporary Jews, who have gone astray from God, "closer to their Father in heaven" (if one may use this talmudic-rabbinic expression). Hartman's aim is accordingly dependent upon another aim: to bring together two groups of Jews that have drifted apart—Jews who observe Torah and *mitzvot* (whom he terms "halakhic Jews") and those who have thrown off the yoke of Torah and *mitzvot* ("nonhalakhic Jews").

But who or what is the "Israel" referred to in Hartman's subtitle? Is this the historical-sacral name of the Jewish people, or an abbreviated form of the name of the author's country, the State of Israel? A careful reading of Hartman's book seems to suggest that, whether implicitly or even explicitly, he intends to identify the two by defining the State of Israel as the framework for the concrete expression of Judaism in our age.

This book, like all of David Hartman's public education or literary work, is infused with a love of Torah and a love of Israel. Both of these loves are nurtured by the author's deep involvement in the practical and spiritual life of historic Judaism and his spiritual affinity with two of its great figures: Maimonides, "the great eagle, the strong hammer, the right pillar" of the Halakhah in all generations from his day up to the present, who is also the greatest figure in Jewish philosophy (which does not mean that "Judaism" necessarily represents a fusion of these two components in one man); and the author's own teacher and mentor, Rabbi Joseph B. Soloveitchik, who embodies the fusion of "halakhic man" and "the man of faith" for our generation. The common feature of these two great men of Judaism, the one who lived six hundred years ago and the other who still lives among us today, is that both are open to the larger framework of human thought in general. David Hartman strives to follow in their footsteps.

Not only the two essays devoted specifically to these two personalities, but also a major portion of the material from other essays in the book, deal with theological questions that transcend concerns of the Jewish people and its Judaism in the present. Indeed, even the author's contemporary message is grounded upon these two eternal foundations.

I

It is to the great merit of the author and an important achievement of his book that, as a "modern" man of Torah appealing to "modern" Jews, he does not succumb to the widespread tendency of "modern" Jewish thinkers who seek to demonstrate the beauty of Judaism to "the nations of the world" (including the contemporary Jewish people) in terms of their own conventional notions of beauty, while intentionally obscuring that distinctive character of Judaism which appears strange to the Gentiles, and to most Jews today as well. David Hartman stands firmly on the rock of Judaism—Halakhah—and explains its significance to both the strangers and the alienated. He depicts the acceptance of the yoke of Torah and *mitzvot* (divine commandments) as a lifelong program that is characterized, not by the element of "the yoke," but rather by the element of joy (the joy of *mitzvah*) and commitment (hence the title of the book). Hartman integrates the life-program of the Jewish individual with the mission of the Jewish people, whose history is defined primarily as a series of successes and failures in shouldering the responsibility for this commitment.

As a man of faith, David Hartman knows that accepting the yoke of Torah and *mitzvot* means accepting the yoke of the kingdom of heaven. In other words, the Torah's "intended goal" (in the words of Maimonides) is the worship of the Lord and not the worship of man—that is, not the service of man, whether as an individual or as a collectivity (society, nation, or humanity). In other words, Judaism is not humanism.

In his discussion of Maimonides, Hartman emphasizes the central element in Maimonides' philosophy; namely, that man is not the goal of creation, because the goal lies beyond the contingently created world and beyond the realm of empirical truth. Nevertheless, his exegetical and educational approach begins with the restoration of man as a member of the Jewish people, a restoration that leads man to know and worship the Lord. This is the approach of "from studying Torah not-for-its-own-sake, one is led to studying Torah for-its-own-sake"—an educational approach which many of our sages accept and which even Maimonides recommends. Hartman seems to ignore the problematic features of this approach, or in any event, he obscures its severity, namely, the danger of inverting the relationship between the means (the restoration of man or of the Jewish people) and the end (the worship of the Lord), the danger of viewing religion as a means to satisfying material, spiritual, or psychic human needs and to realizing human values.

In contrast to the method of inculcating Torah for-its-own-sake through involvement in Torah not for-its-own-sake, the rabbinic sages also developed the idea that Torah for-its own-sake is a "life-sustaining drug," while Torah not-for its-own-sake becomes a "lethal drug." As for the didactic problem of educating toward faith, perhaps David Hartman should have noted that Soloveitchik does not share Maimonides' estimation of the method of studying Torah "not-for-its-own-sake." Long before them all, the prophet ended his prophecy with the shocking sentence: "For the paths of the Lord are straight; the righteous will walk upon them and the wicked will stumble upon them." In other words, one can stumble on the paths of the Lord if one's walking is not directed toward worship of the Lord but rather—even if unconsciously—becomes a disguise for satisfying one's own needs. And in terms of Judaism and the Jewish people, the great danger is that of turning the religion of Israel into an instrument of "redemption," that is, of satisfying national instincts and interests. Precisely a book that deals seriously with the problems of Judaism and the Jewish people and its state as they exist today must not ignore the dark side of this issue.

This leads us to David Hartman's historiography, which gives religious significance to history. Among the different layers of faith during the various periods and in streams of Judaism, he attributes special significance to the belief in the Lord as the God of history and in His revealing Himself in the history of the People of Israel. On this he chiefly founds biblical faith; he also reaches in this way a religious understanding of the Jewish people's national-political renaissance and of the existence of the State of Israel. Hartman thus follows in the footsteps of Judah Halevi on the one hand and of Rabbi Kook on the other. Herein lies a point of profound controversy between us.

The controversy between myself and David Hartman is deepest with regard to the issue of reward. He distinguishes between: (1) the biblical stratum of faith, which holds that divine providence immediately directs historical events and therefore posits a direct link between the observance of the Torah and the historical fate of the People of Israel; and (2) the postbiblical stratum, which recognizes the "natural course of the world" and postpones reward to the World to Come. To this he also ascribes the rise and crystallization of the ideal of worshipping the Lord "for its own sake," in contrast to the idea of worshipping the Lord in order to realize individual or national interests in the realm of concrete reality.

Although this analysis can be supported by countless texts from the Torah and the Prophets, it ignores the general principle that animates all of these texts. The essence of the biblical philosophy of history is not that faith in God is grounded in His revelation in history. Rather, the fundamental fact is that the Lord's mighty hand and awesome power—whether as punishment or reward—which were revealed to the entire People of Israel, did not lead the people to faith. The divine deliverance experienced in the exodus from Egypt, the wandering in the desert, and the conquest of the land, and even the actual revelation of the Divine Presence on Mount Sinai, did not suffice. Likewise, God's revelation through the Holy Spirit's descent upon the best of the People of Israel, the prophets, was also a total failure. Even though God spoke directly through them, the prophets of Israel did not reform even a single person. The objective signs and wonders did not bring about the sign and wonder of knowing the Lord in subjective consciousness.

The biblical narrative even teaches us that the greatest savior and conqueror that arose in Israel, Jeroboam son of Joash, a king who "restored Israel's border from Mevo Hamat to the sea of the Aravah," who "restored Damascus and Hamat to Judah and Israel" (i.e., beyond the borders of the Whole Land of Israel), was a king who "did not abandon the sinful ways of Jeroboam son of Nebat" and who "caused Israel to sin." Yet the kingdom of this savior was doomed to destruction by the prophet of his generation. Or again, the righteous king, Josiah, by virtue of whose work Torah was not forgotten in Israel, fell in the prime of life in battle against Israel's enemies and thereby lost the independence of the Kingdom of Judah. This too reflects divine providence in history, but it is not designed to bring man to religious faith. On the contrary, only very deep religious faith can bring man to accept history as part of the world of the Holy One, blessed be He.

Let us look carefully at the larger picture of history as portrayed in the Bible, from Creation until the beginning of the Second Temple period, the time of God's manifest intervention in the course of human history. We discover that its climax is not redemption but, rather, the existence of one hundred and twenty-seven countries and their nations, including the Jewish people, under the rule of a gang of drunk-ards and lechers led by Ahasuerus, king of Persia. On the other hand, during the scores of subsequent generations during which the masses—not just the chosen few—cleaved to the Lord and His Torah with all their hearts and all their might, the Jewish people saw no signs and wonders, no prophets arose among them, and they were not even redeemed; yet they believed. Neither biblical history nor subsequent events reveal a correlation between the faith of the individual (or the people) before the Lord and the historical fate of that individual (or people).

David Hartman sees all of "biblical faith" in terms of the prayer "If you will surely hearken" (Deut. 11:13ff.), which promises worldly blessing to those who worship the Lord; he seems to ignore the preced-ing prayer, *Shema Yisrael*, "Hear, O Israel" (Deut. 6:4), with its categor-ical imperative to love the Lord without the reinforcement of any sanctions. The fact that these two prayers, so different in spirit, both derive from the Torah teaches us an essential feature of faith, which Maimonides articulates with incomparable clarity. (Maimonides does not offer a philosophical exegesis, but rather a straightforward interpre-tation of the Scripture's plain meaning.) Although the "intended goal of the Torah" is worship of the Lord in accordance with knowledge of His divinity, the Torah "allows" [!] man to worship the Lord in the hope of reward, and to refrain from transgressions out of fear of punishment (see Maimonides' Introduction to *Perek Helek* and *Guide of the Perplexed* III:27–28). It follows that, precisely in this respect, biblical faith and the faith of the rabbinic sages take the same line.

Hartman does not at all realize that equating faith in the Lord with faith in "the God of history" constitutes a devaluation of religion. It is to know and to worship the Lord, not in the sense of "The Lord is God," but as the manager of human deeds and events, just as one may conceive of the prime minister as one whose status is essentially de-fined by the function of running the affairs of the citizens of the state. In other words, a human collectivity, or even humankind as a whole, becomes the supreme goal and value, while God becomes the manager of their affairs, a kind of supreme prime minister or supreme judge—that is, a God who fulfills a function with regard to the world and man. It is thus clear how sincerely believing Jews—including David Hart-man—attach religious significance to the Jewish people's reborn national-political independence, which they identify as a rebirth of Ju-daism, or at least as the beginning of such a rebirth. Does not Hartman realize that Judaism is thus reduced to the level of faith exhibited by Pharaoh's sorcerers, who saw the finger of God in certain events in human reality? He would appear not to realize this, for he reports the religious excitement that seized him in the aftermath of the Six-Day War—in other words, because the Jewish soldier demonstrated his supremacy over the Arab soldier; as well as his spiritual turmoil in the wake of the Yom Kippur War—in other words, when the Arab soldier began to demonstrate parity in fighting ability with the Jewish soldier.

I protest with all my spiritual and emotional powers against the concluding paragraph of Hartman's book, which begins with the (in my opinion, horrifying) sentence: "making contact with the Land of Israel, one is led to make contact with the God of Israel."[1] Why does our author not realize that he is falling into the very pitfall that he criticizes on the previous page: namely, the idolatry of nationalism, statehood, and earthliness, which threatens to replace the Judaism of worshipping the Lord? Can he not see that this transformation has been taking place at breakneck speed among the Jewish people, and that this current has already swept away a major portion of the Jewish people for whom Torah and *mitzvot* have become instruments of patriotism? There is no substance in Hartman's discussion of Zionism as "the continuation of Judaism" and of the State of Israel as "the rebirth of Judaism" because, instead of dealing with reality, he merely offers a vision of the future which has no grip on reality.

The faith that leads to the worship of God for its own sake never was and never will be the product of a particular historical reality or specific events in the history of man. Faith is anchored only in man's readiness to worship the Lord in the world as it is; directing the believing person's consciousness toward "redemption" is a trick of the evil impulse, which diverts man's attention from the task laid upon him. On the empirical level, David Hartman, like many other religious Jews today, errs in discerning signs of religious revival among the Jewish people in the wake of the historical events of the last generation. The process of mass flight from Judaism has not ceased because of or even been slowed by the national-political revival, either in the Land of Israel or in the Diaspora. The phenomenon of individuals returning to halakhic practice has nothing to do with the "beginning of redemption"; it is, rather, an expression of spiritual struggles that can arise within individuals in any place, at any time, and under any historical circumstances. Israel's return to its God will only come about from an awakening of the Jews themselves, not by virtue of the victories of the Israel Defense Force. There is today no sign of this awakening.

What I have said about the "God of history" applies equally to the "God of nature" and the "God of ethics," categories of religious thought which David Hartman also likes to use. The common feature of all these concepts is that God is conceived through functions ascribed to Him—in other words, from the perspective of human interests; this is the essence of serving God "not-for-its-own-sake." I am surprised that Hartman, who has such a deep understanding of the faith of Maimonides, disregards the decisive significance of the second law in *Hilkhot Yesodei Ha-Torah*, which states that God's divinity is neither defined nor conditioned by the existence of the world, let alone by anything within the world. He surely knows and appreciates Maimonides' enormous intellectual efforts to show that the belief in God is independent of the belief in the world's creation (which he did not include among the Thirteen Principles of Jewish faith). Maimonides strives to base faith upon a knowledge of the Lord's divinity rather than upon any function ascribed to Him.

In the metaphysical debate over creation versus eternity, Maimonides sides with those who believe in the world's creation, but not because creation is essential to Jewish faith. Instead, it is a useful concept chiefly among those believers who are unable to know God through the truth of His existence but only through the function of creation ascribed to Him, and whose faith in the Lord and His Torah would otherwise be shaken. Hartman depicts Maimonides' (qualified) preference for the doctrine of creation as a basic postulate of faith. As a matter of fact, Maimonides' preference derives merely from religious opportunism (I use this term without any pejorative connotations); it is not grounded in faith, but rather, serves the needs of faith.

Yet why turn to Maimonides when we have a prayer book which includes the following passage in the Morning Prayers: "You existed until the world was created and You have existed since the world was created." In the same prayer book, we also find: "Lord of the world who ruled before any creature was created." Over what did He rule? We must answer: He is not a ruler by virtue of the world over which he rules, but by His very nature; and He is the God of a faith that obligates the worshipper to "direct his heart toward heaven"—toward heaven, and not toward the satisfaction of the material and spiritual needs of himself or his people, humanity, or the world.

II

David Hartman strives with all his heart and all his might to bridge the great gulf that bifurcates the Jewish people today: the division between halakhic Jews who observe the Torah and *mitzvot* and maintain the traditional way of life of historic Judaism, and nonhalakhic Jews who have thrown off the yoke of Torah and *mitzvot* and maintain a "modern" life-style. Both groups are Jews, both see themselves as part of the Jewish people, but there is a barrier between them which threatens to turn them into two separate communities with distinctive cultures and values. The growing separation between them extends to the formation of mutual feelings of alienation and even animosity. This process, if it continues, will bring about the destruction of the historic Jewish people, whose existence both sides wish to maintain, and thereby destroy the Judaism of which this people was the bearer. How can this destruction be prevented? How can those who have drifted apart be brought closer? How does one generate mutual understanding and coexistence? How does one create a single Jewish people and a single Judaism, which will be recognized by both groups as their shared framework despite their great differences?

Hartman sees the cause of the tragedy in mutual misunderstanding, which can be corrected through explanation. This misunderstanding stems from ignorance, on the one hand, and the refusal to know, on the other. Hartman is a man of Halakhah; he knows that Halakhah was the fundamental pillar of Judaism throughout the generations and its chief—albeit not exclusive—manifestation in history. Halakhah also contains the possibility of solving the problems of Judaism's renewal from one generation to the next, but religious Jews did not take advantage of this possibility when history forced them to confront modernity. The halakhists abhorred the modern world from the outset and refused to acquaint themselves deeply with its values in order to see which of them deserved to be integrated into the world of Judaism. This confrontation was circumvented because halakhic Judaism enclosed itself and turned itself into a sect cut off from the reality of most Jews, who were swept away by modernity. The nonhalakhic majority, on the other hand, having discarded Halakhah as a normative authority, quickly lost all contact with the world of Halakhah. Many Jews became completely ignorant of its values, which are significant for every person who desires to live as a Jew even if he is not ready to accept the yoke of the *mitzvot*.

Hartman calls for dialogue between the two groups, for the sake of preserving the unity of the nation and saving Judaism from the deterioration threatening both sides. The motivation for this dialogue lies in the shared wish to ensure the continued existence of the historical Jewish people and of Judaism, which is dear to both groups. They therefore must reach a closer mutual understanding. Halakhah must become open to the modern world, which is today the existential framework of the Jewish people. As Maimonides did in his day, halakhic Judaism must recognize and integrate the values and achievements of modern culture as "the beauty of Japheth in the tents of Shem," in order to break down the walls of its self-created prison and thereby to resurface as a living, edifying, orienting option for the Jewish people. As for "the nonhalakhic Jews," Hartman tries to coax them into recognizing and understanding the significant conceptual content of Halakhah so that it can serve as a common language in our discussion of the religious act.

Hartman's vision of a "meeting of hearts" in the wake of dialogue is a false consolation. If "hearts" are the symbol of spiritual and emotional content, then one might say that our real problem is organizing a "meeting of bodies," which no dialogue can bring about. Hartman knows as well as I do that Halakhah is practically oriented. There is a vast gulf between "halakhic Jews" and "nonhalakhic Jews," not because of abstract disagreements about faith or divergent evaluations of the different components of Judaism, but rather because those differences of opinion carry implications for the Jew's real existence. In this area too, practice, rather than interpretation, is the main thing. The halakhic Jew accepts the yoke of Torah and commandments with its obligatory way of life because he sees it as the worship of God, and in the worship of God he sees the normative component in the Jewish person's life. The halakhic way of life will not be accepted by an individual who does not see the worship of God as the central value, because he will not acknowledge God and His worship, nor will it be accepted by the person who does not regard the observance of Torah and commandments (a life according to the teachings of the Halakhah) as a concrete expression of the worship of God. Indeed, psychologically he is incapable of accepting it because it deprives him of some of those pleasures to which, according to the modern system of values, the individual is entitled. Moreover, it forces upon him obligations whose significance he cannot understand. The two life-styles remain alien to each other and not parallel; those who pursue them cannot live together even if "dialogue" leads them to "understand" one another.

I would like to illustrate this point with an actual dialogue. During the intermediate days of Passover, I was summoned to a conference for the senior officers of the Israel Defense Force. The conference dealt with the very same topic that concerns Hartman: "Judaism, the Jewish People, and the State of Israel." The discussion was permeated by a sincere desire for mutual understanding and the participants' strong wish to make a positive evaluation of the other side's values. When one of the officers noted with great emotion that we must not forget that we are in the midst of Passover, which is "a national spiritual treasure that all of us have in common, a symbol of our spiritual legacy, and the beginning of our people's history," I reminded him of the fact that if I visited his home on that same day, I could not even drink a glass of water with him. Thus, Passover actually divides us rather than unifying us. Even with regard to the normative content of Passover we have nothing in common, because for the officer and his friends its significance is sentimental, while for me and my family it is existential: this is a week during which we live differently than all other weeks of the year.

In the emotional debate that ensued, the fact was acknowledged that in the current framework of our people and state, an observant Jew cannot eat at the same table with a nonobservant Jew. Moreover, families from the two camps cannot intermarry (and this has nothing to do with the marital laws legislated by the Knesset), because one of the partners sees the laws of sexual purity and ritual immersion as norms that obligate him personally, while the other partner is not prepared to bind himself to this discipline, which he regards as pointless. There is also no possibility of full cooperation in the field, the factory, or the office, not to mention the public services, on account of the Sabbath. All this is true even when a relationship of mutual understanding exists between the two sides!

To the emotional question What unites us today as a Jewish people? I had no answer except, "The Israel Defense Force, the symbol of our national-political sovereignty, and our will to protect it." If a tank in which one soldier puts on phylacteries every day while the other never saw phylacteries is hit by an antitank missile, both soldiers are killed together. But I am not interested in knowing whether we can die together, but rather whether we can actually live together. That question, which I could not answer, Hartman was also unable to answer, although he lets us grasp at the straw of faith. I say "straw," because true faith (worship of the Lord for its own sake) is concerned with the present and not with a hypothetical, utopian future.

Will and Significance:
A Response to
Leibowitz's Critique

T he diverse approaches to Judaism may be characterized in terms of three fundamental models. These models are offered, not as labels for specific periods of Jewish history, but as analytical tools that may shed light on different ways of internalizing Judaism in both the modern and medieval eras.

In the first, the self-sufficiency model, the believer feels no need to interpret Jewish religious belief and practice in ways that would make it intelligible to those outside its own particular framework. Judaism is regarded as complete unto itself; its categories of thought—both cognitive and practical—are internally justified and therefore may be incomprehensible to those outside the framework of a halakhic way of life. Adherents of this model often believe that their refusal to explain Jewish belief and practice in terms of universal categories is most authentically Jewish.

The second model, that of universality, is diametrically opposed to the first. It insists that Jewish self-understanding should be expressed in categories of thought and principles of action intelligible to a universal audience composed of believers and nonbelievers, Jews and non-Jews. Universality thus becomes the ultimate criterion by which to justify and explain Judaism. Judaism may be justified and explained only if it can be shown to serve a universal purpose and may be appreciated by a universal audience. In contrast to adherents of the self-sufficiency model, universalist Jews often emphasize the ethical significance of symbolic ritual, thereby indicating the universal significance of particularly Jewish rituals and practices.

The third model may be described as a synthesis of the other two. Its adherents acknowledge the particularity of many aspects of Jewish thought and practice and do not seek to recast Judaism as an enlightened ethical culture. At the same time, however, they believe that Ju-

93

daism is not *sui generis* but participates in a universal framework of human reason and sensibility. To use a biblical metaphor, the notion of "man created in the image of God"—the Creator of the universe and of all humankind—serves in Judaism as the ground of the ultimate worth and dignity of all human beings. Yet the same notion is also a necessary component of the particularist attempt to establish the Jewish people and its distinct way of life, namely, Halakhah. The account of universal creation is an integral part of the same biblical story that relates the history of a particular people's redemption from slavery and the establishment of a covenant with its God. The universal God of nature is the same God who delivers a particular people from bondage and enters into an intimate covenantal relationship with them. The Jew who pledges covenantal allegiance to God at Sinai must, therefore, become conscious of his or her status as a being created in the image of God.

The third model is characterized by a dynamic tension between (1) the experience of a particular intimate relationship to God, which is mediated by Sinai and Halakhah, and (2) the realization that Halakhah must serve to actualize the *tzelem Elohim* (image of God) in all human beings. On the one hand, the life of the people of Israel makes the Jew a distinct member of a particular community; on the other hand, as a being created in the image of the universal God of Creation, the Jew lives within a framework of universal ontology and psychology. Since history and nature (i.e., Creation) shape the Jew's religious consciousness, Halakhah reveals both modes of consciousness: the God of Halakhah is at once the historical God of Sinai and the universal God of Creation.

Yeshayahu Leibowitz's philosophy of Judaism is closest to the first model, self-sufficiency.[1] His repeated rejection of the legitimacy of utilitarian or even ethical reasons for *mitzvot* rules out the second model.[2]

The third model must likewise be excluded insofar as Leibowitz rejects the view that Halakhah either actualizes or creates Jewish historical self-consciousness. According to Leibowitz, Halakhah is expressive neither of human psychology nor of historical self-understanding, but rather reflects the pure moment of commitment to serve God. For Leibowitz, however, in the context of halakhic Judaism, worship implies service and vice versa. The significance of the content of Halakhah pales when compared with the definitive act of Jewish commitment—the existential decision to serve God. Though Leibowitz confines service of God to the explicit requirements of Halakhah, the only legitimate reason for halakhic observance is the *decision* to serve God.

My views of Judaism as expressed in *Joy and Responsibility* differ from those of Leibowitz, since I maintain that Halakhah may be described in language that expresses a person's total relationship to God. By contrast, Leibowitz's theocentric approach drives a wedge between consciousness of God and consciousness of self. In light of this dichotomy, it makes no sense to speak positively of self-realization within the context of worship. My own philosophy of Judaism characterizes the covenant not only in strictly legal terms as constituting the normative conditions binding a person to Halakhah, but also in terms of a full interaction of God and the human being such that his or her humanity is neither denied nor ignored, but remains an essential component of the God-human relationship embodied in Halakhah.

It would be instructive to examine Maimonides' philosophy of Judaism in terms of the differences between Leibowitz's and my views on the question of whether service of God and self-realization are mutually exclusive. Does an analysis of Halakhah require some reference to a psychology of the human being? If so, to what degree do the love of God and the internalization of Halakhah complement or exclude one another?[3]

Leibowitz is prepared to acknowledge the religious value of my approach to Judaism, but only within the framework of *she-lo li-shemah* ("not for-its-own-sake," i.e., religious practice motivated by extraneous reasons), not as Judaism *li-shemah* ("for-its-own-sake"). Moreover, he accuses me of not being fully aware of the problems involved in ascribing human significance to religious worship.[4]

Because of their different usages and connotations, the categories *li-shemah* and *she-lo li-shemah* are insufficiently precise to serve as exclusive criteria for classifying and evaluating religious behavior. To begin with, there is the philosophical complexity of explaining what it means to serve God simply because He is God. In fact, a single human act may be based on many reasons; the presence of a *she-lo li-shemah* reason does not preclude the coexistence of a *li-shemah* reason. Moreover, the criteria for determining what constitutes an ulterior motive are not as clear-cut as Leibowitz assumes. What is to be considered an extraneous reason for performing a *mitzvah*? This depends upon how one understands the significance and purpose of the *mitzvah* in question.

In the Talmud and in many places in Maimonides' writings, *she-lo li-shemah* indicates an act motivated by reasons extraneous to the purpose of the act itself. If I give *tzedakah* (charity) so that my sick child will become healthy, or if I study Torah to gain honor from others or to become wealthy, or if I fulfill other *mitzvot* so that God will reward me with wealth or political victory, then my reason for doing the act in question is extraneous to its normative purpose. Such acts of *she-lo li-*

shemah differ markedly from religious acts done for reasons associated with the actual religious significance of particular commandments. For example, I may observe the laws of the Sabbath in order to awaken a sense of my creatureliness—that is, in order to become fully conscious of the fact that God alone is the Creator of the universe and that no human individual may relate as absolute master to anything created by God. By abstaining from acts prohibited on the Sabbath, I dramatically express my allegiance to the God of Creation. I become conscious of the implications of the concept of a Creator God, namely, that human-kind is not the absolute master of nature who can exploit it without restriction.

Religious reasons for performing a *mitzvah* are not constituted exclu-sively by deliberate submission to God irrespective of the content of one's act. What one considers to be the significance of a *mitzvah* will determine how one decides whether particular reasons for doing a *mitzvah* are intrinsic or extraneous to the *mitzvah* in question. The rea-sons for the observance of the Sabbath described above are intrinsic to the *mitzvah* of the Sabbath. By equating this approach to the Sabbath with that of fans who observe the Sabbath so that their favorite team will win a soccer game, Leibowitz reduces the category of *she-lo li-shemah* to absurdity. This category ceases to be religiously useful when it fails to discriminate between the religious value of such different motivations.

Leibowitz reaches this untenable position because of a fundamental premise of his philosophy of Judaism, namely, that there is no human significance to *mitzvot*. According to Leibowitz, it is pointless to seek to uncover how a Jew's commitment to God and Halakhah expresses an understanding of human psychology and human values. Accordingly, any attempt to elucidate the human significance of *mitzvot* is futile and may only be justified as an educative instrument meant to be super-seded by what Leibowitz understands as *li-shemah*: pure worship of God. The goal toward which one must strive involves the negation of the total human self. Leibowitz's religious Jew is not unlike the mystic who aspires to the annihilation of the self.

The self-negating voluntarism of Leibowitz's philosophy counteracts the covenantal sense of mutuality described so insightfully by Joseph B. Soloveitchik. Since Leibowitz refuses to admit psychology into his analysis of Halakhah, he attacks my views whenever they suggest that Halakhah has a bearing on human character.

Since I maintain that the entire human person, not only the human will, enters into the worship of God, I am concerned with formulating a characterology of Halakhah, that is, an analysis of the attitudes, sensibilities, and traits that characterize paradigmatic Judaic postures to life. Although I do not make psychology into a necessary or sufficient condition for explaining religious behavior, I argue that unless certain attitudes to life develop in a person, that person will lack the necessary conditions for living fully according to Halakhah. One who believes in God as Creator, for instance, should recognize one's human limitations, relate to life as a gift, acknowledge otherness beyond one's self, give up a manipulative attitude to life. In other words, belief in the Creation not only entails cognitive commitment to a doctrine regarding the origin of the universe, but also involves an attitudinal orientation by which one organizes one's relationship to oneself, the environment, and the world.

It is in this sense that I understand the Talmud's association of anger and arrogance with idolatry.[5] One who is arrogant or subject to violent fits of rage does not have the proper character for entering into a genuine relationship with God. I do not claim that humility, self-control, and gentleness are equivalent to faith. Indeed, I reject the tyranny of faith expressed by those who paternalistically subsume all ethically sensitive individuals under the category of "believer." My approach is simply to seek out necessary human conditions of faith and to indicate to ethically sensitive people that we have a great deal in common. If the halakhic community should formulate a characterology of its world view which would indicate the type of personality that Halakhah seeks to realize, this would create a universe of discourse facilitating profound mutual understanding between halakhic and nonhalakhic Jews.

Leibowitz argues that I offer vain comfort to the religiously divided community by providing conditions for dialogue, since what divides the community is not the values expressed in Aggadah but the legal rulings of Halakhah. In discussing the festival of Passover with secular Jews, it is pointless, according to Leibowitz, to emphasize the notion of the dignity of free persons, or the connection between liberation from slavery in Egypt and the subsequent covenant at Sinai, or to analyze modern socioeconomic conditions that enslave human beings and thwart the realization of their spiritual potential. It is all pointless, says Leibowitz, because if he were invited to a secular Jew's home during Passover, he would be forbidden, as a halakhic Jew, even to drink a glass of water.

The example given by Leibowitz is dramatic but misleading. As a competent halakhist, Leibowitz surely knows that he could find ways of drinking water in the home of a sympathetic nonobservant listener. Were the secular Jew to provide paper plates, fruits, and other delicacies, Leibowitz could spend many pleasant hours eating and discussing the significance of Passover for both halakhic and nonhalakhic Jews. With the conviction that a nonhalakhic person may gain an appreciation of the halakhic way of life based on mutual understanding, the attempts to create ways for the halakhic and nonhalakhic communities to live with each other would be much greater. I do not deny the existence of important differences separating halakhic from nonhalakhic Jews. Differing values and orientations to life characterize all modern pluralistic societies. I do not share, however, Leibowitz's stance which isolates the halakhic and nonhalakhic communities and closes the doors to mutual understanding and appreciation.

A further issue raised in Leibowitz's critique involves my approach to the God of history, specifically my understanding of the spiritual place occupied by Zionism and Israel in the development of Judaism in the modern world. Let us consider Leibowitz's bold claim that the Bible's account of Jewish history indicates the total failure of great providential events in history to increase Israel's commitment to its covenant with God. His claim that the first chapter of the *Shema* (Deut. 6:4–9) captures the essential meaning of biblical spirituality, and that expecting God to respond to human situations in history is *she-lo li-shemah*, seems contrary to the spirit of the Bible. The difference between rabbinic and biblical approaches to history revolves around the difference between God as a victor in history and as a silent waiting God.

Event-based theology permeates the Bible and the rabbinic tradition. Despite exile and the silence of God in history, the basis in real events was not lost in rabbinic Judaism but was carried in memory. Within the rabbinic tradition, the centrality of the God who manifests Himself in events was retained and continued to influence the living consciousness of the community; historical memories became part of daily normative practices.

Leibowitz points to the success of the rabbis and the medieval halakhists who lived under historical conditions devoid of dramatic events like those described in the Bible. They eradicated idolatry among Jews, which the prophets failed to do. If, however, we examine Maimonides' *Epistle to Yemen* and *Epistle on Martyrdom*, we notice that he encourages the Jewish community to persevere by reinforcing belief in messianic redemption. One may argue that Halakhah could sustain the Jewish community only because that community lived with the profound belief that God was in fact the "prime minister" of history (to use Leibowitz's term), that He participated and shared in Israel's historical suffering, and that He would eventually redeem Israel from *galut* (Exile).

It is difficult to accept Leibowitz's claim that what sustained the religious vitality of the community throughout history was a halakhic formalism unrelated to conditions of history. If the concept of God as the Lord of history were absent, what comfort could the Jews of Yemen have derived from those two epistles of Maimonides?

Moreover, God as Creator (which introduces the principle of divine will) had not only instrumental value for Maimonides, as Leibowitz claims, but provided the philosophical basis for the possibility of the Sinaitic revelation. Without the concept of freedom and will in God, one could not speak intelligently about divine action at particular moments in history. The concepts of *mitzvah* (commandment) and *metzavveh* (commander) require an ontology of freedom. Eternal necessity as understood by Aristotle would undermine the very framework of Halakhah.[6] Maimonides' *Treatise on Resurrection* is an argument for the legitimacy of the logic of divine freedom. While Maimonides was not interested in miracles, he was concerned with establishing the logical possibility of miracles, for if the categories of freedom and spontaneity were not applicable to God, then covenantal Judaism would be undermined in the eyes of the community.

Creation thus produces a framework for living with historical hope. Creation provides the ground for understanding God's manifestation in historical events.

I also disagree with Leibowitz regarding the place of events and communal experiences in religious consciousness. My claim is that the Jew serves God with his or her total personality. The notions of divine independence and uniqueness are not incompatible with the covenantal relational framework. Acknowledging that God is independent and that the universe does not exist to serve humankind alone—these constitute important aspects of human maturity. Accepting "otherness" and independence is the ground for mature love. So long as another person is seen as an instrument to satisfy one's needs, mature love is impossible. Nevertheless, Maimonides' position on the independence of God can be fully maintained by one who seeks to bring the entire human personality into the relationship with God and who believes that divine commandments are designed for the full realization of the human personality.

One can be receptive to the needs and wishes of one's beloved, yet also evaluate the content of these needs and wishes. It is true that the commitment of love may sometimes require one to perform actions whose value one may fail to appreciate. But this does not mean (as Leibowitz seems to imply) that when one seeks to evaluate the significance of the beloved's wishes, one violates the independence of the beloved. Maimonides did see an antithesis between the notion of a God whose commands are aimed at developing ethical dispositions and the notion of a God whose existence is independent of the creation of the universe. To regard Maimonides' effort to formulate *taamei ha-mitzvot* (the reasons for the commandments) within the framework of commandments performed "not for their own sake" is, I believe, mistaken. It is the consequence of the profound error of viewing the independence of God and a human significance of His commandments as mutually exclusive. It is similar to the failure to realize that relationships involve two parties who bring not only independent wills but also complex personalities and interests to love relationships. Love is rarely expressed in blind obedience.

Seeking to respond to God within the framework of one's total life experience—"In all thy ways, know him" (Prov. 3:6)—is not equivalent to a theology of history. I share Leibowitz's skepticism regarding attempts to read "the blueprint of history." Far from suggesting that I understand the workings of the Lord of history, I claim only that people respond to God from the living context of the events they experience. I attempted to write a philosophy of religious response rather than a description of how God governs the world.

When I wrote that the Six-Day War and the events connected with it served as catalysts which ultimately led to my *aliyah,* I did not argue for the claim that when Israeli soldiers win, God may be said to be triumphant in history, or that when Israel is humiliated, God has been defeated in history. My claim was merely that particular events sensitize people to dimensions of spirituality which would otherwise go unnoticed.

The Six-Day War was an event that awakened members of the Jewish community to their common destiny. The profound enthusiasm that followed the war was an expression of great relief that a tragedy of massive proportions did not occur. Jews were elated; there were deep feelings of joy and of community. This experience challenged me to reflect on my relationship to the Israeli community and seriously to examine its shaping influence on the development of modern Jewish religious sensibilities. It awakened in me new spiritual possibilities. In general, it offered the Jewish community in the Diaspora new channels of spiritual growth.

Although the liberation from slavery in Egypt did not permanently redeem Jews from their slave mentality, this did not prevent the Exodus from becoming an event which shaped Jewish spirituality. I maintain, therefore, that one is shaped and influenced by events and that one may legitimately incorporate the significance of events and living memories into one's understanding of the service of God. The claim that

Halakhah makes on the Jew is influenced by his or her sense of solidarity with the community of Israel. Historical memories constitute an important aspect of that which shapes religious consciousness. "In every generation a person must see himself as if he personally went out of Egypt," says the Passover Haggadah.

My connection with the covenant of Abraham and the living faith community of Israel are vital factors in my halakhic life. A living connection with the community can awaken one to the covenantal identity of the Jewish people. It is in this sense that I wrote, "In making contact with the Land of Israel, one is led to make contact with the God of Israel." That statement is not idolatrous, as Leibowitz seems to think. I do not identify God with the Jewish people or with the Land of Israel. What I claim is that the Land and the Jewish people provide the individual Jew with a sense of memory and a living framework which make him or her receptive to the living word of Torah.

Israel is a powerful agency for the renewal of Jewish spirituality because it forces the individual Jew to become responsible for a total way of life in a land that anchors a Jew to his or her historical roots. History can thereby become a shaping influence on the Jew's rediscovery of the depths of experience present in a life inspired by Torah and Halakhah. That we have not yet revitalized the covenantal community in Israel does not invalidate my argument. What I claim is only that in Israel there are unprecedented conditions which may revitalize Jewish spiritual sensibilities.

I appreciate Leibowitz's polemic against making Judaism and Halakhah into instruments for the perpetuation of the Jewish people. Leibowitz is one of those spiritual personages who alerted Jews in Israel to the dangers of making Judaism and Halakhah subservient to nationalistic interests. His message is that Jews, like all other peoples, are vulnerable to the seductions of idolatry and political fanaticism. They are not immune to corruption. In this sense, Leibowitz is a genuine halakhic Jew.

For halakhic Jews, it is blasphemous to make Judaism an instrument for the perpetuation of the Jewish people. One's loyalty to the community, one's decision to perpetuate the living community in Israel, must be grounded not only in common historical fate but, above all, in love of Torah and God. Because Judaism as a way of life is of ultimate significance, the perpetuation of this people assumes significance.

I appreciate Leibowitz's reminding me of how the love of Jews and the love of the land can become a source of modern Jewish idolatry. However, one should not equate idolatry with the search for ethical and spiritual purpose in the *mitzvot*. Nor is it idolatrous to believe that modern Israel can restore something vital to the ongoing spiritual drama of the Jewish people.

Leibowitz's approach to Judaism challenges one to internalize the model of the *akedah* (Binding of Isaac)—that is, unconditional surrender to and worship of God irrespective of the human consequences of this worship. Leibowitz's man of faith can transcend self-interest and the needs of community; he is able to assume a posture of faith irrespective of the conditions of history. In an absurd world of radical evil, or under unpredictable conditions, Leibowitz's man of faith has the courage to affirm the dignity of religious worship.

It must be remembered, however, that Abraham, the dominant figure of the *akedah* model, also exposed the commands of God to the test of moral reasoning: "Far be it from You to do such a thing, to bring death upon the innocent as well as the guilty, so that innocent and guilty fare alike. Far be it from You! Shall not the Judge of all the earth deal justly?" (Gen. 18:25). I believe that Judaism strove to integrate both attitudes.

Although prepared to serve God under any conditions, the halakhic community throughout the exile hoped for the opportunity to express love of God within sociopolitical conditions that would make human self-realization possible. Judaism as a way of life cannot be exclusively built on an *akedah* model of spirituality.

The Zionist yearning for Jewish normalcy is a rejection of the notion that *akedah* consciousness can serve alone as the definitive feature of Jewish identity. *Joy and Responsibility* was an attempt to show that this yearning for normalcy may provide unprecedented opportunities to realize Judaism as a total way of life.

PART THREE

"For Brethren to Dwell Together"

DIVISIONS WITHIN THE COMMUNITY

The Resurgence of Orthodoxy

O ne of the most remarkable and unanticipated features of Jewish life in the post-Holocaust period has been the resurgence of the Eastern European style of Orthodox Judaism, particularly in Israel and North America. During the 1940s and 1950s, people spoke of the impending demise of Orthodoxy. The North American Jewish communities were tending toward the Conservative and Reform movements, which seemed to express a more "American" social identification, while Israel presented an image of an anticlerical socialist Jewish nationalism. Many predicted the eventual disappearance of Orthodoxy and the triumph of modernity and secularism throughout the Jewish world. Orthodox rabbis in America at that time found themselves in a defensive position; their synagogue membership was predominantly drawn from the older generation.

Similarly, in Israel, secular Zionism was triumphant. The state was under the uninterrupted control of secularist Labor governments. The religious Zionist community, which chose to participate in the state, needed to fight defensive battles to protect its own educational institutions. Clearly, the Jewish people were moving away from tradition and abandoning the old patterns of daily life organized around the normative structure of Torah and *mitzvot*.

Since sociologists were writing about the end of traditional society, it was expected that the world of the *yeshivah*, of intense Torah learning and of the all-enveloping framework of the Halakhah, was certainly also on the decline. A new kind of Jew was emerging. In the historiography of secular Zionism, Torah and religion were now superseded by Jewish nationalism and peoplehood. The view of such medieval theologians as Saadiah Gaon or Maimonides, according to which Torah was constitutive of Jewish identity, was seen as losing its relevance. The Sinaitic covenant and halakhic practice were viewed as instrumental values, which had served the historical survival of the Jewish people in the past but had lost their efficacy and vitality in the modern age.

Jewish life was to be organized in accordance with new instruments: commitment to Jewish history and the upbuilding of the Jewish state in Israel, the Hebrew language, the building of the land, army service, and the aggressive pioneering spirit. A cultural revolution of the highest order was succeeding. The Jew of the *beit midrash*, the rabbinic house of study, was overshadowed by the suntanned, heroic pioneer who expressed his passionate commitment to perpetuating Jewish history by building the land and establishing strong defense forces.

As a symbolic gesture toward a waning traditional culture, the Israeli government exempted Orthodox *yeshivah* students from service in the armed forces. This approach was imbued with respect for the memory of one's grandfather: by allowing this small, flickering flame of Torah to continue undisturbed in the little town of B'nei Berak or in certain neighborhoods of Jerusalem, one was lighting a memorial lamp for the victims of the Holocaust. The deep feeling that the religious past had inspired the present moved the government to give some semblance of continuity to this flickering flame, which was on the brink of total extinction.

Such, then, was the apparent situation of Judaism in the mid-twentieth century, both in the Diaspora and in Israel. Hitler had given the death blow to a two-thousand-year-old talmudic civilization whose study of the Law and commitment to the details of religious practice had already been undermined by the spirits of modernity and secularism. A new Jewish people, shaped by modern values, was coming into being, and people were preparing to recite the final Kaddish, the mourner's prayer, for the death of this ancient, once vital, but never-to-be-resurrected halakhic civilization.

In the meantime, however, that seemingly inevitable trend has undergone a sharp reversal. In Israel, North America, and Great Britain, the religious group within the Jewish people exuding the greatest vitality, self-confidence, and numerical growth is right-wing Orthodoxy. Today this is the group that is most filled with enthusiasm and confidence in its ability to shape the future character of the Jewish people.

One of the manifest characteristics of the right-wing Orthodox camp is its absolute refusal to compromise with modern values, such as equality of the sexes, religious pluralism, and the participation of all groups in public life. For them the traditional roles within the Jewish family and community are affirmed as strongly as ever.

The birthrate within this group is extremely high. Many an Eastern European *yeshivah* that was decimated by the Nazis has been replaced by a far larger institution. Never before in Jewish history have so many people been engaged in Talmud study. The leaders of this group are drawn from the talmudic academies: leadership is established through their mastery of the talmudic tradition. Their patterns of behavior represent the norm for child-rearing and for acceptable behavior among these Jews. It is symptomatic that, when a great sage recently died, over 200,000 people followed his bier through the streets of Jerusalem.

Torah-observant communities, bustling families, and powerful educational institutions are emerging with enormous vigor. Israel's government no longer views non-Zionist religious parties such as Agudat Israel as flickering memorial candles, but as powerful pressure groups holding the balance of power between the major parties. The future of the Zionist state is thus significantly influenced by non-Zionist elements, who neither see any religious significance in the national rebirth of Israel nor believe that the political state has any importance for the future of Judaism. While they regard it as permissible to work with the state in order to protect their own educational institutions, they do not celebrate Israel's Independence Day in any religious way or see any value in army service. Ultimately, the Jewish people is conceived of as a Torah people, meant to establish its national existence under a messianic king whose knowledge of Torah and allegiance to its commandments are a precondition for any authentic Jewish political leadership.

This community is so confident of its ultimate victory that it allows itself to manifest an aggressive posture toward all groups that it sees as deviating from the normative tradition of Judaism. There is no cooperation with Conservative, Reform, and Reconstructionist groups; their own rabbis may not even join rabbinic bodies in which non-Orthodox rabbis are members. There are clear barriers preventing any social and religious contacts between traditional Orthodoxy and those groups which have "compromised" with modernity. Accordingly, pressure is exerted in Israel to delegitimize the Conservative and Reform rabbinates. At the heart of the political struggle in Israel over the question "Who is a Jew?" is the Orthodox rejection of conversions to Judaism conducted by Conservative or Reform rabbis. May one converted by a Conservative or Reform religious court claim the right to settle in Israel as a Jew under the Law of Return?

Haggling over these issues, as well as over the legal enforcement of public observance of the Sabbath and dietary observance, now regularly precedes the formation of governments in Israel. Indeed, the first Likud-led government was formed after its predecessor fell following a dispute concerning a violation of the Sabbath.

The single-minded dedication of modern-day Orthodoxy to an insular, ghettolike education, its emphasis upon large families, its commitment to meticulous observance of religious laws, and its repudiation of the Western humanistic tradition, have proved a successful means of resurrecting the Eastern European version of Jewish religious passion.

We are experiencing today a powerful revival of a stream within Judaism which totally repudiates all attempts at integrating itself into modernity, whether this modernity takes the intellectual form of the study of Western literature and philosophy, or the nationalist form of the Zionist revolution and the establishment of the State of Israel. What ever happened to the spirit of modern Orthodoxy, whose guiding philosophy was the synthesis of the tradition with modern thought and experience? How does one explain the radical shift away from the position of Orthodoxy on modern culture in the 1950s and 1960s and back to that of old-style Orthodoxy, which repudiates the value of integration with humanism and liberalism?

During the 1940s and 1950s, Orthodoxy was in a defensive position. Many of the best and brightest Talmud students had been seduced away from their traditional religious heritage by modern ideas; Conservative and Reform Judaism seemed to offer more appropriate religious structures for grappling with the enormous appeal of the liberal democratic world; secular culture offered exciting new possibilities and directions. In that cultural environment, Orthodox intellectual leaders commonly tried to show that halakhic Judaism was compatible with Western intellectual and moral values.

However, this apologetic defense of Judaism is today no longer necessary, because the cultural climate of the 1970s and 1980s is completely different. The triumphalist, self-congratulatory ethos of secularism has been called into question even by the secularists themselves. The widespread sense of personal estrangement and *anomie*, the loss of rootedness in community, the failure of revolutionary movements, the weakening appeal within Israel of secular Zionism as a viable option for Jewish self-understanding: all these new factors encourage Orthodox Judaism to return to insularity.

In this new social and political environment, many argue that Judaism must build from within and must be energized by what has always been the source of Judaism's powerful impulse for religious survival— the total repudiation of alien ethical values and the delegitimization of anything other than traditionally sanctioned knowledge. Of course, Orthodox Jews can participate in the world from an economic point of view. They can engage in disciplines and professions that enable them to sustain themselves with dignity, such as computer science, mathematics, and the natural sciences. However, Western philosophy and literature, which inform the humanistic and secular values of contem-

108

porary culture, must be either ignored or repudiated. The religious community has nothing to learn from this alien intellectual world, and there is no one within that world to whom they need feel intellectually accountable.

Those who ground their sense of values in the claim of the eternal and absolute truth of the Sinai revelation need not be concerned with the moral and ethical standards of the West. Openness to non-Jewish thought—so runs the argument—and concern for synthesis with alien bodies will in the long run prove destructive to Judaism. Only those educational institutions and rabbinic leaders who insulate Halakhah and the community from Western civilization will secure the future.

The Power of a Torah-Centered Culture

To appreciate the power of this argument and its deep resonance within the halakhic community, it is essential that we take note of some of the typical sensibilities of the traditional halakhic personality, in particular, of that major strand within rabbinic Judaism that repudiated alien thought and values. This spirit of ghettoized insularity grew through the development of a halakhic world view that claimed to be intellectually and morally self-sufficient.

In the biblical story of the Exodus and of Israel's sojourn in the desert, God is actively involved in the historical and daily life of the community. He defeats Pharaoh in a dramatic struggle visible to all: "And the Egyptians shall know that I am the Lord when I stretch out my hand over Egypt and bring out the Israelites from their midst" (Ex. 7:5). The Exodus drama shows the Egyptians who is the Lord and the Master of history. Both the Sinaitic revelation and God's sustaining concern throughout the difficult trek in the desert testify to a divinity who is active and visible in the community's life. When such enemies as Amalek seek Israel's defeat, Moses is informed that God will bring victory to his people. All who wish to defeat Israel must be aware of God's protective concern for the community. In return for this protection, Israel must promise exclusive allegiance to their almighty, divine king. Faith in God and the obligation to obey God's commandments are based upon the visible manifestation of His liberating power: "I am the Lord, your God, who brought you out of the land of Egypt and from the house of bondage" (Ex. 20:2).

As a result of the destruction of the Second Temple and the loss of political sovereignty, this portrayal of the visible, triumphant Lord of history had to be rethought. How does a community sustain loyalty to

109

God under political conditions which suggest that He is a defeated, not a victorious, God? How does one make God's presence and His Torah into a living reality when His direct involvement is no longer evident? Where is the living word of God when prophets no longer hear His speech?

The following Midrash captures one way in which rabbinic Judaism rethought its biblical foundations. It seeks to define the "greatness" of the Great Assembly, which was summoned to reestablish the rule of Torah in conditions of political weakness.

> Why were they called men of the Great Assembly? Because they restored the crown of the divine attributes to its ancient completeness. Moses had come and said: "the great, the mighty, and the awesome God" (Deut. 10:17). Then Jeremiah came and said: "Aliens are frolicking in His temple; where then are His awesome deeds?" Hence he omitted the word "awesome" (in Jer. 32:18). Daniel came and said: "Aliens are enslaving His sons; where are His mighty deeds?" Hence he omitted the word "mighty" (in Dan. 9:4). But [the men of] the Great Assembly, who returned to proclaim "the great, the mighty and the awesome God" (Neh. 8:6), came and said: "On the contrary, therein lie His mighty deeds that He suppresses His wrath, that He extends long-suffering to the wicked. Therein lie His awesome powers, for but for fear of Him, how could [our] one nation persist among the nations?"[1]

God, the victorious Man of War, becomes the silent, long-suffering God whose power is no longer expressed in the rapid defeat of Israel's enemies. The vision of history in which all nations were meant to proclaim "the Lord of Israel is King" must be postponed. New forms had to be found to express the vitality and presence of God in the community. A way was needed to make God's relational presence felt in the community despite its political dependency and vulnerability. The theological connotations of political power, so central to the history of all nations, needed to be neutralized.

The rabbinic institution of prayer dramatically reiterated the larger picture of God's intimate connection with Israel's historical destiny. The liturgy reinforced the belief that Israel would eventually be vindicated for its faithful waiting. When God shall reign over all of humanity, the suffering servant, Israel, will no longer be despised among the nations but restored as the mediator of God's kingdom in history. In the messianic era, the nations of the world will proclaim that the God of Israel is king and that He rules the earth from Mount Zion in Jerusalem.

> Thou shalt reign over all whom Thou hast made, Thou alone, O Lord, on Mount Zion, the abode of Thy majesty, in Jerusalem, Thy holy city.[2]

110

Petitional prayer sustained the biblical focus on history and on the community's broader historical aspirations.

Our God and God of our fathers, reign over the whole universe in Thy glory; be exalted over all the earth in Thy grandeur; shine forth in Thy splendid majesty over all the inhabitants of Thy world. May every existing being know that Thou hast made it; may every creature realize that Thou hast created it; may every breathing thing proclaim: "The Lord God of Israel is King, and His kingdom rules over all."[3]

God's relational bond to and loving concern for His people were no longer to be judged by Israel's current condition in history. Despite exile and powerlessness, Israel was still God's elect and the recipient of His special providential concern. Through prayer, a liturgical reality was structured in which God was directly involved with the daily needs of the individual and the community. The following prayer reflects the essence of the central petitional section of the daily *Amidah* (Eighteen Benedictions):

Grant us, Lord our God, wisdom to learn Thy ways; subject our heart to Thy worship; forgive us so that we may be redeemed; keep us from suffering; satisfy us with the products of Thy earth; gather our dispersed people from the four corners of the earth. Judge those who stray from Thy faith; punish the wicked; may the righteous rejoice over the rebuilding of Thy city, the reconstruction of Thy Temple, the flourishing dynasty of Thy servant David and the continuance of the offspring of Thy anointed, the son of Jesse. Answer us before we call. Blessed art Thou, O Lord, who hearest prayer.[4]

But the deep bond between Jews and God was not sustained only through prayer. Daily life was organized around the normative framework of the Torah. Having one's existence enveloped by the Halakhah gave everyday life a deep sense of the ongoing presence of God in the community. As different realms of daily life were brought within the scope of Halakhah, the community extended and strengthened God's authority in the world.

One of the central pillars of Orthodox Judaism is the belief that the Torah emanated directly from God to Moses. Maimonides formulated this doctrine in an uncompromising fashion:

He who says that the Torah is not of divine origin—even if he says of one verse, or of a single word, that Moses said it of himself—is a denier of the Torah.[5]

111

Pious Jews need not believe that the account of the Sinai revelation in the Book of Exodus is sufficient to establish the norms for daily living, for the content of Revelation does not in itself totally define the community's normative life, but only the significance given to action. Nevertheless, the dogma that every word in the Torah emanates from God taught the religious community that their actions are significant only if they are a response to the divine will.

Ongoing revelation, however, is not required to enable one to sense the ongoing commanding will of God in daily Jewish life. On the contrary, in the classical Orthodox tradition, the commanding will of God is mediated by human beings, the Sages who have mastered the tradition through study and loyal practice. The community thus retains a powerful sense of God's presence because it is an interpretative community.

Torah is not only divine law concretized in halakhic norms; it also mediates God's uninterrupted speech to the community. God's living presence with Israel is expressed not only through His normative authority but in the invitation to engage in meditation on His word. "This book of the Torah shall not depart from your mouth, but you shall meditate upon it day and night" (Josh. 1:8). Through Torah, God is not only a commanding will but also a present speaker, calling the community to attentive deliberation and reflection, appealing to the intellect and the imagination to plumb new depths and discover new possibilities of responding to the richness of the divine word.

Meditation on the Torah follows the same pattern described above in relation to the application of Torah law to daily reality. When Jews of the *yeshivah* study Torah, they do not feel obliged to open the Book of Leviticus or reflect on the Ten Commandments (sources bearing the language of direct revelation, "Thus says the Lord") in order to feel engaged by God. They may equally do so while studying and reflecting upon a page of the Talmud containing arguments between Hillel and Shammai, or Rabbi Johanan and Resh Lakish. In fact, direct study of the biblical text occupies a minimal part of the curriculum of advanced *yeshivot*. There were even rabbinic scholars who ruled that the commandment of Torah study may be fulfilled without reading the Bible at all, for the study of Talmud was sufficient to enable the individual to fulfill the commandment to "meditate on God's word day and night."

Whenever Jews study or pray, God is present. One senses His commanding presence in the way pious Jews meticulously observe the Law. The people of Israel, as an interpretative and learning community, mediates and builds the content of Revelation. From the outset of the rabbinic tradition, the Sages made the Torah a living word that expresses the living presence of God's kingdom.

This kingdom of Halakhah did not require the support of victorious armies. In the rabbinical academies of learning, whose debates are recorded in the Talmud and Midrash, God was not depicted as the Man of War who manifests his power through triumphant victories over Israel's enemies. He is instead engaged by the joys of studying Torah. Military heroes of the biblical tradition are now portrayed as Torah scholars who, instead of developing ingenious strategies on the battlefield, engage in subtle arguments around the intricacies of halakhic rulings. God's authority and power in history is not reflected in the way in which Rome, Greece, and Persia respond to His power. He rules in splendor in the House of Study. He rules because of the ability of the rabbinic sages to ensure the community's allegiance to the disciplined framework of the Halakhah.

Any crack in this halakhic world, any doubt that it is intellectually self-sufficient, any flirting with the wisdom of the Gentiles and their values, would have threatened the delicate but powerful rabbinic vision of Jewish nationhood and of Israel's role in history.

> Rabbi Joshua was asked when a father may teach his son Greek knowledge. He answered: "It may be taught at a time which is not part of the day nor part of the night. For it is said: 'This book of the Law shall not depart from your mouth but you shall meditate therein day and night.'"[6]

One may only fit the wisdom of the world into one's program of study at a time that is neither day nor night. This ironic answer grows out of the total claim Jewish learning makes upon its adherents. The culture must be insulated; contacts with Gentiles must be kept at a minimum; special laws must be instituted making social intercourse nearly impossible. The talmudic tractate *Avodah Zarah*, for example, lists a whole series of laws and customs established by the rabbis to limit social intercourse with Gentiles.

In order to generate loyalty to a God who studies Torah rather than conquering in battle, the rabbis reacted with distrust and cynicism toward anything valued by the political powers of the pagan world. Total commitment to Torah study went hand in hand with repudiation of the achievements and political aspirations of Roman civilization. This is illustrated by a story about the rabbinic sage Rabbi Simeon Bar Yohai:

> R. Judah, R. Jose, and R. Simeon were sitting, and Judah, a son of proselytes, was sitting near them. R. Judah commenced by observing: "How fine are the works of this people [the Romans]. They have made streets, they

113

have built bridges, they have erected baths." R. Jose was silent. R. Simeon b. Yohai answered and said: "All of what they made, they made for themselves. They built marketplaces to set harlots in them; baths, to rejuvenate themselves; bridges, to levy tolls for them." Now, Judah the son of proselytes went and related their talk, which reached the government. They decreed: "Judah who exalted [us] shall be exalted; Jose, who was silent, shall be exiled to Sepphoris; Simeon, who censured, let him be executed." So they went and hid in a cave. A miracle occurred and a carob tree and a water well were created for them. They would strip their garments and sit up to their necks in sand. The whole day they studied; when it was time for prayers they robed, covered themselves, prayed, and then put off their garments again, so that they should not wear out. Thus they dwelt twelve years in the cave.

Then Elijah came and stood at the entrance to the cave and exclaimed: "Who will inform the son of Yohai that the emperor is dead and his decree annulled?" So they emerged. Seeing a man ploughing and sowing, they exclaimed, "They forsake life eternal and engage in life temporal!" . . .

R. Phinehas b. Ya'ir his son-in-law heard and went out to meet [R. Simeon]. He took him into the baths and massaged his flesh. Seeing the clefts in his body, he wept and the tears streamed from his eyes. "Woe to me that I see you in such a state!" he cried out. "Happy are you that you see me thus," he retorted, "for if you did not see me in such a state, you would not find me thus [learned]."[7]

This story beautifully describes the contrast between the concern with this-worldly activity, with physical beauty and power, and the quest for eternal life gained through exclusive concern with the word of God. For twelve years, Simeon ben Yohai's body is bruised. It cannot even be seen, as it is covered by sand; he is pure mind. He joyfully accepts his injured physical condition (the abandonment of political power) because his suffering (powerlessness) enables him to be single-mindedly devoted to the study of Torah.

We see here a strong rabbinic tendency to view Halakhah and Torah study as all-embracing and self-sufficient. Many Jews built their traditional culture and communal life around their sacred books; within this text-centered culture, the Jews reflected God's will and majesty by diligent performance of daily *mitzvot* and devotion to the study of His Torah.

Aesthetic experience, too, is channeled into the normative framework of Halakhah, joy into the experience of *mitzvah*. Power is exemplified by subordinating one's passionate instincts to the discipline of law. The celebration of the body, the admiration of physical strength, the splendor and glories of nature—these were things that Jews were prepared to leave to the Gentiles. They may have lived in a world dominated by pagan Rome, but they were taught not to value that world.

114

Everything that is of value could be found within their own tradition: "Turn in it, turn in it, because all is in it."[8]

Intellectual Ghettoization and Messianic Nationalism

The resurgence of Orthodoxy in Israel manifests itself in two distinct forms: one repudiates any religious significance in the State of Israel, and the other regards the state as the beginning of the messianic era. The former is embodied in the traditional Eastern European *yeshivot*, whether from the Lithuanian or the various hasidic traditions. This form of Orthodoxy has generally distanced itself from the normalization process that Zionism sought to bring about through the establishment of the State of Israel. In contrast to the Israeli slogan that the best of our youth go into the air force, it maintains that the best of the youth should go to *yeshivot*. According to the latest statistics, 20,000 *yeshivah* students do not serve in the army.

The tension between adherents of this form of Orthodoxy and those who fully accept and participate in every aspect of Israeli society reached a new level as a result of the 1988 Knesset election. Admittedly, there has always been a non-Zionist or anti-Zionist religious element in Israeli society. But what now generates anger and a potential for a split within the people is the fact that the Zionist parties in Israel's parliament can hardly form a government without ultra-Orthodox parties whose religious ideology is either non-Zionist or anti-Zionist.

The majority of Israelis were deeply angered by the political leaders of both Labor and the Likud, who were prepared to compromise their own ideological principles for the sake of political support from the Agudah and Shas parties. It is widely felt today in Israeli society that the values of normalcy and intellectual openness fostered by the Zionist revolution have been abandoned in order to appease a minority community that neither built this country nor feels responsible to it.

How can the agreement made by Ben-Gurion in the 1950s to exempt a few hundred *yeshivah* students from military service be applied to the situation in 1989? When applied to a vigorous movement such as the new Orthodoxy in Israeli society today, that decision loses its rationale. Rage becomes terribly deep when the issue of army service is raised. Any parent who goes through the pain and agony of seeing the life and health of his child threatened in the army for the well-being and security of his country finds it difficult to feel compassion when he sees *yeshivah* students celebrating the virtues of study. How is it possible to

115

have a community of sharing and mutual respect when part of the community opts out of the problems and sacrifices required in order to create a secure political reality?

Besides the question of army service, the entire way of life that Zionism sought to bring about is antithetical to the values of the ultra-Orthodox. Zionism strove to create a new identity which, through its own self-confidence and dignity, would absorb and integrate the best of human culture into Jewish self-understanding. Israel was to provide Jews with a home and a frame of reference from which they could go out into the world. The revival of Eastern European Orthodoxy is the complete antithesis of Zionism's desire to bring the Jew into dialogue with the world. How is it possible to build a Zionist state if political feasibility requires one to win the favor of those who do not share the fundamental values underlying Western civilization, such as pluralism, freedom of conscience, religious freedom, human rights, autonomy, and egalitarianism?

As a result of its dependence upon this religious community, will Israel move toward some form of political Homeinism in which the ideology of Israel's national political aspirations are governed by religious fundamentalism? Is there not a profound danger of merging extremist nationalist positions with a religious ideology that repudiates the necessity for living in dialogue with the world?

Paradoxically, although the Eastern European form of Orthodoxy repudiates the intellectual values of Western civilization, it is somewhat more flexible regarding the issue of land for peace. Among those religious groups whose perception of the state is nonmessianic, one may find allies for a more accommodating stance on the new political reality of the Palestinians.

Eastern European Orthodoxy allows for some understanding with the Arab world at the same time as it makes it impossible for religious and secular Jews to live in mutual respect and dignity. The implacable demands of the ultra-Orthodox concern issues pertaining to the internal Jewish world, such as the Sabbath and the issue of "Who is a Jew?"; they are prepared to be more flexible when it comes to Jewish-Palestinian discussions.

The other major Orthodox group in Israeli society draws its inspiration from the teachings of Rabbi Kook. He believed that the secular community of the early pioneers was implementing God's redemptive scheme for history. Religious significance could therefore be ascribed to secularism and political power, because the creation of the third Jewish commonwealth was the beginning of our ultimate redemption.

This passionate religious Zionism, which crystallized in Gush Emunim, seeks accommodation with the secular community but refuses to compromise in any way regarding Palestinian claims to sovereignty. For them, the major issue is not Halakhah but Jewish sovereignty over the entire Land of Israel. Although they share with the non-Zionist religious community a total allegiance to Halakhah, they give priority to Jewish sovereignty over the land. They rush to the barricades when territorial compromise is suggested, because accepting peace without full control over the land destroys the very meaning of Israel's return to Zion. Only allegiance to the biblical map guarantees God's involvement in the people of Israel's return to its ancient covenantal land.

The religious influence in Israeli society in the 1980s, therefore, stems from these two sources: the religious Zionist community, which focuses on messianic politics to validate their cooperation with the secular community, and the ghettoized Eastern European *yeshivah* Orthodoxy, which repudiates both intellectually and morally all features of the modern world. Both extremes threaten the future of Israeli society. The first endangers the quest for peace, while the second threatens the building of an intellectual and moral attitude to society that seeks to embrace the values of individuality, freedom of conscience, and pluralism.

Maimonides and Soloveitchik

Two traditional masters of the halakhic tradition, Maimonides in the twelfth century and Soloveitchik in the twentieth century, may provide an alternative frame of reference to both these forms of Orthodoxy. Neither thinker offers a fully developed theology of history; neither offers a necessitarian model of redemption; both neutralize the religious significance of historical events and miracles. Their perception of the Jewish people and history, their belief that the Jewish tradition can appropriate the best of human thought, may point to a new way in which the Jewish tradition could give direction and meaning to Israeli society.

Rabbi Joseph B. Soloveitchik has been the leading Orthodox theologian in North America for the past fifty years. Hundreds of his students at Yeshiva University have shaped what has come to be known as modern Orthodoxy. Through his widely read writings, he has mediated the Judaic tradition for thousands of Jews who sought ways to integrate the classical halakhic tradition with the modern world.

As a student, I recall that whenever the question was raised as to whether a shared universe of discourse is possible between Torah and the Western philosophical tradition, the standard answer was to point to the living example of "the Rav" (the Rabbi). Here was an individual who captivated his students both by his brilliant skills in talmudic dialectics and by his profound knowledge of modern philosophy and theology.

Soloveitchik encouraged his students to believe that the best of human thought need not be closed to one who is passionately claimed by Torah study. Loyalty to the tradition is not bought at the price of sacrificing intellectual freedom and honesty. The tradition taught by Soloveitchik was neither fragile nor unable to deal seriously with the best of non-Jewish thought. In his own writings, Soloveitchik welcomed dialogue with Kant, Kierkegaard, Barth, Scheler, Nietzsche, Heidegger, and William James. The notes of his published works, such as *Halakhic Man* and *The Halakhic Mind*, reveal the compass of his intellectual concerns. No serious philosopher or theologian of the modern period was alien to his intellectual and spiritual imagination. He did not inspect their Jewish credentials to see if they were worthy of serious discussion. In that sense, his attitude toward philosophy corresponds to what Professor Shlomo Pines wrote of Maimonides:

> The fact that, relatively speaking, Maimonides had so little recourse to Jewish philosophic literature is significant. It implies *inter alia* that he had no use for a specific Jewish philosophic tradition. In spite of the convenient fiction, which he repeats, that the philosophic sciences flourished among the Jews of antiquity, he evidently considered that philosophy transcended religious or national distinction.[9]

The difference between Soloveitchik and other contemporary halakhic authorities resembles that between Maimonides and the medieval French rabbis. Rashi, the tosafists, and the other medieval commentators expounded the Jewish tradition within its own intellectual parameters. The thought of Aristotle or al-Farabi did not enter into their articulation of the significance of Judaism. Maimonides, by contrast, offered a bridge to the best of Greek and Arabic philosophical thought for Jews loyal to the halakhic tradition. In a similar manner, Soloveitchik has been the pioneering bridge-builder for those contemporary Jews who seek to integrate modernity into their tradition-rooted spirituality.

Rabbi Soloveitchik's powerful influence on modern Orthodoxy is based on the fact that his life embodies the traditional ideal of total commitment to Torah study. Like Maimonides, because of his mastery of Torah he cannot be ignored. What makes both of them so interesting and perplexing is that it is precisely these two masters of Halakhah who seem to have called into question the intellectual self-sufficiency of To-rah study. Both of them bring the wisdom of the world into the sanc-tum of the rabbinic House of Study, which traditionally had room for Greek wisdom only at a time that is neither day nor night.

Both Maimonides and Soloveitchik expand Jewish understanding of what is valuable in human experience, introducing students of the Jew-ish tradition to currents of thought that had not been legitimized in the traditional mode of Orthodox piety. They challenge Jews to deal seri-ously with world views that appear to be incompatible with the ha-lakhic tradition.

It is interesting to note that the first midrashic statement interpreted by Maimonides in his commentary on the Mishnah is one that had been traditionally used to point to the centrality and exclusivity of Ha-lakhah: "God has in His world nothing but the four cubits of the Halak-hah." This Midrash would seem to suggest that halakhic knowledge and practice exhaust the spiritual vision of Judaism. It does not make any factual claim, nor does it contradict any knowledge drawn from the physics of Aristotle or the causal patterns of nature. If understood lit-erally, this statement would seem to reflect the total self-sufficiency of Halakhah for the Jewish spiritual adventure. Maimonides, however, turns this Midrash on its head by demonstrating that the "four cubits of the Halakhah" suggested by this Midrash include the discipline of philosophy.

Both Maimonides and Soloveitchik point to the urgent need to en-gage in other intellectual disciplines in order to realize the goal of one's own system. Love of God in Maimonides, like the search for authentic-ity, creativity, uniqueness, and religious dignity in the thought of Solov-eitchik, cannot be fully realized unless one opens the four cubits of the Halakhah to disciplines and experiences outside traditional halakhic piety.

The traditional Jewish world was opposed to Maimonides, not be-cause of his decision to undertake a halakhic codification, but because of the manner in which he integrated the significance of Halakhah and an appreciation of philosophy. They opposed him because of his pro-found respect for the thought of ibn-Bajja and al-Farabi; they opposed him because they knew that external sources were shaping his religious sensibility. They feared that, were Jews to accept the larger picture painted by Maimonides, they would no longer have total control over students of Halakhah.

Soloveitchik and Maimonides facilitate the development of a Judaic religious personality whose sense of self is not exclusively defined by the tradition. In legitimizing philosophy, they are not only opening up

119

new books but distancing the talmudic self from its own parameters and allowing alternative perspectives to filter into the intense commitment to halakhic practice.

What counts for truth, for creativity, for existential authenticity, is drawn by them from sources independent of the rabbinic tradition. Of course, there can be no doubt that, for Orthodox halakhists such as Soloveitchik and Maimonides, there is no Judaism without total commitment to *mitzvot* and to halakhic authority. But the picture of the universe and of the human condition sketched by both in order to illuminate the halakhic experience creates an Orthodoxy which can no longer live with the triumphalist certainty that everything valuable can be found within Jewish culture.

Maimonides' *Guide of the Perplexed* and Soloveitchik's *Halakhic Man* and "The Lonely Man of Faith" enable us to recognize that particular traditions are fragmentary and incomplete. One of the major contributions of these two teachers to the future of Judaism lies in their awareness that one's own history does not exhaust all that is of value to human growth. They have taught that one need not fear the perplexity and confusion that come from recognizing that there is more in the world than the "four cubits of the Halakhah," understood in the strict sense.

Both teachers can help the religious Zionist community in Israel break down the cultural edifice of intellectual insulation. Both enable students of Judaism to introduce an "alien vocabulary" into the self-understanding of their own spiritual culture. Only one who is a master of the all-embracing talmudic passion can overcome intellectual exclusivity by demonstrating that talmudic Judaism need not erect an intellectual ghetto separating the committed Orthodox Jew from the world.

Maimonides and Soloveitchik provide traditional grounds for those who seek to integrate the wisdom of the world into the four cubits of the Halakhah. They are also important for religious Zionists who seek a religious appreciation of Israel without claiming that we are moving inevitably toward a final messianic resolution of history.[10]

What Israeli society seeks today from its tradition is Zionism without messianic politics, and a passion for Torah and *mitzvah* without ghetto insularity. Those two great masters of the Halakhah, Maimonides and Soloveitchik, may well serve as teachers for a community that seeks guidance for bringing the religious passion of the third Jewish commonwealth into a dialogue with the best of human culture.

Maimonides' Response to the Challenge of Philosophy

Maimonides was one of the few rabbinic leaders who was a recognized master in both Halakhah and philosophy. The great codifier of Jewish law, whose influence on the development of Halakhah was unique and outstanding, was also one of the great teachers of philosophy and metaphysics. His work *The Guide of the Perplexed* exercised a crucial influence upon the development of Jewish philosophy. In fact, Maimonides posed a serious threat to the antiphilosophical halakhic tendency in Jewish tradition precisely because of his tremendous talmudic erudition. Other serious Jewish philosophers were less threatening because they did not command the enormous respect, halakhically speaking, that Maimonides had in the community. Jews had to confront Maimonides' philosophical views because his halakhic views could not be ignored.

Torah and Philosophy

For Maimonides, Torah differs from other legal systems. Whereas *nomos* (law) is concerned solely with social well-being, Torah is also concerned with knowledge of God, that is, with imparting correct beliefs. In the *Mishneh Torah* Maimonides states that the study of the Law is "a small thing" and that the study of physics and metaphysics is "a great thing."

Although these last subjects were called by the sages "a small thing" (when they say "A great thing, *Ma'aseh Merkavah*; a small thing, the discussion of Abbaye and Rava"), still they should have the precedence. For the knowledge of these things gives primarily composure to the mind. They are the precious boon bestowed by God, to promote social well-being on earth, and enable men to obtain bliss in the life hereafter. Moreover, the knowledge of them is within the reach of all, young and old, men and women; those gifted

121

with great intellectual capacity as well as those whose intelligence is limited.[1]

Although the study of metaphysics is primary and of greater value, Maimonides grants that the study of the Law is prior in time, because practice of the Law leads to social well-being and thus creates the social and political conditions necessary for enabling people to engage in the study of philosophy.[2] In the *Guide*, Maimonides repeats a claim that pervades his total philosophical world view: practice creates reverence for God, whereas knowledge creates love.

> For these two ends, namely *love* and *fear*, are achieved through two things: *love* through the opinions taught by the Law, which include the apprehension of His being as He, may He be exalted, is in truth; while *fear* is achieved by means of all actions prescribed by the Law, as we have explained.[3]

These words provoked criticism. Maimonides was criticized for having elevated philosophy to so high a level. Not only did he undermine the Jewish emphasis on the primacy of practice, but he distorted the tradition's basic concern with the study of Halakhah.

It was not only the primacy that Maimonides gave to philosophy that upset the religious sensibilities of rabbinic Jews. The spiritual sensibility that Maimonides sought to nurture seemed strange and alien to the traditional mind. Maimonides' thinking, it was claimed, strayed far from generally accepted currents within the Jewish tradition. One can readily list several areas of Maimonides' thought that deeply upset traditional halakhists.

Maimonides' attempt at understanding God in ontological terms, as the perfect necessary being and not as the God who freely reveals Himself in events in history, appears to undermine the God of the Jewish tradition. Judaism's event-based theology, as well as God's spontaneity and freedom to reveal Himself in history, stand in utter contrast to a theology of the God of philosophers, the absolute, self-sufficient God who draws human beings to worship by virtue of His perfection. It is in great historical events that one finds the living God of the Bible. In Maimonides' thought, however, history appears to play a very limited role in mediating the religious passion for God. In the eyes of his fellow Jews, accordingly, Maimonides' indifference to the miraculous in history and his focus upon the way to God through the study of nature appeared to undermine the biblical emphasis upon God as the Lord of history.[4]

In Genesis, the Creation story obviously leads up to the creation of the human species and the institution of the Sabbath. God's creation of nature is meant to serve His unique final creation, humankind.

One of the most popular classical commentaries on the Bible quotes a Midrash that asks why the Torah begins with the account of Creation, since it is essentially a book of law. The answer given is that the Creation story is didactic; it teaches that since God is the Creator of the world, He has the right to give the Land of Canaan to whomever He pleases. Therefore, Israel's justification for possessing this land is recorded in the story of the Creation of the world. According to the spirit of this Midrash, were it not for a moral, practical, and anthropocentric justification, the account of the Creation would appear pointless.

Maimonides, however, sees in the Creation story not the centrality of humankind but a theocentric universe; man is insignificant in comparison with the celestial Intelligences and, above all, with the infinite Being who created the universe as a consequence of the overflow of His infinite wisdom and power.[5]

The metaphysical perspective of Maimonides also appears in his exegesis of the passage in Exodus in which God tells Moses that His name is *Ehyeh asher ehyeh* ("I will be who I will be"—Ex. 3:14). A traditional midrashic understanding is that this name reflects a God who announces to Moses and to the people that He will be responsive to their suffering. He is a God who can be relied upon to be responsive in history.[6] The Mekhilta sees this name as telling Moses, "Go and say to Israel, I was with you in this servitude, and I shall be with you in the servitude of [other] kingdoms."[7]

As Buber remarked in his essay "The Faith of Judaism":

Not "I am that I am" as alleged by the metaphysicians—God does not make theological statements—but the answer which his creatures need, and which benefits them: "I shall be there as I there shall be" (Ex. 3:14). That is: you need not conjure Me, for I am here, I am with you; but you cannot conjure Me, for I am with you time and again in the form in which I choose to be with you time and again; I Myself do not anticipate any of My manifestations; you cannot learn to meet Me; you meet Me, when you meet Me.[8]

The Midrash and Buber agree that what Israel most needed to know at that moment was that God would be present with them in their suffering. To Maimonides, the slave people beginning their pilgrimage to become a holy covenantal people needed to know that God necessarily exists.

Accordingly God made known [to Moses] the knowledge that he was to convey to them and through which they would acquire a true notion of the existence of God, this knowledge being: *I am that I am*. This is a name deriving from the verb "to be" [*hayah*], which signifies existence, for *hayah* indicates the notion: he was. . . .

. . . This notion may be summarized and interpreted in the following way: the existent that is the existent, or the necessarily existent. This is what demonstration necessarily leads to, namely, to the view that has never been, or ever will be, non-existent.[9]

What a change in spiritual climate! Maimonides takes a dramatic statement rooted in history, a promise to be ever-present—I shall be there—as a statement of the proposition that God necessarily exists.

In the Jewish tradition, the central focus of the First Commandment, "I am the Lord thy God who brought you out of the land of Egypt," is the liberating power of God in history. For Judah Halevi, as for the Mekhilta, the two halves of this statement are inextricably linked: the experience of the Exodus from Egypt and the reflection on God's miracles in history confirm the reality of God for Israel.[10] To Maimonides, however, the first part of the commandment is intelligible by itself: one can understand the meaning of "I am the Lord your God" independent of the descriptive phrase "who brought you out of the land of Egypt."

The basic principle of all basic principles and the pillar of all sciences is to realize that there is a First Being who brought every existing thing into being. All existing things, whether celestial, terrestrial, or belonging to an intermediate class, exist only through His true existence.

If it could be supposed that He did not exist, it would follow that nothing else could possibly exist.

If, however, it were supposed that all other beings were non-existent, He alone would still exist. Their non-existence would not involve His non-existence. For all beings are in need of Him; but He, blessed be He, is not in need of them nor any of them. . . .

To acknowledge this truth is an affirmative precept, as it is said: "I am the Lord, thy God" (Ex. 20:2; Deut. 5:6).[11]

Maimonides interpreted the First Commandment as establishing divine self-sufficiency, perfection, and autonomy. God is a necessary being, not dependent on anything other than Himself.

Jewish prayer is traditionally characterized by the sense of divine presence and responsiveness to the human condition. Halakhah gives expression to this vital element in Jewish thought through the structure of the daily *Amidah* prayer: three benedictions of adoration, followed by thirteen petitions, concluding with three benedictions of thanksgiving. Fundamental to this experience is the feeling that human beings can pour out their needs to God, that they can bring their requests to a God who is called Our Father, Our King. The God to whom one prays

124

is the God who is with humans in their suffering, the God whose She-khinah (Divine Presence) suffers with Israel throughout their exile.

In contrast to the profound sense of intimacy and free expression experienced by the Jew praying before God stands the religious tone of Maimonides' negative theology (*Guide* 1: 50–60). He emphasizes that there is no comparison between God and a human being. Human language is necessarily deficient regarding God. Any statement which aims at asserting something about God must be transformed into a negative statement: "God exists" becomes "He is not nonexistent"; "God is alive" becomes "God is not dead"; "God knows" becomes "God is not ignorant." Statements describing God's compassion, feelings, and mercy are but human projections in no way attributing passions to God.

> God, may He be exalted, is said to be merciful, just as it is said, "As a father is merciful to his children," and it says, "And I will pity them, as a man pities his own son." It is not that He, may He be exalted, is affected and has compassion. But an action similar to that which proceeds from a father in respect to his child and that is attached to compassion, pity, and an absolute passion, proceeds from Him, may He be exalted, in reference to His holy ones, not because of a passion or a change.[12]

The gap separating the religious world view of the Bible and the Midrash from that of Maimonides is obvious in the latter's treatment of negative theology and, above all, in his statement that true prayer consists in silent reflection. Worship using human language is a compromise; the ultimate religious ideal is to express adoration not through poetic descriptions of God but through contemplative silence.[13]

> The most apt phrase concerning this subject is the dictum occurring in the Psalms, "Silence is praise to Thee" (Ps. 65:2), which interpreted signifies: Silence with regard to You is praise. This is a most perfectly put phrase regarding the matter. For of whatever we say intending to magnify and exalt, on the one hand we find that it can have some application to Him, may He be exalted, and on the other we perceive in it some deficiency. Accordingly, silence and limiting oneself to the apprehensions of the intellect are more appropriate—just as the perfect ones have enjoined when they said: "Commune with your own heart upon your bed, and be still. Selah" (Ps. 4:5)[14]

Julius Guttmann claims that Maimonides ignored the important differences between contemplative communion and moral communion. Husik says that Maimonides was deceived in not realizing that the Bible is fundamentally practical and not theoretical.[15] If we accept the implications of these scholarly views, we are compelled to conclude that Maimonides, the great teacher of the Law, failed to realize that his philosophical love for God was essentially foreign to the Jewish tradition. How could Maimonides have missed so obvious a difference in emphasis and in outlook between the religious experience of God expressed in his legal and philosophical writings, and that of the Jewish tradition?

The task of this essay is to show how Maimonides was able to integrate what appeared to be two incompatible traditions. Our concern is not to discover the philosophical influences on Maimonides' world view. This has been done by Professor Pines in his introduction to *The Guide of the Perplexed*.[16] Our concern will be to indicate internal religious concepts emanating from the Jewish tradition which are supportive of Maimonides' philosophical-religious outlook.

The religious impulses which may have led Maimonides to embrace the philosophical tradition so warmly were twofold. One was the uncompromising attitude of the Halakhah to idolatry, which Maimonides expands to a struggle against heretical belief in general. The other was the central importance given to disinterested love of God in the talmudic tradition.

The Struggle Against Heretical Belief

In the *Guide*, Maimonides claims that "the foundation of the whole of our Law and the pivot around which it turns consists in the effacement of these opinions from the minds and of these monuments from existence."[17] Here Maimonides is referring to the idolatrous opinions of the Sabians. Likewise, in his *Mishneh Torah*, Maimonides writes:

> The precept relating to idolatry is equal in importance to all the other precepts put together, as it is said, "And when you shall err and not observe all these commandments" (Num. 15:22). This text has traditionally been interpreted as alluding to idolatry; hence the inference that acceptance of idolatry is tantamount to repudiating the whole Torah, the prophets, and everything that they were commanded, from Adam to the end of time. . . . And whoever denies idolatry confesses his faith in the whole Torah, in all the prophets, and all that the prophets were commanded, from Adam till the end of time. And this is the fundamental principle of all the commandments.[18]

In codifying the halakhic principle that the prophet has the right to suspend temporarily any norm of Jewish law, Maimonides emphasizes that there is only one case where suspension of a norm, even temporary, is not permitted, and that is with regard to the laws of idolatry.[19] The uncompromising demand to reject idolatry is the central concern of the Halakhah. Toleration of anything that may lead, in any way whatsoever, to embracing idolatry undermines the essential purpose of the Law. Maimonides, therefore, codifies the laws of idolatry in the first book of the *Mishneh Torah*, the *Book of Knowledge*. In his introduction, Maimonides explains the purpose of the first book:

> I include in it all the precepts which constitute the very essence and principle of the faith taught by Moses, our teacher, and which it is necessary for one to know at the outset; as for example, acceptance of the unity of God and the prohibition of idolatry.

As this statement already hints, Maimonides holds that the Halakhah's struggle against false religion embraces more than the worship of idols. In "The Laws of Repentance," Maimonides makes idolatry only one of five categories falling under the general definition of heresy.

> Five classes are termed heretics; he who says that there is no God and the world has no ruler; he who says that there is a ruling power but that it is vested in two or more persons; he who says that there is one ruler, but that He is a body and has form; he who denies that He alone is the First Cause and Rock of the Universe; likewise, he who renders worship to anyone beside Him, to serve as a mediator between the human being and the Lord of the Universe. Whoever belongs to any of these five classes is termed a heretic.[20]

Maimonides classifies together under heretics one who claims that there is no God and one who believes in polytheism, but also one who believes that God has a body and form. This last category evoked the rage of the Rabad:

> Why has he called such a person a heretic? There are many people greater than and superior to him who adhere to such a belief on the basis of what they have seen in verses of Scripture and even more the words of those *aggadot* which corrupt right opinion about religious matters.[21]

The Rabad cannot understand Maimonides' insistence on calling an otherwise pious halakhic person a heretic. How can one who lives sincerely by the Law, who follows all the commandments, and who is committed passionately to every detail of the discipline of Halakhah be classified together with one who is an idolater? How can disloyalty to the Judaic faith be found in the heart of one who is totally loyal to Halakhah?

127

Maimonides was undoubtedly aware of the likelihood of such objections, yet his opposition to false notions of God was uncompromising. Essential to understanding Maimonides' metaphysical treatment of God are chapters 35 and 36 in Part I of the *Guide*. There, Maimonides admits that although he realizes that physics and metaphysics are esoteric disciplines requiring preparation and maturity and are not disciplines capable of being studied by the masses, nevertheless one should not withhold from the multitude knowledge of the fact that God is incorporeal and that He is not subject to passions.

> For just as it behooves to bring up children in the belief, and to proclaim to the multitude, that God, may He be magnified and honored, is one and that none but He ought to be worshipped, so it behooves that they should be made to accept on traditional authority the belief that God is not a body; and that there is absolutely no likeness in any respect whatever between Him and the things created by Him; that His existence has no likeness to theirs; nor His life to the life of those among them who are alive; nor again His knowledge to the knowledge of those among them who are endowed with knowledge. They should be made to accept the belief that the difference between him and them is not merely a difference of more and less, but one concerning the species of existence. I mean to say that it should be established in everybody's mind that our knowledge or our power does not differ from His knowledge or His power in the latter being greater and stronger, the former less and weaker, or in other similar respects, inasmuch as the strong and the weak are necessarily alike with respect to their species and one definition comprehends both of them. . . . Now everything that can be ascribed to God, may He be exalted, differs in every respect from our attributes, so that no definition can comprehend the one thing and the other.[22]

Teaching the masses about God's incorporeality is a central motif in Maimonides' writings. In the same chapter, he writes:

> For there is no profession of unity unless the doctrine of God's corporeality is denied. For a body cannot be one, but is composed of matter and form which by definition are two; it also is divisible, subject to partition.

Maimonides concludes the chapter with the same principle he used in the *Mishneh Torah* to categorize the different forms of heresy:

> But it is not that belief in the corporeality of God or in His being provided with any concomitant of the bodies, should be permitted to establish itself in anyone's mind, any more than it is meet that belief should be established in the nonexistence of the Deity, in the association of other gods with Him, or in the worship of other than He.

Maimonides was philosophically convinced that false belief regarding the nature of God is a heresy at least as reprehensible as idolatry.[23] Hence, he had to face the halakhic implications of this claim. Heresy consists not only in mistaken forms of worship but equally in a mistaken conception of the object of worship. It is constituted not only by how one worships but, more important, by one's thinking about whom one worships. False belief, such as belief in divine corporeality, entails heresy in that, instead of worshipping God, one is worshipping a figment of the human imagination. Hence, correct belief (philosophy) is crucial in order to identify God correctly and thus, to worship Him alone.[24]

The purpose of the Law, however, is to correct mistaken forms of worship.

> The essential principle in the precepts concerning idolatry is that we are not to worship any thing created—neither angel, sphere, star, none of the four elements, nor whatever has been formed from them. Even if the worshipper is aware that the Eternal is God, and worships the created thing in the sense in which Enosh and his contemporaries did, he is an idolater.[25]

Halakhah protects Israel from the mistake that idol worshippers, starting with Enosh, made in developing intermediary worship. It provides a mode of worship which will not lead to the removal of God from human consciousness through the substitution of mistaken forms. In addition to mistaken forms of worship, however, heresy is expressed in mistaken conceptions of God. This is only corrected by understanding how unity and corporeality are contradictory. Only by understanding physics, the nature of change, the relationship between potentiality and actuality, the structure of nature, can one root out a heresy based not upon wrong practice but upon mistaken belief.[26]

Indeed, Maimonides considered mistaken practice to be a lesser heresy than belief in corporeality.

> Now the idolaters thought that this prerogative [being worshipped] belonged to that which was other than God; and this led to the disappearance of the belief in His existence. . . . For the multitude grasp only the actions of worship, not their meanings or the true reality of the being worshipped through them. . . . What then should be the state of him whose infidelity bears upon His essence . . . and consists in believing Him to be different from what He really is? . . . Know accordingly, you who are that man, that when you believe in the doctrine of the corporeality of God or believe that one of the states of the body belongs to Him, you "provoke His jealousy

129

and anger, kindle the fire of His wrath," and are "a hater, an enemy, and an adversary," of God, much more so than "an idolater."[27]

Though the Jewish community has a way of worshipping God which distinguishes it from pagan nations, if Jews lack a philosophical understanding of God's otherness, they will still fail to worship Him and him alone. Paganism will grow in Jewish halakhic soil if one does not understand how unity and incorporeality entail one another.

Maimonides also has an answer to his critics who wished to excuse Jews who held mistaken notions regarding God's incorporeality because the language of the Bible itself suggests that God has a body and that He is subject to passions. He points out that one ought to hold a similarly indulgent attitude with regard to Gentile idolaters, for they worship idols only because of their ignorance and upbringing. Maimonides does not allow for a double standard. He does not permit the tradition's rage against idolatry to be turned outward and not inward as well.

Harry A. Wolfson correctly points out that the Bible taught only that God was other than the world. The idea that corporeality is a negation of the concept of the unity of God is not biblical but rather philosophical.[28] Maimonides' knowledge of philosophy gave him a new perspective on idolatry. As a committed halakhic Jew, he could not keep this knowledge from the community. Aware that the Law did not allow any compromise regarding idolatry, he did not follow the path of many medieval Jewish philosophers in allowing the masses to believe that God was corporeal.[29] Had Maimonides been only a philosopher and not a halakhist, he might have refrained from evoking the wrath of the Jewish community by claiming that pious halakhic Jews with incorrect theological beliefs were worse than idol worshippers. If, as Leo Strauss claims, Maimonides only sought a justification for philosophy but not an interpenetration of philosophy and law, he would never have codified the principle that a Jew who believes that God has a body is a heretic. His insistence that the whole community accept certain elementary truths of metaphysics, even if only on the basis of authority, is grounded in his halakhic commitment to the community and to Halakhah's uncompromising attitude with regard to idolatry.

Maimonides refused to accept *shemirat mitzvot* (observance of the commandments) as a self-sufficient, self-justifying mode of religious life. Such unreflective behavior could give rise to dire heresy. He struggled, therefore, to make the community aware of the fact that *shemirat mitzvot* without a proper understanding of the unity of God could turn Jews into pagans. Uprooting the belief in divine corporeality was a burning issue for Maimonides. How could he form a community of faith with people whose religious life was divorced from God?

Maimonides expressed more tolerance for the idolatrous forms of worship in the pagan world than for false conceptions of God in his own community. While idolaters could worship idols, yet refer to God in their thoughts, those who believed in divine corporeality could not refer to God at all. Belief in divine corporeality is tantamount to nonbelief in God, because nothing in objective reality corresponds to the content of this belief.

Maimonides begins the *Mishneh Torah* with a philosophical discussion of God which sets the tone of the entire work. Halakhah must have a transcendent reference, otherwise it exposes its adherents to heresy.

Maimonides felt a passion to spread philosophical knowledge, even in its most minimal form, to the masses of Jews. Wherever there was an opportunity in his commentary to the Mishnah, he taught what he considered to be correct beliefs regarding the nature of God. Paradoxically, it is only the wisdom of Athens that makes the Torah of Jerusalem a genuine religious system. For traditional observant Jews this was both unintelligible and unacceptable.

Philosophy, then, for Maimonides is an indispensable complement to the Halakhah. Philosophy continues the battle of the Law to uproot the last vestiges of idolatry from the world. In the account of Maimonides, Moses was given two ways to deal with idolatry. One was the practice of Halakhah and the other was teaching the community the truth of God's total self-sufficiency. Moses was told at the beginning of his political mission that the name of God that is to be understood by the community is "I am that I am." Only when Jews are fully able to grasp the distinction between the necessity of God's existence and the contingency of human existence, when they appreciate the radical otherness of divinity, will such idolatry disappear.

A God who is worshipped because of human interests and needs, who is understood and loved because of His similarity to the human, mirrors a culture that is still prone to the sin of idolatry. Moses succeeded in weaning the Jews away from the pagan rituals of Egypt. Moses Maimonides undertook the further task of weaning the community away from a heresy that grows from blurring the difference between the human and the divine. Maimonides' philosophical passion is not, as many claim, arid philosophical rationalism. His motivation to teach philosophy was not that of an elitist intellectual, but that of an observant Jew committed to the principle of "He who rejects idolatry, accepts the entire Torah."[30]

We have thus far shown how philosophy obviates the sin of idolatry. Let us now consider how philosophy leads one to the love of God.

Philosophy and the Love of God

The uniqueness of Torah among legal systems, says Maimonides, is its concern with developing love of God. But love of God, he adds, is nurtured only by philosophical knowledge.[31] Even though he recognized the limitations of the intellect and restricted the scope and nature of human knowledge of God, he nevertheless believed that only knowledge drawn from the intellectual disciplines of physics and metaphysics leads us to love of God.

> This God, honored and revered, it is our duty to love and fear, as it is said, "You shall love the Lord, your God" (Deut. 6:5), and it is further said: "You shall fear the Lord, your God" (Deut. 6:13). And what is the way that will lead to the love of Him and the fear of Him? When a person contemplates His great and wondrous works and creatures and from them obtains a glimpse of His wisdom which is incomparable and infinite, he will straightway love Him, praise Him, glorify Him, and long with an exceeding longing to know his great Name; even as David said: "My soul thirsts for God, for the living God" (Ps. 42:3)[32]

Why are the disciplines of physics and metaphysics indispensable to achieving love of God? Why are the practice and study of the Law necessary but not sufficient conditions for achieving love of God? In order to comprehend philosophy's unique contribution to developing love of God, one must compare Maimonides' understanding of God's relationship to nature with his approach to Revelation. Central to Maimonides' understanding of God's revelation in nature and of the human relationship to the universe, is the realization that humankind is not the center of God's Creation. The world does not exist for our sake; God's creative power and wisdom must not be understood as focused exclusively on the creation of the human species. Hence, a most important religious function of metaphysical reflection is to heal us of the illness of human egocentricity. When reflecting on the cosmos, we realize our own insignificance. Thus knowledge of physics and metaphysics creates humility. Philosophy locates us in a theocentric universe where we cannot but realize our modest and humble place.[33]

Maimonides' treatment of the book of Job in Part III of the *Guide* clearly establishes our place in the hierarchy of beings. According to Maimonides, Job did not receive an answer to the problem of evil; he gained a different perception of existence and of himself, which enabled him to continue living despite his suffering.

> This is the object of the Book of Job as a whole: I refer to the establishing of this foundation for the belief and the drawing attention to the inference to be drawn from natural matters, so that you should not fall into error and seek to affirm in your imagination that His knowledge is like our knowledge or that His purpose and His providence and His governance are like our purpose and our providence and our governance. If man knows this, every misfortune will be borne lightly by him.[34]

Philosophy's presentation of an objective world independent of humankind, where we occupy a most modest position in a hierarchy of perfections culminating in the awesome, ineffable perfection of God, transports us from an anthropocentric to a theocentric universe and thereby gives us the strength to cope with human suffering.

This insight is also present in Maimonides' treatment of the *akedah*, the Binding of Isaac.[35] Abraham, the founder of belief in the God of history, is asked to sacrifice his only son, Isaac (his own future in history), in order to express a relationship to God which, in fact, negates the significance of God's promises to Abraham for history. The experience of the *akedah* symbolically demonstrated that the ultimate goal of Torah lay beyond history. The archetypal act of love of God consists in the ability to abandon history.

Maimonides' treatment of the stories of Abraham and Job reveals his belief in the liberating power of philosophy to direct us to live in history after having discovered an anchor point beyond history.[36] For disinterested love of God to be possible, our understanding of ourselves, the world, and the essential purpose and meaning of life must undergo radical transformations. So long as we are anchored solely in history and are concerned exclusively with human needs, we cannot fully recognize and therefore cannot love a God who does not exist merely for our own sake. Philosophy creates the conditions for love because it enables human beings to appreciate an objective reality independent of human needs.

As in the case of idolatry, here too God's otherness and uniqueness are a central theological motif. Philosophy, and specifically the analysis of unity, noncorporeality, and negative attributes, offers a more exact and rigorous understanding of God's otherness. This intellectual pursuit of the implications of divine otherness constitutes a search for the love of God. For love is expressed in the confirmation of the independent worth of the beloved, and it is only philosophy that gives meaning to our affirmation of God's independent existence. In Maimonides' writings, the yearning quality of love finds expression in learning how the universe reveals the actions of God. Love becomes passionate when the universe is perceived from a theocentric perspective. Knowing what God is not, and how He is radically other than the world, provides the intellectual basis for self-transcending, relational love.[37]

While philosophy points to divine perfection and to divine manifestations that are indifferent to and independent of human needs, the revelation of the Law at Sinai was substantially different. In the *Guide*, Maimonides explains how to interpret the meaning of many laws given at that time.[38] In a manner reminiscent of Hegel's notion of the cunning of reason, Maimonides argues that God takes account of the given conditions of history in furthering His purposes. God revealed a law that recognized the limited capacity of the Israelite community to grasp His will at that time. Although obviously God could have changed the human nature of the Israelites to accord with the practices of a perfect law, Maimonides argues that God preferred not to do so. God chose to adopt the role of the teacher who works with the available materials of history, patiently seeking to overcome the limitations and the shortcomings of the people of Israel.

Revelation of God's wisdom in the Law, as distinct from His revelation in nature, is a response to an imperfect human condition. The Law expresses the divine will from the perspective of human needs: "The Torah spoke in the language of human beings." Maimonides was very comfortable attributing human purposes to the Commandments. He held that the Commandments reflect what is good for a human community.[39] The cosmic significance that mystics attributed to them is alien to Maimonides' attempt to make the Law totally earth-bound.[40]

Torah leads us to a God who speaks only after He listens to our human condition. The text of nature, by contrast, reveals the full manifestation of God's artistry, which is conditioned only by His own infinite wisdom and power and is not in any way inhibited by what the human being can bear or understand. The text of nature is therefore given greater weight by Maimonides in his discussion of the love of God. Nature energizes the passion to seek more and to understand more, although we know full well that this hunger to understand God in a deeper way can never be fully satisfied, given the limitations of the human condition and intellect. The text of Torah for Maimonides is anthropocentric. It shows how to build a healthy moral character and a healthy society and political order. The text of nature teaches us how to go beyond our own condition and glimpse the free, powerful, and aesthetic world of divine self-expression.

Talmudic Antecedents

Maimonides' neutralization of the religious significance of history and of divine interference in the structures of reality, and his emphasis on cultivating a passionate love for a God who draws us to Him by virtue of His perfection and not by virtue of His ability to satisfy our human needs and requests, may have their roots in certain features of talmudic Judaism itself. It is not claimed that these features constitute the dominant orientation of rabbinic Judaism.[41] As Ephraim Urbach has shown, there are many diverse schools of thought within rabbinic Judaism. One important strand within the talmudic tradition, however, provides the basis for a spiritual orientation that makes it possible to bridge the gap between the biblical world of divine immediacy and the postbiblical world, which is silent and unresponsive to the human moral condition.

In the following talmudic text, for example, nature becomes neutralized and, so to speak, demythologized. The biblical world view is reinterpreted so that the Jewish relationship to God is no longer sustained by the visible and public interference of a moral God in the processes of nature and history.

> Our rabbis taught: Philosophers asked the elders in Rome, "If your God has no desire for idolatry, why does He not abolish it?" They replied, "If it was something of which the world has no need that was worshipped, He would abolish it; but people worship the sun, moon, stars, and planets; should He destroy the Universe on account of fools? The world pursues its natural course, and as for the fools who act wrongly, they will have to render an account. . . . Another illustration: suppose a man has intercourse with his neighbor's wife; it is right that she should not conceive, but the world pursues its natural course and as for the fools who act wrongly, they will have to render an account." This is similar to what R. Simeon b. Lakish said "The Holy One, blessed be He, declared, 'Not enough that the wicked put My coinage to vulgar use, but they trouble Me and compel Me to set My seal thereon!' "[42]

To appreciate fully this radical shift in sensibility from biblical thought, one need only compare this talmudic passage with a typical biblical statement:

> If, then, you obey the commandments that I enjoin upon you this day, loving the Lord your God and serving Him with all your heart and soul, I will grant the rain for your land in season, the early rain and the late. You shall gather in your new grain and wine and oil—I will also provide grass in the fields for your cattle—and thus you shall eat your fill. Take care not to be lured away to serve other gods and bow to them. For the Lord's anger will

flare up against you, and He will shut up the skies so that there will be no rain and the ground will not yield its produce; and you will soon perish from the good land that the Lord is giving you.[43]

A key expression in the preceding talmudic quotation is "it is right that . . . should not . . ." (*din hu she-lo*). Stolen grain ought not to grow; a raped woman ought not to become pregnant. Nature ought not to respond and give of its strength and bounty to the consequences of evil. In other words, the expectations that nature and morality are organically related, and that the Lord of history and the Lord of nature are one, are legitimate and worthwhile. Yet, although the talmudic author legitimizes this biblical sensibility, he realizes that it does not accord with what in fact happens. Therefore, he makes the generalization *olam ke-minhago noheg* ("the world maintains its natural course"). (As Strauss remarked, the term used is *minhag*, custom, and not *teva*, nature.[44]) One cannot expect nature to reflect the moral law. Jews cultivate a moral sensibility, a belief that the world "should" express moral distinctions, but they are also taught to accept the nonrealization of such an organic relationship.

This demythologization, which enabled Jews to live in a universe that was strange and unresponsive to their deepest moral yearnings, is very definitely a characteristic of talmudic Judaism. Since the reality of the talmudic writers did not confirm a God who was powerful and victorious in imposing his will upon history, they were compelled to reconsider the meaning of divine power.

> Vespasian sent Titus who said: "Where is their God, the rock in whom they trusted?" This was the wicked Titus who blasphemed and insulted Heaven. What did he do? He took a harlot by the hand and entered the Holy of Holies and spread out a scroll of the Law and committed a sin on it. He then took a sword and slashed the curtain. Miraculously, blood spurted out, and he thought that he had slain himself. . . . Abba Hanan said: "Who is a mighty one like unto Thee, O Jah? Who is like Thee, mighty in self-restraint, that Thou didst hear the blaspheming and insults of that wicked man and keep silent?"[45]

Israel in exile found a way of continuing to use biblical language. Biblical divine power continues to be present, but in a neutralized form as the power of divine self-control. Self-control in the face of blasphemous provocation constitutes the new meaning of "power."

The talmudic Jew inhabited two worlds: one where history and nature reflected God's power and judgments, and another where violence and corruption yielded wealth and prosperity. Titus entered the holy of holies with a prostitute and mockingly challenged God to strike him down. In response to this event, the Talmud points out that Titus failed to realize that divine power often takes the form of divine silence.

The talmudic age testified to divine silence and to the tragic dimension of Jewish history. A major concern of talmudic Judaism was how to continue as a spiritual people in a world that did not confirm biblical expectations. The talmudic sages never gave up the biblical consciousness of God's responsiveness and immediacy. They retained the belief in God's power to reveal Himself openly in history, but they tried to restrict and confine it to memories and to eschatological hopes. In talmudic Judaism, we find the world of divine responsiveness and mutuality ("If you will hearken to My command, I will . . .") not in everyday reality but in institutionalized memories, such as the biblical readings and the ambience of the Sabbath and the festivals.[46]

The crucial question facing the analyst of talmudic Judaism is, How effective was this attempt at restricting the biblical mythic consciousness? Was it successfully neutralized? Did it cease being a live option? Or did it remain just below the surface, threatening to explode in the face of rabbinic sobriety and realism? This is a difficult but necessary problem to resolve. It requires the examination of diverse currents in Jewish mystical and philosophical thought in order to discover the various forms that the interrelationship of biblical and rabbinic thought assumed in Jewish history. One thing, however, is clear. A Jew who internalizes the talmudic suppression of biblical consciousness can build a spiritual life in the absence of responsive historical events.

To the talmudic Jew, whose daily spiritual existence was characterized by loyalty to the Law, God was present in history because His Law is present. Because the Torah and the covenant are eternally binding, it is these and not events in history which constitute the mediator of divine concern. Instead of seeking instances of God's breaking into history, the rabbinic teachers expanded and elaborated biblical law to cover enormously wide ranges of experience. As more of reality fell under the authority of the Law, God's will and influence became more deeply felt.

In order to sustain the development of the halakhic process, talmudic rabbis proclaimed the priority of human reason over latter-day intrusions of revelation in the form of "heavenly voices," by referring to the biblical phrase "(Torah) is not in heaven" (Deut. 30:12). "Heaven" may not interfere in the development of Torah. God gave the Torah to a human community which, using reasoning and argumentation, is autonomous in guiding its development.

137

In a text reminiscent of Spinoza's comparison of the prophet with the philosopher, the Midrash compares the scribe, that is, the Torah scholar, with the prophet:

> They [the scribes and prophets] are like two agents whom a king sent to a province. With regard to one he wrote: "If he shows you my signature and seal, trust him, but otherwise do not trust him." With regard to the other he wrote: "Even if he does not show you my signature and seal, trust him." So of the words of prophecy it is written, "If there arise in the midst of you a prophet . . . and he gives you a sign" (Deut. 13:2), but of the words of the scribes it is written: "According to the law which they shall teach you" (Deut. 17:11).[47]

In the talmudic development of the Law, one does not need prophecy or the intervention of God to confirm the validity of a legal argument. The scholar supplants the prophet as leader of the community, presenting his credentials of intellectual competence to reason and to argue persuasively about the law.[48]

These features of rabbinic Judaism, namely, the neutralization of the organic relationship between humankind and nature found in the Bible, the attempt to curb expectations of divine confirmation in history, and the superiority of human legal reasoning over prophecy, create the conditions for the emergence of a spiritual outlook in which the Jewish relationship to God does not depend on discerning His miraculous presence in history.

The God of Halakhah is similar, *mutatis mutandis*, to the God of Aristotle. For the halakhic Jew, God is perfect, and His wisdom is reflected in the structure of the Law; for Aristotle, God is perfect, and His wisdom is reflected in the structures of reality. In the former case, human reason is adequate to disclose divine wisdom in the Torah; in the latter case, human wisdom can achieve an understanding of God's wisdom in nature. The halakhic Jew is drawn to God through the development of His Torah without the aid of revelation or other nonrational intrusions into history. The passion of the *talmid hakham* (talmudic scholar), like the passion of the philosopher, involves a movement from the human being to God, that is, the passion of prayer. Aristotle's god, who attracts humans by virtue of His perfection, can be loved by rabbinic Jews insofar as the neutralization of the divine in historical events has become part of their religious sensibility. Judah Halevi clearly understood the profound difference between a tradition grounded in revelation and one grounded in reason.[49] The battle between philosophy and revealed religion was not only a question of competing truths; it involved, as well, questions of human adequacy and the legitimacy of human reasoning. Revelation and worship characterize the poles of the profound conflict between a tradition grounded in revelation and one nurtured by human initiative and creativity.

From Maimonides to Modern Israel

The talmudic tradition that we have isolated neutralized the religious need for a God who breaks into history. This particular tradition may have encouraged Maimonides to assimilate the Greek metaphysical tradition into rabbinic Judaism. Maimonides did not necessarily locate the relationship between Jew and God within history. As Urbach has shown, Maimonides went very far in banishing the prophet from any relationship to the development of the Law.[50] He was personally averse to magnifying the place of miracles in the tradition.[51] He did not believe that history would ever offer a permanent solution to the human condition.[52] The Law will be needed even in the messianic world. Human freedom and susceptibility to sin are unchanging features of life. That "the world pursues its natural course" is the quintessence of Maimonides' theory of history.

Accordingly, Maimonides rejects the eschatology of a new Creation and only insists on belief in Creation. Eternity *a parte ante* is rejected in order to introduce a theology of will, which, in turn, makes possible the giving of the Torah. Maimonides did not require a theology of history in which history would end, whether supernaturally or otherwise. He therefore accepted eternity *a parte post* and rejected eternity *a parte ante*.

> I have already made it clear to you that the belief in the production of the world is necessarily the foundation of the entire Law. However, the belief in its passing-away after it has come into being and been generated is not, in our opinion, in any respect a foundation of the Law and none of our beliefs would be hurt through the belief in its permanent duration.[53]

Maimonides' philosophical orientation did not seek to restore God's miraculous interference in the messianic world. He required the notion of God's will to justify the authority of Halakhah. Yet, after introducing a theology of will and thereby making sense of the revelation of the Torah, Maimonides undermines the prophetic eschatological passion by accepting eternity *a parte post*. Like his talmudic predecessors, Maimonides sought to cultivate a passion for God grounded in disinterested love of God.

No doubt this was not the only way to interpret the rabbinic tradition. Certainly, many great masters of the mystic tradition in Jewish thought were also talmudic scholars. The movement from the talmudic tradition to the Greek philosophical tradition was not a logically inevitable one. Yet, one must be very cautious in analyzing the relationship of God to community and history in the Jewish tradition. The problematic and interesting nature of this theme results from the fact that Judaism considers the biblical and rabbinic traditions to be one tradition. The Written Torah (Bible) and the Oral Torah (Mishnah, Talmud, etc.) are seen as one. Once the Jewish spirit united both traditions into a single revelation, it became possible and intelligible to interpret *Ehyeh asher ehyeh* as "I am that I am"—I am the necessary Being—and not as "I will be with you in your suffering." Because Maimonides was a master talmudist, he was bold enough to introduce his legal codification, the *Mishneh Torah*, with four chapters dealing with the primacy of the metaphysical tradition and to claim, in *Hilkhot Talmud Torah*, that the discipline of "Talmud" included the study of both Law and philosophy.[54] Surprising spiritual orientations and sensibilities emerge in a tradition in which one of its most respected teachers, Rabbi Johanan, can say:

> God made a covenant with Israel only for the sake of that which was transmitted orally, as it says, "For by the mouth of these words I have made a covenant with thee and with Israel."[55]

What Maimonides may teach contemporary religious messianists in the modern State of Israel is that the biblical emphasis on God as the Lord of history may not be the only traditional framework for interpreting Jewish communal existence. Our return to our biblical homeland needs to be infused with the talmudic appreciation of "the world pursues its natural course" without losing the passion of biblical personalism. Maimonides' philosophical and halakhic work sought to integrate the halakhic passion for the love of God with a world view that neutralized the tendency to see the redemptive drama of history as the only means through which the community could discover the vitality of the living God of Israel.

Many traditional Jews still believe that the passion for Torah can be nurtured by repudiating the wisdom of the world, insisting that the four cubits of the Halakhah define the universe of the observant Jew. From Maimonides' expansion of the "four cubits" they can learn to include physics and philosophy so that the intellectual ghetto will not be the only way to preserve the love of God and His Torah. The modern State of Israel, seen in the spirit of Maimonides, does not need to be either a political or an intellectual triumphalist celebration of the Jewish people's separation from the world. As Maimonides has repeatedly taught, Torah, in both its halakhic and its aggadic manifestations, was not meant to isolate the Jewish people from intellectual and spiritual participation in world culture. Rather, our Torah was meant to be a sign "of your wisdom and discernment to other peoples, who on hearing of all these laws will say, 'Surely, that great nation is a wise and discerning people.'" (Deut. 4:6).

Soloveitchik's Response
to Modernity

T he creativity of a "Jewish philosopher," as the first half of this expression implies, first unfolds within the intellectual and cultural matrix of the Jewish community. Unlike Descartes, for instance, who endeavored to rebuild philosophy entirely anew, the Jewish philosopher is not concerned with establishing totally new systems of thought,[1] but with clarifying and developing received conceptions.[2] Hence, Jewish philosophy has often been formulated in commentaries to traditional texts. Maimonides' main philosophical work, *The Guide of the Perplexed*, is in important respects a commentary on the Bible.[3] The medium of commentary enabled Jewish philosophers to innovate without discarding the tradition. The value of the tradition was accepted, but its content was analyzed and sometimes transformed.[4]

The second half of the term "Jewish philosopher" implies a love of wisdom, regardless of the source of that wisdom.[5] A philosopher is a thinker who enters into a dialogue, or even a confrontation, with modes of thought not necessarily of his own tradition.

Accordingly, on the one hand, Jewish philosophers are rooted in a tradition and intellectually responsible for the continuation of its values. In this sense, the limits of their path are charted and the overall frame of reference is fixed. The enormous burden of the past rests upon their shoulders; their minds are claimed by their history and by their people. On the other hand, Jewish philosophers participate in a universe of discourse not confined by the boundaries of traditional Jewish experience. As philosophers, they must examine and confront a vast domain of issues; they must face the challenges of modes of thought that are not their own. They must build an intellectual and spiritual bridge between their particular tradition and other contemporary cultures. As Jewish philosophers, they evaluate cultures in general with an eye to their potential contribution to the fabric of contemporary Jewish experience.

142

This attempt to bridge cultures is a difficult and painful process. Many people simply do not consider it essential to their lives. For others, however, Jewish philosophy is a most significant intellectual task. Through the confrontation with "foreign" thought patterns and ideas, they become aware of the points of contact and collision between the Judaic tradition and the modern world. The modern Jewish philosopher is compelled to ask "Can I guide Jews first from the tradition to the contemporary world, and then back to their roots? Can contemporary thought enrich the soil of these roots? Is it possible to inhabit two spiritual worlds?" This was the spiritual and intellectual dilemma of Maimonides once he opened his mind and soul to Plato, Aristotle, and al-Farabi.[6]

Contemporary Jews face essentially the same dilemma. Torn between their Jewish roots and their esteem for some other cultural framework, they seek to weave these conflicting elements into a single fabric. It is to this confrontation that modern Jewish philosophy addresses itself. In the writings of Rabbi Joseph Soloveitchik, it appears on page after page.

The Contemporary Problem

In order to clarify the type of problems that Soloveitchik has dealt with, one must first distinguish modern religious problems from those of the medieval world. The major problem of Maimonides, indeed of medieval philosophy in general, was the challenge posed by reason to religion, that is, reason-based knowledge versus revealed knowledge. The medievalist knew of two sources of truth: one grounded in the authority of tradition going back to Revelation, the other based on the autonomous workings of human reason, namely, logic and Aristotelian science. A typical question of medieval philosophy was, To what degree is one's tradition compatible with the truths of science and metaphysics? Maimonides, for example, examined Jewish normative and cognitive frameworks in the light of Aristotelian physics and psychology.[7]

Fundamentally, the problem of medieval Jewish philosophy was an epistemological one. The medieval world cannot be understood without an appreciation of the importance it attached to identifying the sources of knowledge. The medieval world was a world of faith, where the Bible was considered a reliable source of objective knowledge. The Bible was not read merely for spiritual edification or psychological insight, but in order to gain access to reality. Consequently, the medieval

143

thinker faced the problem of how to deal with other sources of knowledge; for if he admitted their legitimacy, conflicts could arise. For instance, a philosophical understanding of the God of nature might conflict with the idea of the God of history mediated by one's tradition. A central question of medieval philosophy, then, was how to integrate competing sources of truth.

The greater problem facing Soloveitchik and other recent religious philosophers, however, is not that of competing sources of truth. What, then, is Soloveitchik's religious problem? What troubles him spiritually? What kinds of problems is he trying to solve? The answer may be found at the beginning of his essay "The Lonely Man of Faith."[8]

Soloveitchik says he was never seriously troubled by the conflict between the scientific theory of evolution and the biblical account of Creation, nor by the contradiction between the mechanistic view of the human mind and the biblical concept of human freedom. Moreover, he consciously ignores the challenge presented by biblical criticism, which altered the course of Western religious thought in the last century when it cast systematic doubt upon the divine authorship of the Bible. However, writes Soloveitchik,

> while theoretical opposition and dichotomies have never tormented my thoughts, I could not shake off the disquieting feeling that the practical role of the man of faith within modern society is very difficult, indeed, a paradoxical one.[9]

Whether the world is a billion years, a million years, or five thousand years old is not a religiously disturbing question. What tormented Soloveitchik was the fact that the contemporary "man of faith" appears to be an anachronism. The issue that perturbed him was not the truth of religion but rather the current relevance of the religious person.[10] His questioning is not directed toward the theoretical realm, but emerges as the consequence of a personal, spiritual struggle with a self-confident and rapidly developing technological society. Soloveitchik is concerned with rehabilitating the significance of religious people in a society that appears to have no need of them. Religion seems irrelevant, or at best marginal, to contemporary life. Religion has not been refuted; it has been ignored. Secularization has reduced religion to a fragmentary, partial, and insignificant element of life.[11]

The contemporary world view shows indifference to the religious option. Consequently the religious person

> looks upon himself as a stranger in modern society which is technically-minded, self-centered, and self-loving, almost in a sickly narcissistic fashion, scoring honor upon honor, piling up victory upon victory, reaching for

the distant galaxies, and seeing in the here-and-now sensible world the only manifestation of being. What can a man of faith like myself, living by a doctrine which has no technical potential, by a law which cannot be tested in the laboratory, steadfast in his loyalty to an eschatological vision whose fulfillment cannot be predicted with any degree of probability, let alone certainty, even by the most complex, advanced mathematical calculations— what can such a man say to a functional utilitarian society which is *saeculum*-oriented and whose practical reasons of the mind have long ago supplanted the sensitive reasons of the heart?[12]

As this quotation reiterates, the challenge that science poses to religion today is not rational or epistemological in nature; the real challenge is the attitude to life that is engendered by technological society. The successes of science generate human feelings of pride, while mastery of one's environment eliminates feelings of dependence and helplessness and the need for God or religion. In the light of this modern attitude toward religion, the task of Soloveitchik and of other modern religious philosophers is to describe the inner spiritual life of the religious person in a manner that commands respect. Soloveitchik is not concerned with solving problems of truth, but with vividly portraying a viable religious position in the face of an alien technological world view. He addresses the challenge of religious anthropology, not of religious epistemology.

The focus of this type of religious philosophy is on the "man of faith" himself. If religion is grounded in human dependence on God, but the modern person no longer feels the need for God or religion, the fundamental anthropological (human-centered) question becomes, Can a religious framework in a technological society stress human adequacy and independence? More specifically, can Judaism meaningfully address people for whom spirituality can no longer be based upon dependence on God?

As a modern Jewish philosopher, Soloveitchik asks whether technology poses a threat to Judaism and whether Judaism can validate its existence as a positive phenomenon in the modern world. He chooses to evaluate the effect of technology on Jewish experience in terms of the inner sensibilities of the religious human being.

Religious Man and Technological Society

At this juncture, suffice it to say that there is a tension between the dignity provided by technology and the religious yearning for human redemption, which cannot be satisfied by technological achievement.

Soloveitchik formulates this tension in typological categories: Adam the First (of Genesis 1) is the model of dignified technological man, while Adam the Second (of Genesis 2) typifies existential man who is lonely and longs for redemption.

In general, Soloveitchik views technology as a valuable and positive phenomenon. With the successful exploration of outer space, some religious circles accused modern humankind of arrogance and hubris. A Russian cosmonaut mockingly commented that when he flew through outer space, he looked in vain for God and the angels. A. J. Heschel's reaction was, "What is the value of conquering outer space when man has not yet conquered inner space?" Soloveitchik's response, however, was that any undertaking of intellectual curiosity that enhances human mastery of the natural environment is religiously valid. Human feelings of pride and adequacy resulting from technological and scientific achievements are not, as such, threats to religion. On the contrary, the world of technology validates an important element of the religious outlook.

> Even this longing for vastness, no matter how adventurous and fantastic, is legitimate. Man reaching for the distant stars is acting in harmony with his nature which was created, willed and directed by his Maker. It is a manifestation of obedience to, rather than rebellion against, God.[13]

Soloveitchik interprets the biblical tradition not only as validating technological progress but also as explicitly prescribing the acquisition of power and dignity, and he interprets the first biblical account of Creation in this light. He argues that human beings possess dignity only if they overcome helplessness in the face of uncontrollable natural forces. Human dignity is a religious imperative that is validated by the Creation story of Adam the First in the first chapter of Genesis.

The Bible begins with an account of the creation of nature and man in seven days. Man is created in the image of God and is told to conquer and subdue nature. According to Soloveitchik, this is a divine mandate for man to harness, control, and master nature in the fullest possible manner. He interprets man's creation "in the image of God" as implying that just as God is a creator, so man is, in essence, a creative being; just as God is the Master of the cosmos, so, too, must man master the natural forces of the cosmos.

> There is no doubt that the term "image of God" in the first account refers to man's inner charismatic endowment as a creative being. Man's likeness to God expresses itself in man's striving and ability to become a creator. . . . God, in imparting the blessing to Adam the First and giving him the man-

146

date to subdue nature, directed Adam's attention to the functional and practical aspects of his intellect through which man is able to gain control of nature.[14]

In the religious anthropology of Adam the First, the creative impetus in man is a divine gift; the active expression of human creativity is a divine demand. In contrast to religious outlooks that view God as the sole creator and man as the passive recipient of God's beneficence, Soloveitchik believes that God's creative activity sets a pattern for human emulation.[15] The Creation story has a normative message. It becomes a moral imperative for human action; it prescribes human dominance over nature.

Man's confrontation with nature is a relationship of power. Since nature is indifferent to human needs, human beings must uncover and harness the secrets of nature in order to survive. Nature's gifts are painfully extracted, not freely given. If man is to satisfy his basic needs and overcome his inherent weaknesses vis-à-vis the cosmos, he must conquer nature. Not to do so is to remain helpless and lacking in human dignity.

> The brute's existence is an undignified one because it is a helpless existence. Human existence is a dignified one because it is a glorious, majestic, powerful existence.[16]

Soloveitchik goes a step further and connects dignity with "the halakhic category of responsibility."

> Dignity of man expressing itself in the awareness of being responsible and of being capable of discharging his responsibility cannot be realized as long as he has not gained mastery over his environment. For life in bondage to insensate elemental forces is a non-responsible and hence an undignified affair.[17]

Because modern technology has widened the range of human capabilities, it has increased the scope of human responsibility. A child is less responsible than an adult largely because of being less able to act effectively. Likewise, modern man is morally more culpable than medieval man because he is capable of doing more.

Soloveitchik validates the world of technology for it invests man with power, dignity, and responsibility, which are fundamental religious values within his tradition. Jewish law, representing a spiritual way for human beings to relate to God, assumes human freedom to choose and the ability to realize one's spiritual obligations. To the Apostle Paul, this assumption was an unwarranted presumption. Man, he held, is inadequate and invariably guilty; the way of spirituality must point from God to man. Early Christianity's challenge to Judaism centered on this fundamental point; it negated human adequacy and argued that God must actively intervene in human life in order to liberate man from failure. The symbols of the Incarnation and the Crucifixion stressed man's complete dependence upon God. Not only was man inadequate to elevate himself spiritually through the Law, but the Law itself was a burden impossible to fulfill, which only intensified man's feelings of guilt and inadequacy. Rather than ennobling man, the Law testified to his degradation. Therefore God Himself had to provide a direct means of redemption within the human world, in spite of sin and regardless of merit. Paul suggested that God's "experiment" with the Law had served only to convict human beings of their guilt; therefore God offered humanity a new option, namely, spiritual salvation through divine grace—a gift of salvation for an undeserving being. Divine grace would replace the Law, and implicit in this "good news," as Paul called it, was the negation of Jewish law and its development.

The Jewish community, however, stubbornly insisted on seeking a spiritual way not through grace but through the halakhic development of normative legal spirituality. Rabbinic Judaism developed a text-oriented culture grounded in the belief in human adequacy and competence to construct a dignified life. Halakhic Judaism assumed the prerogative to build a collective religious life independent of divine intervention.

Jewish law is determined by human beings, not by miracles; Jewish legal spirituality does not depend upon heavenly interference. When God Himself interferes in the rabbinic house of study and tells the sages how to decide the Law, they reply: "Excuse us, but it is written in the Torah that one must follow the majority." The rabbis tell God, as it were, that man alone must decide his religious destiny[18]. Moreover, God provided man with a spiritual system in which human beings must struggle to resolve human dilemmas. Rabbinic Judaism marks the weaning of man away from dependency on revelation.

For Soloveitchik, the source of the belief in human competence and independence is learning. The halakhist who studies and masters the Talmud feels intellectually competent to deal with social and spiritual problems. In temperament, halakhic scholars are spiritual activists and builders; they do not regard themselves as passive, weak, or insignificant.[19]

Because halakhic spirituality is not rooted in human dependency and helplessness, modern technology may challenge but cannot deliver a mortal blow to the halakhic outlook. Soloveitchik responds affirmatively to the expansion of scientific knowledge because his spiritual world is based on a foundation of human competence and intellectual independence.

The Quest for Meaning

The functional "how" question preoccupies Adam the First, who is created at once man and woman ("Male and female He created them"—Gen. 1:27) for the function of reproduction ("Be fruitful and multiply"—Gen. 1:28). In contrast, Adam the Second, who is lonely until he encounters Eve, is concerned with "why," with the existential question of meaning. He seeks to know the purpose of existence. He does not seek to discover laws governing the uniformities and causal connections in nature, but is interested in the unique and wondrous aspects of ordinary events. Soloveitchik spells out the difference as follows:

> While Adam the First is dynamic and creative, transforming sense data into thought constructs, Adam the Second is receptive and beholds the world in its original dimensions. He looks for the image of God not in the mathematical formula or the natural relational law but in every beam of light, in every bud and blossom, in the morning breeze and the stillness of a starlit evening. In a word, Adam the Second explores not the scientific abstract universe but the irresistibly fascinating qualitative world where he establishes an intimate relation with God.[20]

In contrast to Adam the First, who is confident and assertive, Adam the Second is receptive. His dilemma is that he cannot fully accept himself as he is, "since loneliness is nothing but the act of questioning one's own ontological legitimacy, worth, and reasonableness.[21] The questioning of one's sufficiency, the deep sense of loneliness, and the longing for confirmation by another are key features of the religious sensibility of Adam the Second.

Loneliness is the central motif of the second account of man's creation (Genesis 2). The overcoming of loneliness is the underlying and pressing drive of Adam the Second ("It is not good for man to be alone"—Gen. 2:18). According to Soloveitchik, loneliness must be understood "not in utilitarian but in ontological terms: it is not good for man to be lonely (not alone), with emphasis placed upon *to be*."

> "To be" is a unique in-depth experience of which only Adam the Second is aware and it is unrelated to any function or performance. "To be" means to be the only one, singular and different and consequently lonely. For what

149

causes man to be lonely and feel insecure if not the awareness of his uniqueness and exclusiveness?[22]

When Adam the Second looks upon nature, he senses an abyss between himself and the cosmic order. In the consciousness of this separation, he discovers his existential uniqueness and utter isolation. As
he becomes aware that there is no being in Creation like him, the focus
of his attention shifts to the singularity of his "I." Adam the Second
cannot overcome his inner isolation by conquering the external world.
He stands irrevocably apart from nature, separated by an abyss of self-
consciousness.

In contrast to the majestic life-style of Adam the First, Adam the
Second longs for what Soloveitchik terms a "redeemed existence." The
very search for redemption brings self-defeat. For Soloveitchik, if man
is to break out of the self-enclosed vicous circle of isolation, he must
accept self-defeat. That is, he must accept the inability of the self to
validate itself; he must realize that the self is not whole. It is not only
singular, but also partial and incomplete. This realization compels
Adam the Second to seek a special kind of companionship by which to
build community.

> At this crucial point, if Adam is to bring his quest for redemption to full
> realization, he must initiate action leading to the discovery of a companion
> who, even though as unique and singular as he, will master the art of com-
> municating, and with him, form a community.
> This new companionship is not attained through conquest, but through
> surrender and defeat. "And the eternal God caused an overpowering sleep
> to fall upon the man." Adam was overpowered and defeated—and in defeat
> he found his companion . . . it was indispensable for Adam the Second
> to give away part of himself in order to find a companion. . . . For Adam
> the Second, communicating and communing are redemptive sacrificial
> gestures.[23]

"Overpowering sleep" refers to that state when man is will-less; it is
only out of this posture of total surrender and receptivity that man can
form an in-depth relationship. Similarly, in-depth communication is
not a function of will; there is a dimension of speech which does not
deal with solving problems, but which expresses the communion of
two human beings.

According to Soloveitchik, communication finds its fullest expression when two people meet in a framework of common commitment.
Real communication is not the product of practical technique but the
result of a total life commitment where giving is a mode of being. It
does not entail mastery over the natural environment, or control over

others, but requires self-mastery; such self-mastery is the basis of communication with other human beings and with God.

Man's exposure to his fellow human being finds expression in a new experience of God. As is well known, God is called "Elohim" in Genesis, chapter 1, and "Adonai" (the Tetragrammaton) in Genesis, chapter 2. In this change of names, Soloveitchik sees a transition from Adam the First, who knows only *Deus absconditus*, the hidden silent God of nature, to Adam the Second, who meets *Deus revelatus*, the God of revelation. The Elohim and Adonai experiences of God, accordingly, reflect two conceptions of man and of human relationships. Just as the goal of a majestic existence is self-sufficiency, so the God of Adam the First represented an independent, self-sufficient, and inaccessible being. Elohim is manifest in the impersonal forces of nature. And just as Adam the First's encounter with Elohim is impersonal, the corresponding relationship between man and woman is functional and utilitarian. In the single-minded, egocentric quest for majesty, intimate communication with another is a distraction; Adam the First needs a co-worker, not a confidant.

In contrast to Elohim, Adonai represents the God with Whom one may have a personal relationship. In his search for redemption, Adam the Second meets, not the God of the distant skies, but "the God of earth, i.e., the God of Men," who addresses him in his singularity. Adonai is depicted in relational categories such as "Father, Brother, Friend." Adam the First's experience of Elohim is one of silence within the majestic cosmic order; Adam the Second's perception of Adonai is one of dialogue and intimate fellowship.

> Only when God emerged from the transcendent darkness of He-anonymity into the illumined spaces of community-knowability and charged man with an ethico-moral mission, did Adam *absconditus* and Eve *abscondita*, while revealing themselves to God in prayer and in unqualified commitment, also reveal themselves to each other in sympathy and love on the one hand and common action on the other. Thus, the final objective of the human quest for redemption was attained; the individual felt relieved from loneliness and isolation. The community of the committed became, *ipso facto*, a community of friends—not of neighbors or acquaintances. Friendship—not as a social surface-relation but as an existential in-depth relation between two individuals—is realizable only within the framework of the convenantal community where in-depth personalities relate themselves to each other ontologically and total commitment to God and fellow-man is the order of the day.[24]

Commitment to the covenant of Sinai becomes the bridge connecting Adam the Second, Eve, and Adonai, by crystallizing Adam the Second's feelings and by confirming the legitimacy of what he seeks. In spite of a silent cosmos, there is room for genuine communion; in spite of the loneliness of the single self, communication and community are possible; in spite of being lonely, one can experience the loving response of another. In-depth communication, communion born of self-surrender, and the consequent acceptance by another constitute the existential ground of the convenantal commitment to community.

Soloveitchik's prototype of a genuine religious community is the covenantal halakhic community. While guided by explicit halakhic norms, the framework is infused with the aggadic experience of Adam the Second. The covenant is at once a formal legal framework and a profound existential experience.

There are three closely related features of the covenantal experience which can be characterized as responses to Adam the Second's existential dilemma and which together form the basis for community.

1. Adam the Second is horrified by the absurdity of a silent natural order, which exposes his cosmic insignificance. He feels he is but a worthless speck in an infinite, unresponsive universe. In the covenantal experience, however, this cosmic relationship is reversed; man becomes aware of standing in the presence of the Infinite and of listening to and speaking with God. In acknowledging the significance of man in this way, the covenant creates the conditions for communication.

2. Deeply aware of his singularity, Adam the Second tends to become imprisoned in an "I" consciousness. But because God's communication, that is, the covenantal message, is addressed not to man as an individual but to a community, Adam the Second is forced out of himself and into a domain of sharing and empathy. The covenantal experience entails a "we" consciousness.

3. Adam the Second asks, What is the purpose of all this? What message is embedded in the cosmos? The covenantal experience embodies a message; it is a normative message that commits one to values and goals. Purpose and commitment, message and norm, go hand in hand.

These three elements, communication, "we" consciousness, and commitment to a normative message, are the defining features of the covenantal community in which "the individual intuits his existence as worthwhile, legitimate, adequate, and anchored in something stable and unchangeable." The covenantal community is the experiential matrix in which man's inner worth is confirmed.

Halakhah and Aggadah

The interdependence of the individual and community is symbolically reflected in the relationship between Aggadah as internal religious meaning and Halakhah as communal norm. (Aggadah is the story form of midrashic literature; Halakhah refers to positive law and legal analysis.) The human condition as described by Soloveitchik indicates an approach to the internal dimensions of religious experience, Aggadah, whose outward garb is Halakhah. The inner dynamics of Adam the Second, his awareness of singularity and loneliness and his longing for a redeemed existence, constitute a contemporary Aggadah. Even though the longing for redemption is grounded in the consciousness of man's individuality, redemption can only be realized through community. A redeemed existence for Adam the Second is ultimately a communal form of existence; the individual and the communal religious norm are inextricably bound together. In essence, Halakhah is at once both a response and an expression of the in-depth religious sensibility of Adam the Second. The religious sensibility, by nature essentially subjective and private, crystallizes in the objective and public terms of the Halakhah; the individual's inner spiritual life finds expression in the shared experiences of community.

The covenantal community, however, has two aspects: it is both a prophetic as well as a prayer community. Soloveitchik's definition of the covenantal community includes the assertive dignity of Adam the First, and the longing for redemption of Adam the Second. The foundation of communal purpose is shared commitment to the divine norm as communicated by the prophet. The divine norm creates a partnership giving God and man a common stake in human history. This partnership is initiated by God, who approaches the human community by sending His prophet. The community is faced with a threat to its very existence, however, when it becomes apparent that the last prophets have spoken and the lines of communication with God are silent. The Men of the Great Assembly called by Ezra rose to the challenge:

> At a later date, when the mysterious men of this wondrous Assembly witnessed the bright summer day of the prophetic community full of color and sound turning to a bleak autumnal night of dreadful silence unilluminated by the vision of God or made homely by His voice, they refused to acquiesce in this cruel historical reality and would not let the ancient dialogue between God and men come to an end. For the men of the Great Assembly knew that with the withdrawal of the colloquy from the field of consciousness of the Judaic community, the latter would lose the intimate companionship of God and consequently its covenantal status. In prayer they found the sal-

vation of the colloquy, which they insisted must go on forever. If God had stopped calling man, they urged, let man call God. And so the covenantal colloquy was shifted from the level of prophecy to that of prayer.[25]

This passage forms the heart of Soloveitchik's conception of the prophetic and the prayer communities. Prayer became dominant, says Soloveitchik, when prophecy ceased; prayer became prophecy in reverse. The direction of the covenantal dialogue shifted; rather than God addressing man, man addressed God. In response to God's silence in history, the prophetic community was transformed into a prayer community.

This yearning for covenantal intimacy can be initiated either by God through revelation or by the community through prayer.

Prayer is the continuation of prophecy and the fellowship of prayerful men is *ipso facto* the fellowship of prophets. The difference between prayer and prophecy is, as I have already mentioned, related not to the substance of the dialogue but rather to the order in which it is conducted. While within the prophetic community God takes the initiative—He speaks and man listens—in the prayer community the initiative belongs to man: he does the speaking and God, the listening. The word of prophecy is God's and is accepted by man. The word of prayer is man's and God accepts it.[26]

How does Soloveitchik know that God is responsive to man's call? Is it not possible to claim that the absence of prophecy signals that God has abandoned the community, that He is no longer available in any relational sense? Not so, in Soloveitchik's portrait of "covenantal man." Rather, God now energizes His covenantal partner to believe in his own ability to initiate. The absence of prophecy does not signal God's rejection of covenantal man, but rather the call for him to become the active partner in the relationship.

This indifference to history, characteristic of a certain way of looking at the halakhic experience, enables us to understand how, for Soloveitchik, God is never absent from the Judaic religious life. Prophecy moves into prayer; God can be addressed as "Thou." The Halakhah commands one to pray every day. In *Halakhic Man*, Soloveitchik's earlier essay, he argued that the *mitzvah* validates human dignity because God could not command if there were no faith in the human ability to implement His commands. Here, he claims that there can be no *mitzvah* of prayer unless God is always present in a personal mode, capable of being addressed in the intimate language of the second person singular.

The movement from prophecy to prayer parallels the movement from the prophet to the rabbinic sage of the *beit midrash* (talmudic academy). God no longer pronounces on the development of the Halakhah. He wants His human partner alone to take responsibility for its content. Similarly, God does not determine the intensity of the relationship, but seeks from His covenantal partner *his* calling out. In that sense, there is a deep parallelism between the way that prayer replaces prophecy and the way that the Torah scholar in the development of the oral tradition follows the mode of the prophetic revelation in formulating Torah and *mitzvot*.

This is not an event-based theology, in which one reads the signs of history to see if God is present or absent. Instead, it is a tradition in which one formulates a normative world, in which one feels the presence of God through Torah, prayer, and *mitzvot*. Prayer replaces prophecy. God is present, because for the "lonely man of faith" to abandon the possibility of prayer is to destroy the very foundations of the religious intimacy that is central to his whole mode of being. The world of the personal, of total normative commitment, of sacrificial love, could not surface as a human possibility were prayer not a permanent possibility in human experience. God must be present for the lonely man of faith.

This is a far-reaching theological argument. It would appear that Soloveitchik's covenantal man decides upon God's presence or absence. Buber would argue that Soloveitchik has impaired God's freedom. One could present a significant argument for the need for miracles, the need for grace, to read the signs of the calling, to decipher God's decision regarding our relational needs. This is not the mode in which Soloveitchik, the halakhist, chooses to describe God's relational presence in Jewish history. A tradition that validates learning as a path for developing God's ongoing revelatory presence controls the content of God's word. Moreover, this tradition posits a notion of divine presence which flows from the certainty of the human religious quest, rather than from external validation through miracle.

Just as there is no separation between the written and the oral tradition, so there is no separation between the prophetic, revelatory moment and the prayer moment. There is no effective difference between a biblical outlook, which reveals God's presence through miraculous, redemptive drama, and a prayer-oriented outlook that hands over the categories of creation, revelation, and redemption to those who seek a covenantal faith experience.

Halakhic Jews and History

How does covenantal man comprehend the meaning of historical events, and how does he understand God's presence in history? The answer of halakhic Judaism to these questions constitutes the strength of the halakhic system, but also its greatest potential weakness.

The problem emerges when God's redeeming presence, once deeply felt in Jewish history, is no longer felt or discernable. The horror of divine silence becomes manifest during periods of historical catastrophe. Postbiblical history does not appear to confirm the dramatic presence of God, which is so graphically expressed in the Bible. Christianity claimed that God's apparent noninvolvement in Israel's history revealed divine rejection of the Jewish people. Buber, using the metaphor of "the eclipse of God," claimed that, like an eclipse in nature, God's absence from history was merely temporary and we must await His return.[27]

Soloveitchik, the halakhist, turns to man to seek a proper response to God's silence in contemporary history. Soloveitchik points out that the Men of the Great Assembly instituted prayer when God was no longer ostensively present in history: when history became "unillumined by the vision of God or made homely by His voice, they refused to acquiesce in this cruel historical reality and would not let the ancient dialogue between God and men come to an end."

The Men of the Great Assembly decided that if God would not address man through prophecy, men would address God through prayer. But in order to have any sort of conversation or dialogue, the presence of two parties is required. The Men of the Great Assembly may have wished to address God, but how did they know that God was listening? How did they know that He was even interested in their prayers? On what basis does Soloveitchik claim that the Men of the Great Assembly "refused to acquiesce" and "insisted" that the dialogue go on?

Buber could never have made such a statement. The difference between Buber and Soloveitchik provides a basic insight into the halakhic approach to God's presence in history. To a halakhist, God is present insofar as the law is binding. The validity of the *mitzvah*, that is, the obligatory force of the commandment, brings God's presence into the human orbit of experience. The commandment mediates the presence of the commander. For the halakhic Jew, the *mitzvah* mediates God's active presence in history.

Events, then, became somewhat unimportant for the spiritual life of halakhic Jews because they did not seek God in historical events. Halakhah shifted away from an event-based theology. Even today, halakhists are generally not interested so much in formulating theologies of history as in maintaining the functioning of the framework of *mitzvot*.

Herein lies the fundamental difference between Buber and Soloveitchik. Buber, the religious existentialist, focused on an event-based theology and insisted on responsiveness to God's spontaneity; Soloveitchik, the halakhist, formulated a *mitzvah*-grounded theology immune to the fluctuating conditions of empirical history. In his book *Moses*, Buber finds the focus of Jewish spiritual life in the singular, dramatic historical encounters between Israel and God. According to the religious existentialist, the divine-human encounter is the crux of religious experience and the hub of religious life. On a communal level, these experiences constitute a historical I-Thou encounter between Israel and God. Also as a solitary individual a person may experience an I-Thou meeting with God. In either case, the unmediated experience of God's presence is crucial. Therefore, Buber speaks of an ongoing revelation. Since religious life centers around direct encounters with God, the cessation of revelation would signal the end of religion. Buber developed a theology of history to account for God's involvement in and withdrawal from history; there are moments of darkness (eclipse) when God is absent, as well as moments when He is present. To Buber, these moments of presence are decisive, for the spiritual life is nothing without I-Thou encounters with God.

The spiritual life of the halakhist, however, does not depend upon such moments of divine presence. The halakhist's meeting with God is not dependent upon fleeting moments of history, but upon fixed patterns of behavior. Even during the blackest moments of history, the halakhist wakes up in the morning, puts on his *tefillin* (phylacteries), and says, "Blessed art Thou, Lord our God." He can still address God because historical events do not mediate his addressing the divine Thou. He says "Thou" because he feels the force of the *mitzvah* in his daily life. Through the *mitzvah*, he experiences God's presence.

The Men of the Great Assembly secured the authority of the commandments, thereby preserving dialogue with God for future generations. As long as the community kept the commandments, it could, in principle, speak with God just as the prophet did. As long as the community preserved the prophetic message and was committed to its fulfillment, the community could share in "prophecy" within the framework of the prayer community. It is in this sense that Soloveitchik can say, "Prayer is the continuation of prophecy and the fellowship of prayerful men is *ipso facto* the fellowship of prophets."[28] No event in history can undermine that framework or destroy that fellowship.

Because halakhic man was spiritually grounded in *mitzvot*, and not

157

in historical events, Jews were able to withstand the cruelty of exile for thousands of years. Jews in exile were painfully aware of the abyss between accounts of past historical redemption and the bleak reality of persecution in the present. Yet they could still address God.

Had the Jews been Buberian disciples, they could hardly have survived; the events of history would surely have crushed them. But they were not existentialists awaiting spontaneous encounters with the eternal Thou. They were people who studied Torah and who, when they performed a *mitzvah*, felt that God was with them. The greatness of halakhic Jews was commitment to Law, which in effect made them immune to history. The tragedy of halakhic Jews, however, is that Halakhah failed to respond adequately when the Jewish people consciously reentered history.

After the Emancipation, the Jewish people felt the attraction of history. At least as individuals, Jews were invited to move from the margins of society into the mainstream of the political and cultural life of the nations. More important, the Emancipation paved the way for Zionism and the birth of the State of Israel. The halakhic community, however, was prepared neither for the Emancipation nor for the State of Israel. Halakhic spirituality ensured that events in history did not seriously affect the Jewish community, for potentially that could injure communal solidarity and destroy the individual's faith. History meant catastrophe; history was the enemy, the subversive enticer. The halakhic community also feared new turns of events because of its experience with the delusions of premature responses; Jewish history is replete with false messiahs. It therefore recognized the danger of permitting the Jewish community to be dependent on the capricious fluctuations of historical events.

Despite these fears, however, two dramatic events forced the majority of Jews to reshape their lives: the Holocaust and the creation of the State of Israel. In the wake of these events, history could no longer be neutralized or ignored. Soloveitchik was also faced with this challenge. After the Six-Day War, many Jews sensed the redemptive presence of God. How was the halakhic leadership to react? Soloveitchik's response was muted: while he noted that the State of Israel could reawaken Jewish sensibilities in Jews who had seemed lost to assimilation, he counseled waiting. He based his reaction on a passage in the talmudic tractate Shabbat, which states that when the miracle of Hanukkah occurred, the rabbis "waited a year" before proclaiming the Festival of Hanukkah. He concluded that this generation of Jews must also wait before declaring a festival celebrating God's redemptive presence in history. This sober response was far removed from the theologically aroused response of numerous Jews seeking ways of pointing to God's presence in such "epoch-making events."[29]

The halakhic sensibility is not at ease in contemporary Jewish history. It is too keenly aware of the vicissitudes of history to risk mistaking appearance for reality, that is, of seeing God's redemptive power in events that may subsequently be reversed. One need only note the contrast in moods after the Six-Day War and after the Yom Kippur War.

Events are precarious blocks with which to build one's spiritual outlook. Nevertheless, Jews must face the painful possibility that the halakhic neutralization of history may secure Judaism, albeit at the expense of the participation of large segments of the Jewish people. Halakhah may be a viable response for a lonely man of faith, yet be a dead letter for a Jewish community that stakes its very life upon the precarious ground of the State of Israel.[30]

The dilemma confronting the Halakhah becomes obvious: can the sober sustaining power of halakhic spirituality unite with the volatile drama of the return of the Jewish people to its ancient homeland? Can we celebrate the rebirth of Israel yet not lose sight of the rabbinic skepticism regarding the significance of singular events on changing Jewish history?

The drama of Israel and the rebirth of a people after decimation by the Holocaust has generated a profound sense of wonderment and a belief that everything is possible if we only will it. There is a messianic fervor that infuses so much of our religious passion for Israel. Precisely in this atmosphere, Soloveitchik's sober affirmation of Israel may play a role in keeping our society both passionate and sane.

159

Soloveitchik's
Religious Hero

The intellectual climate of the early twentieth century was characterized by a deep confidence in the human ability to confront, and eventually to remove, any obstacle in the way of human happiness. Inspired by the remarkable advances in scientific inquiry and technology, people became convinced of their ability to fashion the world as they desired. Unlike the contemplative ideal of philosophers such as Aristotle and Spinoza, the ideal of the late nineteenth and early twentieth centuries was action-centered. Bacon's dictum "Knowledge is power" captured the imagination of modern humanity eager to expand its newly discovered strengths.

In light of this self-confident ethos, traditional religion appeared to be anachronistic, if not reactionary. If religion is a prescientific position vis-à-vis life, based on human helplessness in the face of the uncontrollable and the unknown, then modern science and technology render religion obsolete. Petitional prayer is pointless in the modern world if judged in terms of its efficacy, say, as a response to sickness in competition with medical science. If a religious attitude to life is marked by passivity and surrender to one's fate, then religion ceases to be a live option for the modern human being.

Accordingly, the critique of religion in the nineteenth and twentieth centuries focused not so much on the cognitive claims of religious beliefs as on the type of human being that religion cultivates. The crucial issue was not to prove or disprove God's existence or to question the need for belief in God in the light of scientific theory. The attack on religion grew out of a concern with liberating human beings from the debilitating influences of religion.

Modern critics of religion supposed that, in order to reinforce human initiative, it was necessary to uproot religious commitments that engendered passivity and self-negation. The revolt was not so much against God as it was against a religious anthropology that undermined the unfolding of human powers and creative potential. Scientific and

160

technological advances in the nineteenth and twentieth centuries confirmed the need for a modern conception of humankind which could
strengthen belief in human adequacy and the ability to bear responsibility for history. The main aim of many philosophical anthropologies
was to counteract religious ideologies which undermined the belief that
the human being is a responsible agent capable of transforming the
human environment.

Ludwig Feuerbach, who influenced Karl Marx, described religion as
a form of human alienation. In *The Essence of Christianity,* he formulated
the thesis that religion was a grand projection of human powers onto a
mythical, superhuman God. The more human beings attributed to
God, argued Feuerbach, the less they attributed to man. Given such an
inverse relationship, the belief in God's perfection automatically de-
creased belief in human worth. Human beings not only created God in
their image, but also emptied themselves of all the virtues that they
attributed to God; the more man glorified God, the more man became
impoverished. According to this view, divine glorification is in fact an
externalization and alienation of what rightfully belongs to man. Man
feels inadequate, impotent, and guilty for being creative. The consequence of attributing love and righteousness to God is belief in human
sinfulness and depravity. Adoration of God diminishes man's self-
respect.

It is in this context that Soloveitchik expounded his theology. The
challenge facing Soloveitchik was not to develop a metaphysical or
epistemological defense of Judaism, but rather to counteract a prevailing belief that Judaism was incompatible with the human-centered
ethos of modernity. Let us begin by looking at the way Soloveitchik
brings the traditional halakhic Jew into the world of modernity.

I

The hero of the East European (especially Lithuanian) Jewish intellectual tradition was the *talmid hakham,* the scholar totally immersed in the
study of talmudic texts. Such a figure, of which Soloveitchik's grandfather was a pristine example, stands in sharp contrast to the triumphant man of action of the modern age.

The picture of the traditional *talmid hakham* engaged in intense legal
argumentation is an easy target for the type of critique of religion discussed above. What better example is there of the reactionary, debilitating influence of religion than the student preoccupied exclusively with
talmudic texts and oblivious to the world of ordinary human affairs?

Engrossed in erudite jurisprudential texts, he seems passive and utterly devoid of prophetic Judaism's urgent moral and political passions. He appears to be a paradigmatic example of the alienated individual, a fossil who has substituted scholarship for life. He lives as a recluse whose philosophy of life may be summarized succinctly by the talmudic statement that after the Temple was destroyed, "God only has in His world the four cubits of Halakhah."[1] The limits of the traditional talmudic student's world rarely appear to extend beyond the talmudic universe of discourse.

The core of the dilemma seething in Soloveitchik's first essay, *Halakhic Man*, is whether halakhic Judaism can become a compelling option for individuals influenced by the modern values of spontaneity, autonomy, individualism, and creativity. Unlike Buber, who believed he could bridge Judaism's transition to modernity by a selective presentation of hasidic pietistic anecdotes, Soloveitchik accepted the challenge of focusing on the Lithuanian halakhic mind. Soloveitchik sought to restore dignity to the Lithuanian halakhist who was wholly committed to the rigorous discipline of the Law. Soloveitchik is, so to speak, the poet of the Law. His task is to uncover the "soul" of the halakhist and to reveal the inner workings of a world view maligned and misunderstood by many of his contemporaries.

There are two main areas that make halahic Judaism vulnerable to attack by those committed to the modern ethos. First, Halakhah may be criticized for inducing human passivity. The "four cubits of Halakhah" may, psychologically speaking, constitute the borders of one's world. Halakhah spirituality may foster a form of cultural narcissism focusing on the intricacies of talmudic argumentation and removing the practical affairs of community and history to the periphery of one's field of vision. From the perspective of the man of action, concerned with the material conditions of society, the Torah world appears to be a cloistered retreat at the margins of history.

Many Zionists, for example, saw the world view revolving around the traditional talmudic academy as an obstacle on the Jewish people's path to national-political rebirth. Talmudic Judaism hindered the politicization of Jewish self-consciousness insofar as it offered Jews a substitute for actual history. The ocean of the Talmud was thought to be so vast and captivating that, having once entered it, one could think of little else. It is not surprising, therefore, that early Zionist thinkers often expressed deep antitalmudic sentiments.

Secondly, Halakhah conflicts with the individualistic ethos of modern society by virtue of its emphasis on uniformity and standardization of practice. Halakhah appears to be a straitjacket that crushes individuality by forcing behavioral conformity and discipline. Halakhah, whose scope goes beyond ordinary law and includes moral as well as symbolic-expressive forms of conduct (for example, prayer and ritual), regulates practically all aspects of the individual's life.

Judaism imposes order and regularity on the individual's choices and actions. The Jew encounters the normative stamp of Halakhah in all areas of life. The *Shulhan Arukh*, the code of Jewish law, takes little account of differences between individuals when prescribing how one should act in the intimate precincts of the bedroom or how one should express grief. The subjective feelings of the mourner or of the bride and groom, their concern with their own spontaneous feelings of grief or joy, do not justify deviation from standard halakhic practices. Halakhic rules do not seem to respect the modern notions of uniqueness, spontaneity, and individual realization.[2]

It is for such reasons that many religious existentialists reject Halakhah. They assail Halakhah for suffocating spontaneity and personal feeling by forcing the individual into a Procrustean bed of halakhic uniformity.

Soloveitchik's writings respond to the critique of Halakhah discussed above. His approach to traditional Jewish texts, as well as his choice of subject matter, indicates his interest in counteracting the stereotypical characterization of halakhic Judaism as a rigid, legalistic regimen. Soloveitchik's approach to Halakhah regards the form and structure of halakhic norms as the expressive embodiment of inwardness and subjective spiritual feeling. He seeks to show the relevance of aggadic Midrash, the narrative parable form of rabbinic literature that is often considered merely popular and therefore unworthy of serious analysis.

As an Orthodox leader of the Jewish community, Soloveitchik is uncompromisingly committed to the authority of traditional Halakhah, which he has characterized as a closed formal system of norms. Nevertheless, he broadens the scope of individual religious experience within Halakhah by analyzing halakhic norms in terms of underlying human attitudes and orientations.

Halakhah, for Soloveitchik, may be characterized as a spirituality of tasks. Judaism's affinity with modernity can best be demonstrated not by pietistic hasidic parables but by sympathetic portrayals of scholars, such as Rabbi Haim of Brisk, who grappled with classical talmudic problems, such as, What are the limits and nature of one's liability if one's animal destroys another person's property? If a person builds a fire in his yard and an unexpected gust of wind spreads the fire to a neighbor's property, is he responsible for damages? What constitutes negligence? What conditions affect the extent of liability? Such problems are an integral part of the texts to which students of talmudic academies devote most of their attention. Unlike the main religious texts of many religious traditions, which are devoted to theological, doctrinal, or confessional matters, traditional Jewish literature consists of legal texts whose subject matter cuts across the common distinction between religious and secular issues. Jewish law embraces interpersonal, social, political, and economic as well as ceremonial and liturgical subjects. Torts and criminal law receive no less attention than laws of ritual impurity and prayer.

The common denominator of most of the subject matter studied in talmudic academies is its relationship to concrete behavior and practice. Philosophical speculation on theology and dogma is alien to the mainstream of traditional Jewish study. Traditional talmudic academies (*yeshivot*) cultivated the legal mind whose intellectual rigor and acumen were oriented to disclosing pragmatic, conceptual distinctions and perfecting the skills of cogent legal argumentation. Jewish law was less concerned with doctrinal disputations than with the conditions of liability for fires originating in one's yard or for dangerous pits dug in public thoroughfares. This concern with minute details of mundane daily practice once made Judaism susceptible to charges of legalism and pharisaism, especially when the spirit of the age was preoccupied with otherworldly spirituality. But in the modern world, which emphasizes active involvement in transforming the material conditions of life, Soloveitchik can commend Judaism's rootedness in concrete reality.

Unlike contemplative, mystic forms of spirituality, Halakhah, for Soloveitchik, compels one to become engaged with the concrete problems of daily life. Rather than encouraging one to seek God in solitary moments of private illumination, Halakhah focuses one's attention on concrete behavior and on the mundane details of everyday life. The proper context of religious activity is the marketplace; the problems engaging the halakhic man of faith are practical rather than speculative or doctrinal. Jewish thinkers who continue to feel defensive because of traditional Judaism's legal orientation and who apologetically camouflage the legal tradition in Judaism by exaggerating mystical and pietistic trends in Jewish history fail to grasp the modern relevance of a tradition whose legal-practical orientation is in many ways akin to the modern temperament.

This is not to say that the conceptual analysis of practical issues, which typifies talmudic discussions, cannot become a self-contained intellectual discipline removed from the current practical problems of human societies. The legalist may become enamoured of the intellectual intricacies of practical problems and ignore the painful uncertainty of concrete decision-making. The complex legal concepts involved in human contracts may arouse one's interest as an intellectual puzzle; actual contracts, however, may be less interesting and intellectually more frustrating than hypothetically conceived cases. The danger of study and analysis—even if the subject matter be in principle practical—involves the seductive attraction of intellectual alienation. Intellectual puzzle-solving may become a substitute for involvement in human dilemmas that defy neat, intellectually satisfying solutions. The challenge facing the talmudist is to study a page of Talmud and then to test out its solutions in the marketplace. The student of torts must strive to master complex talmudic discussions of liability with an eye to the "banana peel" inadvertently dropped in the street.

The Jewish tradition's emphasis on *talmud Torah* (study of Torah) may produce a culture of intellectually sophisticated activists, or it may produce a sheltered enclave of *pilpulists* (casuists). Soloveitchik believes, however, that Halakhah can defy this risk.

II

Which features of Judaism encourage Soloveitchik to claim, starting with his essay *Halakhic Man* (1944), that the modern values of creativity and autonomy can grow within a halakhic culture? What is there within the Judaic tradition that anchors the religious person to everyday life?

Halakhic man's spiritual life is nurtured by two central features of the Judaic tradition. One is the *mitzvot*, the practical commandments through which God is revealed to the community. The other is Torah study. The Judaic community's way of life is defined by the entire exegetical tradition, not merely by the Bible's revelatory framework. As portrayed by Soloveitchik, halakhic man lives in intense discussion and dialogue with two thousand years of commentary by Torah scholars who participated in the development and clarification of Halakhah.

Soloveitchik discerns a profound dialectic between revelation and intellectual creativity. Although halakhic man believes that every word of Torah is divine, this word itself becomes his possession. There is both receptivity and creativity in halakhic Judaism. All authority is grounded in divine revelation, yet God Himself submits to the earthly academy's ruling. The Law is shaped, interpreted, and expanded by halakhic man, not by prophets claiming the authority of revelation.

Halakhic man repudiates the assertion that revelatory grace is necessary for interpreting the Torah. This learning tradition enables ha-

165

lakhic man to feel intellectually adequate and totally self-confident. Nothing beyond ordinary human resources is needed to provide normative guidance for the covenantal community of Israel.

Halakhic man's sense of autonomy is not simply a psychological experience arising from his identification with and internalization of God's revealed law. The Torah scholar's sense of autonomy is based above all upon the fact that human judges define the halakhic norm's applicability and content. Soloveitchik illustrates the point with familiar passages from the Midrash.

When the ministering angels ask God on which days Rosh Hashanah and Yom Kippur will fall, when He will judge Israel, He tells them to heed the decision of Israel's own earthly court. As Rabbi Judah inferred from "These are the festivals of the Lord, which you shall proclaim" (Lev. 32:37):

> God said: "Before Israel became My people, the festivals were the festivals of the Lord." But henceforth the festivals are those "which you shall proclaim." (Deut. Rabbah 2:14)[3]

Another passage compares Israel to the son of a king, who had treasure houses filled with every precious thing.

> When the son grew up and came of age, his father told him: "As long as you were a minor, I would watch over everything. Now that you have come of age, I am handing over everything to you." (Exod. Rabbah 15:30)[4]

Soloveitchik comments:

> The Holy One, Blessed be He, has, as it were, stripped Himself of His ornaments—i.e., His dominion—and has handed it over to Israel, to the earthly court. The earthly court decrees, and the Holy One, blessed be He, complies. If the earthly court rules in matters of law and judgment, the Halakhah is always in accordance with its decision, even if the heavenly court should disagree. Halakhic man reigns over all and is esteemed by all.[5]

A world infused with the centrality of the *mitzvot*, which celebrates the joy of studying Torah, a tradition in which human beings move their bodies with the rhythms of song as they study Torah, a tradition that portrays God Himself as a student of the teachings of the rabbis—all these provide halakhic man with a profound sense of rootedness in the world. The world of the human, with all its limitations and imperfections, is where God seeks to be present.

Soloveitchik highlights the earthbound features of halakhic man by contrasting him with another ideal type, *homo religiosus*, who is indeed familiar to Western students of religion. Of the latter, he says:

> *Homo religiosus*, dissatisfied, disappointed, and unhappy, craves to rise up from the vale of tears, from concrete reality, and aspires to climb to the mountain of the Lord. He attempts to extricate himself from the narrow straits of empirical existence and emerge into the wide spaces of a pure and pristine transcendental existence (p. 40). *Homo religiosus*, who thirsts for the living God, demolishes the bounds of this-worldliness, transforms himself into pure spirit, breaks through all barriers, and ascends on high. For him the approach to God consists in a leap from the empirical and concrete into the transcendent and the mysterious.[6]

For *homo religiosus*, the concrete material world is an affront to divinity; the temporal, fleeting moment is the total antithesis of the longing for eternal life. The longing for holiness, redemption, and purity is only consummated to the extent that the finite, temporal human world is totally transcended and absorbed by God's infinite redeeming power. Death is the portal conveying man from a limited, mortal existence to an eternally blessed life of salvation.

Homo religiosus yearns to be released from the chains of matter; he strives to become pure spirit; he longs for a world free of all human contradictions and distractions. *Homo religiosus* feels like a stranger in his body and in human history. He believes that man's task is to liberate God and man from the sinful blemish of temporality, finitude, and concreteness.

> The mystic sees the existence of the world as a type of "affront," heaven forbid, to God's glory; the cosmos, as it were, impinges upon the infinity of the Creator.[7]

Religion and God provide a vital consolation for those who experience the world in this way. The longing for eternal salvation provides a powerful alternative to life's struggles and imperfections. God provides an escape from the limitations of history and the body.

Homo religiosus believes that secular atheism locates man's true home in a fleeting, corrupt realm. By contrast, he believes that theism describes an eternal, perfect abode which represents the true destiny of the human spirit. For *homo religiosus*, ethics and politics merely provide an orientation to this world. Religion, by contrast, offers symbols, rituals, and experiences through which one becomes aware that this world is simply a vestibule to a realm far more ultimate and significant.

Soloveitchik is well aware that halakhic man's attitude to the world seems closer to secular man's than to that of *homo religiosus*. Halakhic

man is not overwhelmed and tortured by the weight of human sinfulness and pride. He is not a spiritual beggar seeking divine forgiveness
for his human limitations. The self-sufficient confidence revealed in the
academy of Torah learning inspires him with the belief that whenever
he knocks at the gates of heaven, he will be answered. The study of
Torah generates the conviction that God is always present for those
who seek Him.

Homo religiosus finds significance when life is wholly infused by eternity. For him, to feel at home in finitude represents a revolt against
divinity; to love temporal existence with a total passion is to fall into
the trap of atheism. To believe in a transcendental eternal God is to see
in human history and in man's finite existence a defect, a profoundly
incomplete fragment.

For halakhic man, by contrast, spirituality does not consist in liberation from the chains of finitude. The revealed commandments
constitute a total way of life that must be implemented within the
social-political frameworks of human history. The God of *mitzvot* and
Halakhah anchors man completely within history and makes him
understand that his true home lies within the temporal.

God is not in His true abode when He is separated from human
history, when human sin, pride, arrogance, and brutality evict Him
from the world. When God is exclusively in heaven, He is in exile. The
true home of the divine is in this world, where God meets man in the
domain of *mitzvot*, proclaiming, "Build for me a sanctuary on earth that
I may dwell within it."

> Halakhic man declares that the true home of the divine presence is in this
> world. The divine presence goes into exile from this world to the hidden
> and awesome transcendental realm. . . . The universal *homo religiosus* pro-
> claims: The lower yearns for the higher. But halakhic man, with his unique
> mode of understanding, declares: The higher longs and pines for the lower.[8]

The spiritual world of halakhic man completely reverses the direction of the passion of *homo religiosus*. Halakhic man proclaims that the
religious person does not need to obliterate finitude. Rather than embracing eternity, the religious person brings eternity into the realm of
finitude. The world is not a pale image of eternity, but the true abode
of the Shekhinah, the Divine Presence.

This consciousness leads to a unique perception of redemption.

> The ideal of halakhic man is the redemption of the world not via a higher
> world but via the world itself, via the adaptation of empirical reality to the
> ideal patterns of Halakhah. If a Jew lives in accordance with the Halakhah,

then he shall find redemption. A lowly world is elevated through the Halakhah to the level of a divine world.[9]

The desire to be liberated from the body and history has often created a religious consciousness that is immune or insensitive to the daily suffering of human beings. Why bother about disease, poverty, and physical oppression if one can find eternal peace? The longing for mystic union with God can become a deceptive way of numbing the religious spirit, preventing it from responding to human suffering and evil.

> *Homo religiosus*, his glance fixed upon the higher realms, forgets all too frequently the lower realms and becomes ensnared in the sins of ethical inconsistency and hypocrisy. See what many religions have done to this world on account of their yearning to break through the bonds of concrete reality and escape to the sphere of eternity. They have been so intoxicated by their dreams of an exalted supernal existence that they have failed to hear the cries of "them that dwell in houses of clay" (Job 4:19), the sighs of orphans, the groans of the destitute.[10]

Moral activism has often been understood as the antithesis to the quest for holiness and redemption. Not so in Soloveitchik's portrait of halakhic man's religious passion.

> Halakhic man is characterized by a powerful stiff-neckedness and stubbornness. He fights against life's evil and struggles relentlessly with the wicked kingdom and with all the hosts of iniquity in the cosmos. . . . [11]

This passion also infuses halakhic man's understanding of religious ritual. The whole of human life, not merely the synagogue, is the arena for worshipping God.

> The primary difference between halakhic man and *homo religiosus* is that while the latter prefers the spirit to the body, the soul to its mortal frame, as the main actor in the religious drama, the former, as has been stated above, wishes to sanctify the physical-biological concrete man as the hero and protagonist of religious life. Therefore, the whole notion of ritual assumes a special form in Judaism. The standard notion of ritual prevalent among religious men—i.e., ritual as a nonrational religious act whose whole purpose is to lift man up from concrete reality to celestial realms—is totally foreign to Judaism. . . . The Halakhah is not hermetically enclosed within the confines of cult sanctuaries but penetrates into every nook and cranny of life. The marketplace, the street, the factory, the house, the meeting place, the banquet hall, all constitute the backdrop for the religious life. The synagogue does not occupy a central place in Judaism.[12]

Halakhic man, as understood by Soloveitchik, is never far from the cries of the oppressed. His consciousness of God's commanding presence never allows him to forget that he is accountable for the social, economic, and political conditions of human society. Covenantal halakhic consciousness is anchored in human history. Such consciousness is responsible to a God Who seeks to be mirrored in the fullness of society. Halakhic man, therefore, never separates moral passion from the life of ritual and worship. Traditional arguments over whether ritual or ethics constitutes the essence of religious life are totally alien to halakhic man.

Homo religiosus, who is primarily concerned with redemption from human finitude, perceives ritual as a preparation for a redeemed otherworldly existence. Halakhic man, by emphasizing how infinity is brought into finitude, sees *mitzvot* not as symbols of a transcendent realm but as normative frameworks that enable human existence to embody the spirit of holiness. Soloveitchik's anthropocentric analysis of *mitzvot* reflects his claim that halakhic man expresses his religious passion within the human world.

III

Soloveitchik's thinking oscillates between an emphasis on the dignity of the individual and the centrality of the community. Halakhic norms, for Soloveitchik, reflect the institutionalization and democratization of spiritual life as well as an appreciation of the unique spiritual capacities of different human beings.

Although appreciating the modern existentialist emphasis on inwardness, authenticity, and spontaneity, he is firmly committed to Halakhah's emphasis on objectification and form.

> Kierkegaard lacked the understanding of the centrality of the act of objectification of the inner movement of faith in a normative and doctrinal postulate system which forms the very foundation of the Halakhah. The Halakhic world of faith is "terribly" articulate, "unpardonably" dynastic, and "foolishly" consistent, insisting that the feeling become thought and experience be acted out and transformed into an objective event.[13]

The *mitzvot* of prayer (*tefillah*), mourning (*avelut*), repentance (*teshuvah*), and charity (*tzedakah*) receive very careful attention in Soloveitchik's writings. By discussing the details of these commandments,

Soloveitchik shows his reader how Halakhah gives expression to the unique and the common, the personal and the communal.

Soloveitchik's treatment of prayer, for example, indicates the dialectical relationship between external form and subjective feeling.

> Prayer is basically an awareness of man finding himself in the presence of and addressing himself to his Maker, and to pray has one connotation only: to stand before God. To be sure, this awareness has been objectified and crystallized in standardized, definitive texts whose recitation is obligatory. . . . However, . . . it remains unalterably true that the very essence of prayer is the covenantal experience of being together with and talking to God and that the concrete performance such as the recitation of texts represents the technique of implementation of prayer and not prayer itself.[14]

One of the risks involved in the institutionalization of religion is that the specified formal conditions of worship will be considered as ends in themselves and formal Halakhah will degenerate into a soulless legalism devoid of personal spiritual meaning. Formal prayer demands attentiveness and concentration, which may suffocate spontaneity and subjective feeling. The formal requirements of prayer may become the very conditions responsible for the absence of genuine prayer—the means may interfere with the realization of the end.

Soloveitchik is fully aware of the fact that Halakhah risked the potentially negative consequences of formalized prayer by refusing to allow prayer to become the exclusive property of a spiritual elite. The tension between the minimal, formal conditions of prayer and the full expression of praying in the presence of God was never abolished. The undeniable danger of standardization is the loss of immediacy and the transformation of personal outpouring of feeling into a routinized recitation of prayer formulae. The tension implicit in halakhically prescribed prayer results from the constant danger that the external form will be taken as a substitute for subjective authenticity. Halakhah took this risk because of its fundamental commitment to the democratization of the spiritual.

Judaism rejected the option of formulating a spiritual way of life for a select few; it sought to institutionalize collective forms of practice so that the community as a whole could share meaningful religious experiences. Spiritual elitism, in which the saintly few were venerated by the self-disparaging masses, was counteracted by halakhic norms which the majority of the community could fulfill. Judaism democratized the spiritual by formulating minimal standards of conduct attainable by all Jews regardless of their socioeconomic and intellectual differences.

> If we were to eliminate the norm from the prophetic God–man encounter, confining the latter to its apocalyptic aspects, then the whole prophetic drama would be acted out by a limited number of privileged individuals to the exclusion of the rest of the people. Such a prospect, turning the prophetic colloquy into an esoteric-egotistic affair, would be immoral from the viewpoint of Halakhic Judaism, which is exoterically-minded and democratic to its very core. The democratization of the God–man confrontation was made possible by the centrality of the normative element in prophecy. Only the norm engraved upon the two tablets of stone, visible and accessible to all, draws the people into this confrontation.[15]

The Jew after Sinai did not perceive himself as the spiritual descendant of Abraham alone, but as a member of the covenantal community of Israel. The paramount importance of community forces the "lonely man of faith" to submit to collective forms of worship and religious expression. Subjective passion must defer to the standardized discipline incumbent on each and every member of the halakhic community.

Although community plays a central role in the Halakhah, Soloveitchik constantly insists that it never lost sight of the dignity of the single individual. To support this claim, he shows that the many halakhic laws, such as the regulations of mourning, are based on the unique value of the individual. In contrast to Leibowitz, Soloveitchik indicates that Halakhah's basic concern is spiritual inwardness, not behavioral conformity. In our time, Soloveitchik brings the heroic sensibility of modern existentialist thought into the collective framework of halakhic life.

Heschel's
Religious Passion

Heschel's Response to Events

A braham Joshua Heschel was a man of thought and action. His models were the prophets, who were outraged by social injustice and exploitation. His soul was set aflame by the urgency of the moment; he was shocked by the brutalization of the human spirit and passionately affirmed the ultimate significance of a single human life. He also denounced the trivialization of human institutions and the climate of banal mediocrity which, he believed, was suffocating the soul of modern man.

Heschel's lyrical command of the English language and his un-self-conscious use of evocative metaphors were not substitutes for concrete action. He personally bore witness to the "cash value" of his impassioned eloquence. As a proud, committed Jew, he demonstrated that intense love for a particular people and its religious tradition need not blind a person to the legitimate needs of others. His tireless efforts to end the war in Vietnam, his marching with Martin Luther King in the civil rights struggle, flowed naturally and beautifully together with his urgent plea for Russian Jewry and his concern for the security and moral well-being of Israel.

Unless one is attuned to the lyrical-poetic style of Heschel's prose, one may feel frustrated in trying to follow his arguments. The philosophically oriented reader is bound to have difficulties with Heschel's writings, which often contain loosely connected apodictic statements, not rigorous reasoning. Nevertheless, learning how to read Heschel is a worthwhile endeavor.

To appreciate fully Heschel's thought, one must read his books as if one were listening to a moving *niggun* (melody); one must read slowly and intermittently so as to allow the depth of his insights to take root in one's soul.

Devoting days on end to composing beautifully worded lines, Heschel sought to master a style of writing whose impact would approach that of music.

> Listening to great music is a shattering experience, throwing the soul into an encounter with an aspect of reality to which the mind can never relate itself adequately. Such experiences undermine conceit and complacency and may even induce the sense of contrition and a readiness for repentance. I am neither a musician nor an expert on music. But the shattering experience of music has been the challenge to my thinking on ultimate issues. I spend my life working with thoughts. And one problem that gives me no rest is: do these thoughts ever rise to the heights reached by authentic music?[1]

Heschel lived in a world that was crumbling. His one hope was to captivate his readers with a stirring melody that would arouse and inspire. Rather than attempt to persuade by clever argumentation, Heschel chose to enchant with a great melodic line that would haunt the soul of the sensitive reader.

In accordance with his view that Judaism affirmed the sanctity of time over space, he was quick to respond to the major historical events of his time. There was always an event or series of events which impelled Heschel to write.

In response to the Holocaust and the decimation of East European Jewry, he wrote *The Earth Is the Lord's*, wherein he tried to capture the spirit and values of this dying civilization.

Though some have found fault with Heschel's selective, idealized picture of East European Jewry, one should evaluate the style and substance of his essay in the light of his passionate concern to rescue Judaism from the assimilatory tendencies of modern Jewish history. Heschel felt the burden of generations on his shoulders; his task was to revitalize and renew interest in Jewish thought and practice. Unlike nineteenth-century *Wissenschaft des Judentums* writers who sought, as some have said, to give Judaism a dignified burial, Heschel strove to save it from dying by breathing new life into it.

> In this hour we, the living, are "the people of Israel." The tasks, begun by the patriarchs and prophets and continued by their descendants, are now entrusted to us. We are either the last Jews or those who will hand over the entire past to generations to come. We will either forfeit or enrich the legacy of ages.[2]

Immediately after the Six-Day War, Heschel took upon himself the role of helping Israel to overcome its political isolation. He tried to correct the view that the rebirth of Israel and the Jewish people's love and concern for Jerusalem were no more than a modern manifestation of biblical tribalism.

Heschel believed that loyalty to Israel, which in the modern world is the most powerful expression of Jewish particularity, contains within itself a message of hope and concern for all of humanity.

> The ultimate meaning of the State of Israel must be seen in terms of the vision of the prophets: the redemption of all men. The religious duty of the Jew is to participate in the process of continuous redemption, in seeing that justice prevails over power, that awareness of God penetrates human understanding.[3]

> The modern world, haunted by the bleak perspective of the twentieth century, has been given a concrete symbol of hope by the return of this people to its land.
> Pagans have idols, Israel has a promise. We have no image, all we have is hope. Israel reborn is a verification of the promise. The promise of redemption of all people involves the presence of this people in this land.[4]

Although the visible life of Israel is largely secular, Heschel regarded the Zionist call to return to the land as a resurgence of biblical spirituality.

> Israel reborn is an answer to the Lord of History who demands hope as well as action, who expects tenacity as well as imagination. . . . It is a land where the Bible is at home. . . . When you think of Israel, you think of events, of breakthroughs in history. . . . What is holy about the Holy Land? It is not only because its space is filled with frozen echoes of a voice heard in the past. Israel is a prelude, an anticipation. . . . The State of Israel is not only a place of refuge for the survivors of the Holocaust, but also a tabernacle for the rebirth of faith and justice, for the renewal of souls, for the cultivation of knowledge of the words of the divine.[5]

The world must understand that Israel has not been established merely because of Western guilt for the Holocaust. The rebirth of Israel reestablishes the living power of the biblical message for humanity.

Heschel asks, Where was it ever seen that a people staked everything on a promise? Where is there greater allegiance to the covenant with God than in this people's willingness to return to a Middle East in which everyone says, "You are unwelcome, you do not belong, you are a post-Holocaust phenomenon." Where can one find greater loyalty to the biblical promise than in the willingness of three million people to put all their eggs in one basket and to affirm: "We will live in the land of the promise. We are faithful to the biblical roots of our national identity"? They have returned to the Middle East only because they have been haunted by a memory which was founded on a prophetic dream and a divine promise: "I am the Lord your God, who brought you out of the Land of Egypt. I am in search of you, My people. I am only if you are in history. Your return to visibility mediates my concern for the human condition."

Israel's return to statehood has brought God's living presence back to history. "Next year in Jerusalem" has at last become a reality. That vow is no longer restricted to the domain of sermons and prayers. A new echo of God's concern for history has been heard as Israel returns to its ancient homeland. It is not a loud voice, but in this age of still-ness, despair, and darkness, any echo of eternity is all we can hope for.

> Israel reborn is an explicit rendering of an ineffable mystery. The Presence is cloudy, but the challenge is unmistakable.[6]

The Individual and God

Heschel was convinced that philanthropy and membership in Jewish institutions could not stem the tide of assimilation which threatened to sweep over the Jewish community in America. He believed that unless individuals were gripped by the spiritual power of Judaism, Jewish life would eventually die out.

> Jewish thinking during the last three generations has had one central preoc-cupation. . . . The group, the community and its institutions, received all our attention. The individual and his problems were ignored. We saw the forest, but nothing else. We thought about community, we forgot the per-son. The time has arrived to pay heed to the forgotten individual. Judaism is a personal problem.
>
> We have built organizations, but how Jewish is their membership? Our synagogues are beautiful, but the homes are a wilderness. We have devel-oped forms of living socially as Jews. Jews attend Jewish meetings, be-long to Jewish organizations, contribute to communal and national funds. But when left alone, or retired in our homes—they are poor in religious spirit. . . .
>
> If the individual is lost to Judaism in his privacy, the people are in danger of becoming a phantom. . . . Unless a person knows how to pray alone, he is incapable of praying within the congregation. The future of congrega-tional prayer depends on whether the Jews will learn how to pray when they are alone.[7]

Heschel was less concerned with how Jews acted within the collective framework of Jewish institutions than with how they acted in the privacy of their homes. He persistently attacked institutions such as the modern synagogue for their deadening effect on the individual's quest for spiritual meaning.

Heschel, like Soloveitchik, had little respect for those theologians and rabbis who market religion in terms of peace of mind and repose from the burdens of daily life. He refused to sanction conceptions of Judaism wherein God was not the central focus. Heschel unequivocally repudiated counterfeit prophets. True prophets, he believed, reveal divine pathos; they are not merely social reformers who reflect a humanistic ethos. Rather, true prophets mirror the divine impatience with social injustice and human mediocrity.

Heschel sought to restore this theocentric perspective on human affairs by embedding a concern for social justice within a passionate belief in God. He showed that involvement in human affairs takes on a new urgency when we see the human condition through the eyes of God.

Although Heschel emphasized the need for a sympathetic identification with God, it is noteworthy that the God he referred to is not the transcendent, impersonal Infinite of the mystics but the "human" God of the Bible. The prophetic experience of divine pathos differs from mystical ecstasy insofar as the concrete relation between God and Israel informs the prophet's sublime religious encounters. The prophet's emphatic identification with God is made possible by the vivid, lifelike characterization of God that shapes the religious person's consciousness. Unlike Maimonides, Heschel was not afraid of attributing human emotions to God. He sought relational intensity with God, not a pure, conceptual idea of the perfect being. Consequently, Heschel's writings are full of anthropomorphic depictions of God.

Maimonides tried to bring dignity and conceptual rigor to the uniqueness and transcendence of God. Heschel was concerned with making God a living reality for modern Jews who were embarrassed by faith. He sacrificed conceptual rigor for the sake of experiential intensity.

Halakhah and Aggadah

Heschel stands in stark contrast to those Judaic thinkers that regard the detailed specifications of Jewish law in Halakhah as the essence of Judaism. The implicit danger of emphasizing the obligations and prohibitions of halakhic Judaism is the loss of interest in God as the vital center of religious life.

Out of sheer punctiliousness in observing the law, one may come to be oblivious to the living presence of the Lord.[8]

Because Halakhah is so vast and detailed, one may lose sight of the *telos* of this elaborate religious enterprise, namely, the covenantal relationship between God and Israel. One can, for example, become so immersed in the myriad details of the laws of the Sabbath that one forgets that the Sabbath is a symbolic celebration of the world as a divine creation. Therefore, for Heschel, it was crucial to reestablish the importance of Aggadah, the theological and experiential underpinnings of the halakhic system.

Yeshayahu Leibowitz, by contrast, argues that Halakhah, rather than theology, constitutes the essence of Judaism. He notes that Judaism prescribes explicit rules of conduct without formulating an official dogma or theology. Halakhah is therefore the common denominator underlying the great variety of religious orientations in the Jewish tradition. According to Leibowitz, traditional Judaism was shaped essentially by the talmudic rabbis, not by the biblical prophets. Those who changed the community's way of life and ensured its continued existence were not God-intoxicated visionaries, but rather practice-oriented talmudic teachers who elaborated a comprehensive structure of normative behavior.

In contrast to Leibowitz, Heschel believed that the secret to reviving Judaism in the modern world lay in joining the prophet's theocentric passion to halakhic commitment. He sought to guide Jews back to Halakhah by way of the prophets, who showed the community how to live in response to God's concern for man.

> From a rationalist's point of view it does not seem plausible to assume that the infinite, ultimate supreme Being is concerned with my putting on Tefillin every day. It is, indeed, strange to believe that God should care whether a particular individual will eat leavened or unleavened bread during a particular season of the year. However, it is that paradox, namely, that the infinite God is intimately concerned with finite man and his finite deeds; that nothing is trite or irrelevant in the eyes of God, which is the very essence of the prophetic faith. . . .
>
> If we are ready to believe that God requires of me "to do justice," is it more difficult for us to believe that God requires of us to be holy? If we are ready to believe that it is God who requires us "to love kindness," is it more difficult to believe that God requires us to hallow the Sabbath and not to violate its sanctity?[9]

Heschel addressed an audience that had become estranged from traditional Judaism and had to be persuaded that Judaism warranted serious consideration.

In seeking to revive his reader's hunger for transcendence, Heschel dramatically depicts a characterology of the man of faith.

> We are in greater need of a proof for the authenticity of faith then of a proof for the existence of God. . . .
> We have to press the religious consciousness with questions, compelling man to understand and unravel the meaning of what is taking place in his life as it stands at the divine horizon. By penetrating the consciousness of the pious man, we may conceive the reality behind it.[10]

Heschel protested against those who relegated Aggadah to a minor position in relation to strictly legal exegesis. Heschel sought to reverse this legalistic attitude and to cultivate an approach where the Law could mediate, not mitigate, the God-intoxicated passion of the prophets.

> The modern Jew cannot accept the way of static obedience as a short-cut to the mystery of the divine will. His religious situation is not conducive to an attitude of intellectual or spiritual surrender. He is not ready to sacrifice his liberty on the altar of loyalty to the spirit of the ancestors. . . . His primary difficulty is not in his inability to comprehend the *Divine origin* of the law; his essential difficulty is in his inability to sense *the presence of Divine meaning* in the fulfillment of the law.[11]

Heschel's book *The Sabbath* reveals his unique approach to Halakhah. The book stands in stark contrast to other works on the Sabbath, which offer an exhaustive explanation of the thirty-nine categories of work (*melakhah*) prohibited on the Sabbath, as well as their numerous subcategories and legal extensions.

Heschel's important insight was that modern Jews needed to discover a compelling Aggadah of the Sabbath before they could relate to it seriously. They would have to gain an understanding of what it means to be enveloped by a sacred day. Only then would they begin to appreciate the significance of the rules and detailed regulations of the Sabbath.

For example, Heschel does not discuss the laws prohibiting the use of money on the Sabbath in terms of the halakhic category of *muktzeh* (objects one is forbidden to handle on the Sabbath). Instead of using this technical halakhic terminology, he writes of the need to free man from the idolatry of material possessions.

The Sabbath, according to Heschel, ushers in a new reality that transcends the traditional laws of Sabbath observance. His concern was to explain what happens to us when our consciousness is completely enveloped by a sacred day. *The Sabbath* introduces the reader to the poetry of this special day. Heschel writes about eternity in time, about the Additional Soul (*neshamah yeteirah*) which was said to enter a person on the Sabbath, about the positive spiritual dimensions of *menuhah* (rest), about the significance of stillness and declaring a truce between oneself and the world, about the architecture of time and the art of rest. Heschel piles one illustration upon another in this vein. He describes the Sabbath as a day on which one refrains from using technological instruments, which are all too often used as weapons of conflict; as a day for being with oneself; as a period of detachment from vulgar busyness; as a respite from worshipping the idols of technological civilization; as a cease-fire in the economic struggle with one's fellow man. The seventh day is an armistice in the cruel struggle for existence; a genuine truce from personal and social conflicts; peace between human beings and between humans and nature; a day on which a person avows his or her true independence. This type of language differs enormously from dry, formal, halakhic descriptions of the Sabbath.

Heschel believed that one must appreciate the poetic dimensions of a spiritual way of life before one can regard its "prose" seriously. For Heschel, living by *mitzvot* is poetry, for Leibowitz it is prose. For Leibowitz, Halakhah requires decision and discipline; for Heschel, one cannot pray without the sensibility of the poetic imagination and without the aesthetic sense of wonderment and surprise. Leibowitz claims that it is an heroic act of will to surrender oneself to halakhic discipline; the individual's personal sensibilities have no place on the altar of halakhic regularity. Heschel also recognized the importance of regularity and discipline in halakhic life, but his explanation of its importance does not negate the aggadic, poetic sensibility he sought to cultivate. This is how Heschel describes the relation between inwardness and regularity:

> Prayer becomes trivial when ceasing to be an act in the soul. The essence of prayer is *agada, inwardness*. Yet it would be a tragic failure not to appreciate what the spirit of *halacha* does for it, raising it from the level of an individual act to that of an eternal intercourse between the people Israel and God; from the level of an occasional experience to that of a permanent covenant. It is through *halacha* that we belong to God not occasionally, intermittently, but essentially, continually. Regularity of prayer is an expression of my belonging to an order, to the covenant between God and Israel, which remains valid regardless of whether I am conscious of it or not.[12]

For Heschel, prayer is the orienting framework for understanding *mitzvot*. "What is a *mitzvah*, a sacred act? A *Prayer in the form of a deed*."[13]
For Leibowitz, prayer must be subsumed under the rubric of *mitzvot*.

Prayer has no unique status, no unique experiential mode. The same attitude of acting out of duty found in all *mitzvot* is the intention one brings to prayer. To understand what Heschel means by the life of *mitzvot*, one must carefully study his notion of prayer.

Although Heschel recognized the importance of communal prayer in the synagogue, he nevertheless believed that praying alone teaches the soul how to listen to its own urgent need for God's presence. He therefore provides a new experiential language that prepares the individual to overcome the modern embarrassment at surrendering oneself totally in the moment of prayer.

Heschel believed that the study of Judaic texts was insufficient to revitalize the Jewish soul in the modern world. He measured the quality of Jewish learning by its impact on the prayer experience.

> This is the way of finding out whether we serve God, or an idea of God—through prayer. It is the test of all we are doing. What is the difference between Torah and *Wissenschaft des Judentums*? If an idea we have clarified, a concept we have evolved, turns into a prayer, it is Torah. If it proves to be an aid to praying with greater *kavanah*, it is Torah; otherwise it is *Wissenschaft*.[14]

Halakhah and Existentialist Anthropology

Even if Heschel's halakhic anthropologies are faithful reconstructions of the *telos* of Judaism, or are at least compatible with a great deal of halakhic thought and practice, the question still remains: Does his work adequately capture the type of commitment required in order to shoulder the burden of Halakhah? Does Heschel adequately prepare his readers for the rigorous demands of actually living according to the Halakhah? Does Heschel's aggadic portrait of the Sabbath prepare a person to deal with halakhic details of Sabbath observance? I think not. Though Heschel may help one understand prophetic anthropology and halakhic teleology, he fails to provide a complete account of what is involved in living according to the discipline of Halakhah.

It is one thing to persuade a person whose imagination has been captivated by an Aggadah of Judaism to try to live by the Halakah. Whether that person will be able to sustain the delicate tension between Halakhah and Aggadah is another thing entirely. Soon after a person begins to live according to an halakhic way of life, he or she invariably discovers what conformity to a comprehensive legal system entails.

Though the *telos* of a legal system and the values it was originally meant to realize are often reflected in its normative details, law differs from morality by virtue of being formal, systematic, and subject to official rules and procedures. The official reasons for obeying a law may differ from the rationale underlying the original enactment of the commandments. The complexity and technicality of Halakhah may exasperate those who are drawn to Judaism by the captivating music of Heschelian Aggadah.

A philisophy of Judaism that takes Halakhah seriously must reveal the dialectical relationships betwen Halakhah and Aggadah. It is not sufficient to present the Sabbath as eternity in time or to describe abstention from work in terms of inner peace and freedom. The subjective meaning of rest and stillness is only one aspect of the traditional experience of the Sabbath. The other aspect is collective, not individual.

In embracing Halakhah, the Jew enters a religious community committed to a normative system where Halakhah and Aggadah are not always perfectly balanced. Halakhah is, in many respects, self-sufficient and independent of Aggadah. Thus, the paths charted by Halakhah and Aggadah may not always point in the same direction. The modern philosopher must grapple with a series of difficult issues: What is the relative weight of Aggadah and Halakhah in situations of conflict? Is there an internal logic of Halakhah that is not controlled by aggadic teleology? How do we deal with halakhic developments that seem entirely indifferent to aggadic motifs? How much room is there within the halakhic system for individual choice? Does Halakhah necessarily collectivize our consciousness, or does it leave room for the singular halakhic individual?

Maimonides understood that Halakhah regulates collective behavior, while ignoring, in many cases, the individual's unique needs and sensibilities. An existentialist Aggadah, as developed by Heschel and Soloveitchik, will run into grave difficulties with a Halakhah that ignores the unique, singular individual. The emphasis laid by Heschel and Soloveitchik on the polarities and dialectical tensions in Judaism does not adequately resolve the difficulty in creating a halakhic culture in a modern world that values spontaneity, autonomy, and individuality. Neither thinker has shown where the individual has room to choose actions that are not validated by the formal canons of halakhic justification. The *akedah*'s religious passion, which inspires total surrender to God's will, if used excessively to justify the gap between halakhic rules and personal sensibilities, will undermine the claim that Halakhah nurtures the value of the unique individual.

In all fairness, this type of tension between the logic of collective life and the individual's personal sensibility is not restricted exclusively to

182

halakhic Judaism; it is a perennial conflict facing all human institutions. Any long-standing human institution must confront the fact that the goals and aspirations underlying its establishment lose their force once the institution begins to develop. A marriage may initially serve as a vehicle for the expression of love and mutual commitment, but under the weight of daily responsibilities and habit it may become little more than a routinized, self-perpetuating institution.

The anarchistic claim that all institutions generate human alienation is all too often borne out in fact. Institutions tend to become self-justifying objects of veneration that no longer need to validate themselves in terms of the values they were meant to serve. The problem that Halakhah faces is but one instance of a problem confronting all human institutions. Can human beings establish institutions that take structure and detail seriously without losing sight of their intended ends and guiding values? Once human aspirations and values become objectified in lasting, organized frameworks, the processes of estrangement and alienation begin to have their deleterious effects.

Notwithstanding these difficulties, Heschel's work is valuable because he illustrates the crucial polarity that religion must encompass in order to remain a live option in the modern world. By rehabilitating an anthropology of Halakhah, and insisting on personal religious meaning, he has provided an important corrective to the behaviorist-institutional emphasis of traditional Judaism. Future developments in the philosophy of Jewish law must show how the collective-social thrust of Halakhah can accommodate the God-intoxicated pathos of Heschel's aggadic spirituality.

Kaplan's Critique of
Halakhah

T he central concern underlying Mordecai Kaplan's philosophy of Judaism is the survival of the Jewish people. A basic presupposition of Kaplan's outlook is that Judaism is the creative product of a people seeking to perpetuate itself. Jewish assimilation in the modern world signals the urgency of formulating an approach to Judaism which could revitalize the people's will to survive.[1] Given the modern humanistic-activist ethos, he believes this goal can best be served by expounding a persuasive interpretation of Judaism which would indicate how Judaism serves human interests and unfolds human potentialities. Whereas Soloveitchik seeks to uncover the activist orientation of the classical halakhic Jew, Kaplan attempts to formulate a distinctly modern interpretation (reconstruction) of the dynamics of traditional Judaism, employing those elements which are amenable to a functionalist interpretation.[2]

In Kaplan's theology, God is not conceived as the unique Being who freely created the universe, but rather, as an immanent Power pervading the world. Thoroughly incarnate in the world, God may be identified with the manifold forms of human expression and productivity. The concept of God becomes a convenient way of referring to human aspirations and creativity. Otherworldly spirituality is considered fantasy and illusion; the otherness and transcendence of God are notions to be discarded. Any notion suggestive of the supernatural character of God must be replaced by concepts that highlight human potentialities and achievements.[3]

For example, Kaplan inverts the usual understanding of the meaning of the Sabbath. As traditionally understood, the Sabbath involves a suspension of humankind's creative manipulation of nature and an acknowledgment of God's supremacy. By abstaining from our ordinary mastery over nature and society, by relinquishing our right to control and manipulate our environment, we proclaim that God alone is the rightful master of the universe.[4] According to Kaplan, however, the modern Jew's perspective on the Sabbath ought not to be theocentric; the central focus of the Sabbath need not be the acknowledgment of the supremacy of a transcendent God.[5] Kaplan reverses the theocentric orientation of the Sabbath by humanizing the notion of God. Accordingly, he claims that the imagery of God as Creator is designed to turn our attention to our own creative powers. Rather than relinquishing their role as active shapers of their environment, Jews on the Sabbath symbolically reaffirm their majestic calling to be creators. The true import of the Sabbath is not the information it imparts about a free, transcendent God who created the universe, or about the relationship between creature and Creator, but rather the symbolic affirmation of human creative potential.

Kaplan's interpretation of the Sabbath is thoroughly functional. When on the Sabbath we proclaim our belief in one God Who created the universe, we are signifying that evil cannot permanently inhibit the human quest for salvation. In keeping with Kaplan's immanentist approach, salvation is constituted by the full realization of human potential and the integration of psychic energies, that is, by the positive development of a healthy, productive personality. The unity of God and the negation of dualism are interpreted as dramatic metaphors which express human optimism and repudiate fatalism in the face of obstacles limiting human development. That God alone is the ultimate ground of being implies that nothing which blocks the realization of human potentialities is permanent and unchanging. Evil is not an ultimate datum of reality, or, to use Aristotelian or medieval terminology, evil has no positive ontological status. The functional interpretation of this metaphysical statement is that human beings can effectively remove the crippling conditions of history that thwart human development. God's unity is less important as a metaphysical truth than as a catalyst energizing human optimism and initiative. The doctrine of creation repudiates fatalism and passivity; it supports and reinforces belief in the efficacy of human creative endeavors.[6]

Kaplan reduces many features of biblical and rabbinic theology to pragmatic-functional dimensions. Theology is interpreted in terms of the underlying human needs which it meets. When their physical survival was endangered, the Jews depicted God in terms of His power; when not wholly preoccupied with survival, they emphasized the moral nature of God which supported and reinforced particular human ideals and aspirations. God-centered supernatural concepts are thus transformed into human-centered functional discourse. The point of departure and the limits of Kaplan's interpretative framework are exhausted by the human condition. God-talk is admissible to the extent that it explains or influences projects and values serving humankind alone.[7]

Kaplan's approach is not entirely without rabbinic antecedents. Rashi's commentary to Genesis begins with Rabbi Isaac's question, Why does the Torah begin with a description of Creation rather than with Exodus 12, where the first commandments appear? As a classical halakhic Jew, Rabbi Isaac conceived of the Torah in terms of a normative way of life. Since the Torah is primarily a book of commandments, it should have commenced with law rather than with descriptive narrative. His question indicates a predominantly functional approach to Judaism, although, of course, unlike Kaplan's, his functional orientation centers around the normative framework of Halakhah.

The history of rabbinic Judaism testifies that in Judaism, practice has often taken precedence over theology. Despite differences of theology and religious doctrine, the characteristic common to traditional Jewish societies throughout two thousand years of history was conformity to Halakhah. Jews were less concerned with what one believed than with how one behaved. Unlike their Christian counterparts, Jewish scholars were involved primarily with the explication and development of law rather than with philosophy and theology.

The primacy of practice above theology is clearly expressed in the following Midrash attributed to Rabbi Hiyya ben Abba:

It is written, "They have forsaken me and have not kept My law" (Jer. 16:11)—i.e., would that they had forsaken Me but kept My law, since by occupying themselves therewith, the light which it contains would have led them back to the right path.[8]

The judgment, "Would that they had forsaken Me but kept My law," expresses a fundamental postulate of rabbinic Judaism: practice is more influential on human character than belief. As perceptive students of human psychology, the rabbis were skeptical of the lasting influence of ideological or doctrinal beliefs not rooted in practice.[9] Unless ideas are expressive of a firm "material substructure," they may become a weak and fragile "superstructure" unable to withstand the winds of change. Although Rabbi Hiyya ben Abba did not negate the importance of belief in and consciousness of God, he expressed the conviction that there are times in history when correct theology is less important for a person's religious development than correct practice. Though the ideal religious personality must integrate thought and action or, to use Aristotelian terminology, must acquire the intellectual as well as the practical virtues, there are times when practice must take precedence over belief.

The Midrash quoted above justifies a temporary suspension of faith in God so long as one practices His Law. One may claim that Jewish practice is legitimate even if it is not accompanied by correct doctrinal belief. "Would that they had forsaken Me but kept My Law" legitimizes Jewish practices and symbolic behavior during periods in history when theological skepticism is rampant. Given the abandonment of theological concepts in modern scientific discourse and the ghastly manifestations of evil in the twentieth century, which have led to widespread theological skepticism, one may argue that the attitude expressed in the above Midrash is particularly relevant to modern Jewish history. The tradition may be said to legitimize intellectual attempts to revive Judaic practice by suspending or ignoring theology. The modern Jewish philosopher may call for a "suspension of the theological."

Although this midrashic deferment of theology differs markedly from the articulation of a new philosophy of Judaism incompatible with fundamental beliefs of traditional Jewish theology, it shows that the functionalist approach to Judaism expressed by thinkers such as Kaplan is not entirely foreign to the Jewish tradition. It highlights the pragmatic-functional orientation which typifies a good deal of classical Judaism. The fact that Jews were not taught to recite catechisms and that differences in dogma alone rarely led to sectarian splits in the community reflects the predominantly practical orientation of traditional Judaism. Membership in the community was not based so much on dogmatic-cognitive affirmations as on behavioral conformity to the community's normative practices.[10]

The Bible itself often emphasizes the functional import of theological descriptions. For example, the concept of God as Creator of the universe is used to rationalize the reclamation of property in the Jubilee year: "But the land must not be sold beyond reclaim, for the land is Mine; you are but strangers resident with Me" (Lev. 25:23). With regard to the release of laborers in the Jubilee year, the Torah rationalized this practice in terms of the description of God as Redeemer. "For it is to Me that the Israelites are servants: they are My servants, whom I freed from the Land of Egypt, I the Lord your God" (Lev. 25: 54–55). Theological descriptions entail normative consequences; acceptance of God as Creator and Redeemer goes beyond cognitive affirmation and makes a significant difference in practice.

Midrashic interpretation, like the Bible, often makes practice the focus of biblical theology.

"You shall walk after the Lord your God" (Deut. 13:5). But how can a person walk after God? Was it not written: "For the Lord your God is a consuming fire" (Deut. 4:24)? It means, walk after His attributes (*middot*)—just as He clothes the naked, as it is written: "And the Lord God made garments of skins for Adam and his wife, and clothed them" (Gen. 3:21)—so too, you clothe the naked; God visited the sick, as it is written (after Abraham's circumcision): "The Lord appeared to him by the terebinths of Mamre" (Gen. 18:1)—so too, you visit the sick; God comforted mourners, as it is written: "After the death of Abraham, God blessed his son Isaac" (Gen. 25:11), so too, you comfort the sick; God buried the dead, as it is written: "He buried him (Moses) in the valley . . ." (Deut. 34:6), so too, you bury the dead.[11]

Statements about God serve as models for human imitation. Knowledge of God not only constitutes knowing that something is the case but also knowing how one ought to behave. Consequently, Midrash was unabashedly anthropomorphic in its depictions of God. "What does God do after having created the world?" is a typical midrashic question. The answer to this particular question, namely, that God is busy arranging human marriages, may appear scandalous and simple-minded, as if God had nothing better to do.[12]

Rabbinic anthropomorphic descriptions of God, however, should not be viewed as primitive theology, since the point and use of such a Midrash were not speculative and philosophical. In keeping with the practical human orientation of rabbinic Judaism, midrashic writers used theological language as paradigmatic models for human behavior. *Imitatio dei* (the imitation of God) made theology interesting. In order to make God a standard for human beings to emulate, talmudic teachers humanized theology. The "God of the philosophers" is beyond human emulation; *imitatio dei* is logically absurd if God is pictured as the sublime, transcendent being with regard to whom "silence is praise" (Ps. 65:2). The more God is pictured in anthropomorphic terms, however, the more He becomes subject to human imitation.[13] Accordingly, midrashic writers were blatantly anthropomorphic and did not hesitate to ascribe all-too-human feelings, emotions, and needs to God. The revelation at Sinai became the paradigmatic model for teachers who, in teaching Torah, were imitating the God who revealed Torah to His people at Sinai. In contrast to the fear and trembling of the biblical account, classic midrashic portrayals of the Sinai revelation picture God as a loving and patient teacher.[14] This anthropomorphic depiction of God was so real and concrete that the Talmud could ask whether one may accept payment for teaching Torah, since God—the teacher *par excellence*—taught Torah to Israel gratuitously.[15]

Although Kaplan's functional interpretation of theology may be said to have traditional antecedents, it reflects above all the ethos of the American experience. The overriding spirit of American philosophy, as formulated, for example, in William James's *Pragmatism*, was future-oriented and optimistic, grounded as it was in the faith that ideas must make a difference in practice. The openness and excitement of the frontier spirit were reflected in James's insistence that ideas be analyzed in terms of their "cash-value." Concepts must make a significant difference for human choices and attitudes. The frontier spirit was dominated by the restlessness of the man of action who inhabited an environment that was new, unfinished, and responsive to his efforts. The frontier spirit encouraged originality and innovation. Its borders were open; its ethos encouraged human ingenuity and bold experimentation. Thought was not considered an escape from a finished reality but, rather, an instrument for productively answering the challenge of a new and untried reality.

To the American, Europe represented the Old World which discouraged innovation and experimentation. Hegel claimed to have grasped the entire picture of human history. His task as a philosopher was to stand back and delineate the stages of the soon-to-be completed process of history. Philosophy was the culmination of history insofar as it embodied the cognitive dimension of the absolute. The Whole could be grasped and become incarnate in philosophical consciousness. Hegel addressed his thought to deciphering the Whole; he thereby reflected the spirit of a world nearing completion. In contrast, William James and John Dewey inhabited a frontier society; their world was just beginning to take shape.

Such philosophical thought, which regards intelligence as an instrument with which to change reality, shares in the activist spirit of youthful America. The ethos of the frontier was mirrored in the distinctive catchwords of American philosophy, for example, "cash-value," "instrumental intelligence," and "pragmatism." Only philosophical differences that were embodied in practice were deemed worthy of attention. The American mind was intimately tied to action.[16] Philosophy in America reflected a new faith in the human ability to establish the kingdom of heaven on earth. The spirit of young, expanding America interpreted many human problems in ways that made them amenable to technological solutions. There was nothing that human intelligence could not solve. Social and environmental problems awaited human ingenuity. Suggesting that there were limits to human efforts was tantamount to heresy.

Kaplan's thought reflects the perspective of a young European boy captivated by the spirit of early twentieth-century America. He is not

189

wearied by the repetitions of history, nor is he hardened by tragedy or by manifestations of radical evil. His world view reflects the innocence of America and the optimism of the rugged frontier.

Kaplan loved America. He organized a nondenominational prayer book expressing and celebrating the modern American faith in human powers and initiative. Kaplan also loved Judaism, and sought to formulate an approach to it that would enable it to flourish in America. He desired to rid religion of authoritarianism, convinced as he was that democracy had created the optimal conditions for the flowering of the human spirit. His love of America was not the product of blind nationalism so often characteristic of the immigrant's attitude to the New World, but, rather, expressed his enlightened appreciation of the American spirit.[17]

Like Kaplan, Soloveitchik focused on a religious attitude to life that encouraged the expansion of human powers. Soloveitchik was not frightened by the growth of technology and science. On the contrary, he argued that passivity in the face of natural catastrophe undermined the rightful dignity of man. According to the creation story of Genesis 1, as interpreted by Soloveitchik in "The Lonely Man of Faith," helplessness in the face of disease and natural disasters is inimical to the dignity implicit in man's creation in the image of God, the creative master of nature *par excellence.* Human dignity is destroyed by subservience to natural forces. Promethean man must stand before nature and declare, "I can solve the problem of hunger; I can cure disease; I can overcome obstacles limiting my knowledge and control of nature."

The jetliner, to Soloveitchik, enhanced human esteem in that it overcame spatial limitations. According to Soloveitchik and Kaplan, "majestic man," "dignified man," and "technological man" are not necessarily Marx's atheistic man. The notion of the Creator God does not represent the sublimated, creative aspirations of human beings, but rather serves as an impetus to human strivings to become creative like God.

Figurative characterizations of God may be models which encourage human imitation. Though in worshipping God man becomes conscious of what he is not, he also gains an appreciation of those divine characteristics which he can emulate in his own life. Man is told to be like God: "And God created man in His image. . . . God blessed them and said to them: 'Be fruitful and increase, fill the earth and master it. . . .'" (Gen. 1:27–28); "You shall be holy, for I, the Lord your God, am holy" (Lev. 19:2). Although the divine attributes of power and creativity are not analogous to human power and creativity in all respects, the overlap of these attributes is sufficiently large for man to view God as a model to be imitated.[18]

While Soloveitchik and Kaplan both responded to the Marxist critique of religion by focusing on Judaism's emphasis on human activism, there is a crucial difference between them. Soloveitchik also contrasted Genesis 1 with Genesis 2, where we read about man who is existentially lonely and in need of an in-depth relationship with God. Kaplan's approach to Judaism, however, lacks this contrasting religious component. Though Kaplan does refer to some reality other than man ("cosmic process"), his world view remains thoroughly humanist. Kaplan makes God so immanent that it is difficult to avoid the conclusion that his theology is little more than an elaborate metaphor celebrating human powers. Is there a reality corresponding to his concept *God*, or are references to God satisfied by substituting the term *man*? Whatever the human implications of the notion of the unity of God, the question remains: Who is said to be one? If, when talking about God, one is in fact referring to man, why use God-talk at all? If theology is ultimately a human projection, why complicate and confuse matters by using a concept which seems to refer to a reality other than man?[19]

Though Kaplan's functional approach to theology is akin in certain respects to traditional modes of interpretation, the crucial difference between Kaplan and classical Jewish commentators is that the latter never believed that their functional, anthropomorphic interpretations were exhaustive. Although rabbinic teachers on occasion proposed functional interpretations of theological statements, they always qualified anthropomorphic descriptions of God with expressions such as *kivyakhol*—"as it were." In the Bible itself, though God was depicted in human terms, making images of God was expressly prohibited. Analogously, the poetic license granted to midrashic writers to depict God in human terms was clearly circumscribed by the firm belief in a transcendent, divine reality beyond all human characterizations.[20]

As Ephraim Urbach indicated in *The Sages: Their Concepts and Beliefs*, there was no consistent or definitive rabbinic theology. Even with regard to functional, doctrinal matters, such as the notion of providence, it is difficult to infer a consistent formulation of such doctrinal beliefs on the basis of traditional rabbinic sources.[21] For example, ben Azzai states in Avot 4:2, "The reward of a *mitzvah* is the *mitzvah* itself," thereby discouraging one from seeking rewards in the material conditions of one's life. Yet in Berakhot 47a, the same ben Azzai states that longevity is dependent on how one utters "Amen" during prayers. One may interpret these conflicting statements in terms of the different audiences which ben Azzai addressed. The rabbis were less concerned with precisely formulating correct dogma and theology than with motivating practice and enlivening Jewish religious experience.

191

In the absence of official, well-formulated dogma, the rabbis used theological and doctrinal concepts to further their religious, pragmatic interests, often at the expense of consistency and logical continuity. It would be a mistake, however, to focus exclusively on this feature of rabbinic thought and to characterize rabbinic approaches to religious language in terms of contemporary noncognitive pragmatic theories. Though the cognitive content of religious concepts may not have been explicitly spelled out by rabbinic teachers, there were limits beyond which interpretation became illegitimate. Jewish mysticism, for example, was boldly anthropomorphic, even using sexual symbolism in referring to the numerous forms in which God manifested Himself. Nevertheless, behind the graphic anthropomorphic imagery was the notion of the *Ein Sof*, the Infinite, which was beyond human language and cognition.

A serious critique of Kaplan's thought must clarify whether his analysis of religious language provides an account of what Heschel called "the sense of the ineffable," or whether his approach leaves one thoroughly anchored within the human framework. Are all descriptions of divine attributes exhaustively interpreted by indicating their practical human implications? Is knowledge of God only knowledge of how human beings ought to behave and of the attitudes to life that they ought to adopt? Is there not some reality answering to the name "God"? Is there not a point at which human internalization of divine characteristics stops and one is forced to acknowledge, perhaps by silence, the sublime reality of God?

Kaplan's thought suffers from an excessive desire to correct what he felt to be the weakness of twentieth-century Judaism, namely, nonexperiential faith. To use William James's terminology, Kaplan struggled to make religion a momentous live option. He strove to make Judaism serious and relevant to modern Jews by eliminating dogma and compulsive obedience and by emphasizing its functional, experientially vital aspects. A system of ideas and practices is worthy of attention when it makes a difference to the way people live. In order to achieve this end, Kaplan devoted great efforts to elucidating an approach to Judaism which could "work" in the modern world.

My criticism of Kaplan is not based on what he says, but rather on what he leaves unsaid. I greatly admire his emphasis on the centrality of peoplehood in Jewish thought and his attempt at restoring the importance of experiential functionalism to theological discourse. Religious belief which fails to affect daily life is sterile. Acceptance of the yoke of heaven (*kabbalat ol malkhut shamayim*) which does not lead to acceptance of the yoke of commandments (*kabbalot ol ha-mitzvot*) is foreign to traditional Jewish thinking.

If someone translates traditional religious concepts into a mode of discourse which works, then, from a pragmatic perspective, this undertaking is legitimate. If, however, Kaplan claims to be writing a philosophy of Judaism in order to reconstruct and perpetuate Judaism, then he must ask himself whether his functional interpretation adequately expresses Judaism's emphasis on the otherness of God.

In contrast to Kaplan's writings, Maimonides' philosophy of Judaism is marked by a polarity which is characteristic of traditional Jewish thought. On the one hand, Maimonides adopts a functional approach to Halakhah which highlights the human-centered orientation of divine revelation of Torah:

> The Law as a whole aims at two things: the welfare of the soul and the welfare of the body. As for the welfare of the soul, it consists in the multitude's acquiring correct opinions corresponding to their respective capacity. . . . As for the welfare of the body, it comes about by the improvement of their ways of living one with another. This is achieved through two things. One of them is the abolition of their wrongdoing to each other. . . . The second thing consists in the acquisition by every human individual of moral qualities that are useful for life in society so that the affairs of the city may be ordered.[22]

Maimonides rejected mystical, theocentric interpretations of the commandments. Save for certain details, such as the type and number of sacrifices, where some degree of arbitrariness is inevitable, Maimonides claimed that one may discover the utility of all the commandments—including *hukkim* (statutes), for which many argued that there were no discoverable utilitarian reasons.[23]

On the other hand, Maimonides stressed the importance of philosophy which, as opposed to the anthropocentric orientation of Halakhah, was theocentric. Philosophy led the reflective student from a framework wherein humankind was at the center to a framework where God alone was the focus of attention. According to Maimonides, when one examines Halakhah and *mitzvot*, one discovers a God concerned with and responsive to the human condition; when, however, one studies physics and especially metaphysics, one discovers a universe where the significance of the human species fades before the awesome power and wisdom of God. Herein lies the perpetual tension in Judaism between a religious posture facing "downward" to earth, and a religious posture straining toward the transcendent source of being.[24]

193

Maimonides explains Job's silence after the whirlwind episode in terms of Job's having attained a perspective on life according to which humankind is dwarfed by the infinite perfection of God.[25] God is not wholly immanent in the universe but transcendent and beyond human categorization. Job's defiant insistence on comprehending the universe was placated and superseded by a theocentric religious outlook whose logic was irreducibly other than the standards of human rationality. Functional interpretations break down in the face of a world view wherein humankind is but a trivial component. Job finally became aware of the mystery of a nonrational universe revolving around the notion of a transcendent God. When his angle of vision had changed, the problem of evil was dispelled rather than resolved. The whirlwind episode indicated to Job that evil was but one aspect of a universe which transcended human comprehension. Having glimpsed the awesome, unfathomable mystery of a universe created by a transcendent God, Job fell silent.

In Kaplan's universe, God and humankind are locked into the same anthropocentric framework of experience. There is no *mysterium tremendum* as understood by Rudolph Otto in *The Idea of the Holy*. There is no experience of silent awe before the ultimate mystery. Everything in Kaplan's religious picture of life is reducible to ethical categories and optimistic, activist attitudes. Judaism, however, is more than ethics and the realization of human potential. It also includes the humility and shame felt by a person who contemplates God's creation and wisdom, as captured in the formulation of Maimonides:

> When he ponders these matters, he will recoil affrighted and realize that he is a small creature, lowly and obscure, endowed with slender intelligence, standing in the presence of Him who is perfect in knowledge.[26]

Kaplan's account of religious experience is wholly Promethean. His religious attitude to life involves the constant affirmation of the creative potential of man and of man's ethical character. Kaplan's philosophy is "Jewish" insofar as "Six days a week you shall labor" is "Jewish"; it is not "Jewish" insofar as it fails to capture the religious meaning of "but the seventh day is a Sabbath of the Lord your God: you shall not do any work" (Ex. 20:9–10). Six days of work express the worth of human labor and of the creative unfolding of human powers. The total picture, however, does not consist entirely of *hol* (mundane time) wherein the Jew is active and productive; the Sabbath is not simply a symbolic instrument serving the rest of the week. The Sabbath inaugurates a framework of *kodesh* (holy time), which is set off from the rest of the week by the restrictions it places on a Jew's control and manipulation of the environment. Halakhah imposed limits on one's control of one's environment and thereby created the conditions for transcending self-centeredness and encountering God within the context of a genuine nonutilitarian framework. According to Kaplan, however, even on the seventh day the universe is perceived in terms of human needs and interests.

I do not agree with Kaplan's argument that Halakhah cannot be taken seriously by modern Jews because of the diminished credibility of the notion of supernatural revelation. According to Kaplan, when supernaturalism receded in importance, the sole justification of traditional Judaism lost its force.

In response to Kaplan, I maintain that his characterization of Halakhah is incomplete and misleading. The viability of Halakhah did not depend solely on divine, supernatural revelation. Halakhah's normative claim on the lives of its adherents was not experienced solely in terms of direct imperatives emanating from God. Phenomenologically speaking, commitment to Halakhah was not characterized by a continuous theophany; Jews did not regard their common forms of practice solely as straightforward divine dictates. Halakhah was experienced, as well, as a framework expressing a historical people's spiritual aspirations. It was shaped and mediated by the covenantal community of Israel and its sages.

God may be said to address Israel through its scholars and not only through its prophets. The wise man, the *talmid hakham*, mediates the Law after the end of the biblical period: "The wise man takes precedence over the prophet" (Baba Batra 12a). The scholar whose credentials are legal expertise and knowledge expands Torah by introducing new content, which then becomes part of Torah. The benediction "Blessed art thou . . . who teaches Torah to His people, Israel" may also be recited when studying the oral law, which postdates prophecy and divine revelation.[27] Halakhah, both procedurally and phenomenologically, is in many respects removed from supernaturalism; it may be more accurately described as a historical people's response to a primary religious event. Some Kabbalists went so far as to limit primary revelation to the *alef*, the first letter of *anokhi* (I) of the First Commandment, and to characterize the rest of Torah as interpretation.[28] In other words, though the primary source of Torah is revelation, the norms and practices that constitute the greater part of Halakhah reveal the unmistakable imprint of human mediation.

Soloveitchik's claim that the God-man relationship shifted direction when prayer replaced prophecy as the mediating framework for the

195

covenantal relationship suggests a way for us to characterize post-biblical rabbinic Judaism.[29] Living by Halakhah leads a person to God (prayer); it need not be experienced only as an imposition from above (prophecy). Halakhah is not only responsive to God's legislative authority; it is also a dramatic, symbolic framework expressive of the human yearning for God.

Unqualified submission to divine will is but one moment of the halakhic Jew's religious experience. Halakhah is also a rich, multifaceted way of life expressive of the human spiritual quest for meaning and holiness. Kaplan missed this point by assuming that Halakhah was no longer a live option because modern man could not believe in the literal significance of supernaturalist concepts. We have seen, however, that the supernatural origins of Halakhah pale in comparison with the component of human interpretation. Thus Halakhah as "prayer" (Soloveitchik) or as "man's quest for God" (Heschel) is indeed a live option for the religious person today.

An important difference between traditional interpretation and what Kaplan called reconstruction is that the former does not propose to speak with finality about the past. Instead of announcing that his views constitute the final word on the tradition, the traditional interpreter respects the gap between his creativity and the full, multifaceted meaning of the original text. By guarding the literal integrity of the text, the interpreter keeps alive the possibility that different audiences will appreciate the full force of the text independent of his commentary. Rather than uttering supposedly eternally valid judgments, the interpreter retains the delicate balance between loyalty to and innovative use of the past.[30]

The characteristic rabbinic attitude to doctrine as well as to authoritative texts reveals a subtle dialectic between innovative freedom and conservative loyalty. Rabbinic commentary expresses the attitudes of both subservience and dependence. Unless one is sensitive to the subtle interaction of change and continuity in the historical evolution of traditional ways of life, one will fail to understand the complex nature of traditional Jewish thought. There is no simple way of describing the cause-and-effect relationship between past and present.

An analysis of rabbinic use of biblical material would reveal this twofold attitude to the past. Even where the innovative, interpretative freedom of the rabbis is most evident, the influential force of the original material is somehow retained. For example, the rabbis often demythologized biblical concepts without completely neutralizing the effects of the original mythic material. The conservative-innovative dialectic is revealed in the following talmudic discussion on the meaning of divine providence:

> Philosophers asked the elders in Rome, "If your God has no desire for idolatry, why does He not abolish it?" They replied, "If it were something of which the world had no need that was worshipped, He would abolish it; but people worship the sun, moon, stars, and planets; should He destroy the Universe on account of fools! The world pursues its natural course, and as for the fools who act wrongly, they will have to render an account. Another illustration: Suppose a man stole a measure of wheat and went and sowed it in the ground; it is right (*din hu*) that it should not grow, but the world pursues its natural course and as for the fools who act wrongly, they will have to render an account. Another illustration: Suppose a man has intercourse with his neighbor's wife; it is right that she should not conceive, but the world pursues its natural course and as for the fools who act wrongly, they will have to render an account." This is similar to what R. Simeon b. Lakish said: "The Holy One, blessed be He, declared: 'Not enough that the wicked put My coinage to vulgar use, but they trouble Me and compel Me to set My seal thereon!'" [31]

According to a literal understanding of the Bible which describes God's direct involvement in history and nature, stolen grain ought not to grow and adulterous women ought not to conceive. The rabbis' understanding of what ought to occur in nature is determined by the biblical mythos in which nature and morality are organically related: "Your brother's blood cries out to Me from the ground!" (Gen. 4:10): "And the earth vomited forth its inhabitants" (Lev. 18:25). Nevertheless, the rabbis state, *olam ke-minhago noheg*, "the world pursues its natural course." Conditions of fertilization are independent of morality; grain, whether stolen or not, grows in soil if the biological conditions for growth are satisfied; human conception occurs when a sperm cell fertilizes an egg cell, regardless of the moral circumstances of intercourse. Though the rabbis maintain a moral posture vis-à-vis nature by insisting that nature *ought* to be responsive to moral factors, they are aware of the apparently amoral laws governing empirical reality. Natural occurrences are not characterized by morally sensitive causal connections nor by miraculous interventions of God.

Although the biblical account of creation attributes the pains of childbirth to Eve's sin, and the Bible repeatedly affirms a direct connection between favorable weather conditions, abundant crops, and serving God "with all your heart and soul" (Deut. 11:13), the rabbis referred to in this talmudic passage acknowledged that the regularities observed in nature appeared to be independent of religious-ethical human behavior. Even though the naturalistic realism expressed in this passage is rationalized in terms of God's decision not to destroy the world "on account of fools," that is, in mythical, theological terms, the net effect of this divine decision not to interfere with natural regularities is a demythologization of nature. The rabbis did not, however, demythologize their belief that nature ought to be governed by moral laws, nor did they abandon their eschatological hope that the power of God in nature and in history would become manifest at some time in the future ("and as for the fools who act wrongly, they will have to render an account"). The biblical religious sensibility was not wholly reconstructed. It remained an important shaping influence on one's overall attitude to life. While the "is" was demythologized, the "ought" was determined by the Bible's ethico-religious conception of nature.

The classical Jewish mode of intellectual creativity was commentary, which gave generations of Jews the opportunity to interpret their intellectual heritage creatively within the context of a tradition. The method of commentary, whose spirit informs the writings of many traditional Jewish philosophers as well, contains two vital elements: *peshat* and *midrash*. *Peshat* refers to the strict, "simple" meaning of the text, which the commentator attempts to elucidate as faithfully as possible. *Midrash*, on the other hand, refers to imaginative interpretation of text, which aims at uncovering secondary layers of meaning often loosely connected with the literal meaning. *Peshat* may be characterized as attentive listening, while *midrash* involves imaginative interpretation and creative use of texts.

Commentary thus involves a balance of potentially contradictory attitudes. *Peshat* demands of the commentator the subordination of personal interests and feelings to the text, while *midrash* frees the commentator to uncover personally meaningful insights and attitudes within the given text. The dialectical tension between continuity and change lies at the heart of commentary and explains how Jewish creativity was able to express vastly differing religious orientations without severing its connection to the past.

In contrast to rabbinic Judaism's twofold attitude to its sources, that is, creative reinterpretation together with faithful preservation, Kaplan proposed a radical reconstruction of traditional modes of discourse. He was not satisfied with interpretation within a tradition, but sought to reconstruct the past, rewriting it entirely according to the beliefs of the present.

Some will always assume a deprecatory attitude toward the attempt to reinterpret the Jewish values from a modern, functional standpoint on the

198

ground that Jewish religion would attain a form that its Jewish forebears would not recognize. They argue that, since our aim is to maintain the continuity of Judaism, we are defeating that aim when we impose modern categories of thought upon the literature and institutions of Judaism. A basic error in approach is at the root of this contention. It proceeds from the assumption that those who are to determine whether or not the continuity of a culture is maintained are its founders or initiators, and not its spokesmen in the generations following. Those who make that assumption, therefore, believe that since the founders are no longer alive when the problem of continuity arises, we must be possessed by their spirit and act as their proxies in deciding whether the adaptation of the culture to the exigencies of the times preserves the identity of the culture or not. This is essentially the point of view of all the orthodoxies that have acted as a dead weight upon human progress. The only ones to decide whether the continuity of a culture is maintained are those who are actually confronted with the problem. The past or its proxies can no more pass judgment upon the present than the child can sit in judgment upon the man.[32]

Kaplan's interesting and bold claim expresses one vital aspect of Jewish spirituality: "This is my God and I shall adore Him"; it does not, however, do justice to the other pole of Jewish spirituality: "The God of my fathers, and I shall exalt Him" (Ex. 15:2). Kaplan's reconstruction of the past upsets the delicate balance between change and continuity and thus lacks the bridging quality of traditional commentary. The chain of tradition may be unable to bear the stress of "reconstruction."

An additional aspect of Kaplan's thought with which I take issue is his definition of Judaism as a civilization. Were Kaplan simply indicating that Judaism is more than a faith system composed of religious dogma and ritual practices, he could merely be restating what is manifest to anyone familiar with traditional Judaism. Anyone familiar with the Talmud knows that the subject matter of talmudic discussions transcends the narrow confines of strictly "religious" issues and involves personal, social, moral, economic, and political matters—what are often labeled "secular" issues. Judaism is a comprehensive way of life which includes symbolic ritual and ethics as vital components of a normative framework embracing both individual and collective behavior. That broad range of components is exemplified by chapter 19 of Leviticus. Beginning with the general injunction, "You shall be holy, for I, the Lord your God, am holy" (Lev. 19:2), it continues: "You shall each revere your mother and father, and keep My Sabbaths: I the Lord am your God" (19:3); "Do not turn to idols or make molten gods for yourselves: I the Lord am your God" (19:4); "You shall not steal, you shall not deal deceitfully or falsely with one another" (19:11); "The wages of a laborer shall not remain with you until morning" (19:13); "You shall not insult the deaf, or place a stumbling block before the blind" (19:14); "You shall not render an unfair decision; do not favor the poor or show deference to the rich; judge your neighbour fairly" (19:18); "The stranger who resides with you shall be to you as one of your citizens—you shall love him as yourself" (19:34); and "You shall not falsify measures of length, weight or capacity. You shall have an honest balance, honest weights. . . ." (19:35–36).

Kaplan's statement that Judaism is a civilization, however, suggests more than that Judaism is a comprehensive way of life. It serves, at least potentially, as a rationalization for an undiscriminating devotion to the people of Israel, a devotion that weakens the critical force of Judaism. Although he made the Jewish people the central concept in his philosophy of Judaism, he rejected the notion of the Chosen People. He refused to accept this notion even in a demythologized form, believing that it was chauvinistic and antidemocratic and thus had no place whatsoever in American Jewish life. Seeking totally to obviate any dangerous effects of this concept, he spoke of Judaism as a vocation and advocated Judaism's becoming a type of ethical culture of the Jewish nation.

Judaism is undoubtedly more than a religion in the conventional sense. Peoplehood has always been an essential component of the religion of Israel. Maimonides, in his codification of Jewish law, *Mishneh Torah*, regards identification with the historical community of Israel as a *conditio sine qua non* of halakhic Judaism. In *Hilkhot Teshuvah* (3:20), he states that if a Jew separates himself from the community, even if he does not commit any other halakhic transgression, he has violated a cardinal principle of Judaism and thus "has no portion in the world to come." Torah Judaism is unrealizable outside the context of the people of Israel. This is the essential force of the notion of the Chosen People. "You are my witnesses" (Isaiah 43:10) and "I will dwell amidst the children of Israel and I will be their God" (Ex. 29:45) express the fundamental idea that germinates into the core concept of Kaplan's philosophy of Judaism. The religion of Israel is inseparable from the people of Israel.

Judaism, however, is not simply the aggregate total of what Jews do and create; it is a framework by which to evaluate critically Jewish patterns of behavior and institutions. In the light of Kaplan's orientation to Judaism, one could argue that the State of Israel is the embodiment of the notion that Judaism is a civilization. Unlike Jews in the Diaspora, Jews in Israel are not confined to ghettos but are responsible for a total society. In Israel, the sphere of Jewish activities includes labor unions, welfare institutions, art, literature, public transportation, an army, a navy, and an air force—even the vernacular, Hebrew, is distinctively

Jewish. May not Israel, then, be considered the realization of Kaplan's notion of Judaism as a civilization?

One of the cultural dangers facing contemporary Jewry stems from the confusion of religion with nationalism. A common Israeli secularist argument is that whereas Judaism and its symbols served a purpose in consolidating Jewish identity in the Diaspora where Jews were a minority, in Israel, where the overwhelming majority of the population is Jewish, there is no point in maintaining allegiance to traditional Jewish beliefs and practices.[33] Yeshayahu Leibowitz has assumed the role of the gadfly stirring up the Israeli establishment by repeatedly stressing the danger of equating religion with nationalism. Leibowitz protests against the idolization of statehood and attacks those who ascribe religious significance to the establishment of the State of Israel. In contrast to Kaplan, who reconstructs Judaism in terms of a radical humanism, Leibowitz stresses the irreducibly nonrational meaning of Halakhah. Not only is Judaism distinct from nationalism but, according to Leibowitz, Halakhah is a unique normative framework whose justification is independent of ethical, humanistic, and utilitarian considerations. Leibowitz drives a wedge between Judaism and all those values underlying Kaplan's reconstruction of Judaism.

Leibowitz's extreme position notwithstanding, it is safe to affirm that Judaism is not simply an instrument serving to perpetuate the Jewish people, but is a normative framework in terms of which one may assume a critical posture with respect to the given conditions of history and society. Torah contains standards that indicate how the Jewish people *ought* to live; it is not simply the cultural product of how Jews *in fact* live. It is, therefore, important to determine whether and how Kaplan's understanding of Judaism can retain the critical dimension of Judaism without becoming a blanket endorsement of the prevailing conditions of Jewish civilization.

The individual Jew must love Judaism because he loves the Jewish people, and love the Jewish people because he loves Judaism. This is the tension with which the Jewish thinker must grapple. It appears that Kaplan focused primarily on the former statement, thereby weakening the productive tension between commitment to the people of Israel and to the God of Israel.

The Reconstructionist version of Judaism as an evolving religious civilization initiated a Copernican revolution in the interpretation of the Jewish spiritual heritage. Rejecting the assumption that the Jewish people must be maintained in order that their religion may live, Reconstructionism declares: *The Jewish religion must be maintained in order that the Jewish people may live.*[34]

Kaplan neutralized the tension between peoplehood and Torah or, in other words, between the immanent and the transcendent principles of divinity. In so doing, he undermined the critical function of Judaism.

Although I agree with Kaplan's elevation of the concept of peoplehood to a position of prime importance in his analysis of Judaism, I refuse to allow for the possibility of the Jewish people's becoming the object of a modern form of idolatry. What serves the Jewish state or contemporary Jewish civilization ought not to become the sole criterion of authentic Judaism. There must be a tension underlying Jewish commitment; one should not sacrifice the Jewish people to God or to Torah, nor should one abandon God and Torah in favor of the glorification of the Jewish people.

Kaplan weakened the dynamic tension underlying Judaism by seeking a complete translation of Judaism into the human-centered, functional discourse of modernity. My main critique of his orientation is its failure to recognize the limits of such a translation. God both is and is not intelligible to human beings. The crucial point which modern philosophers of Judaism must bear in mind is that affirming this *prima facie* paradox need not depend on one's becoming articulate in metaphysics. One may legitimately affirm the transcendence of God even if one cannot formulate this notion to the satisfaction of the metaphysician or theologian. It is a mistake to assume that if one cannot propound a rigorous metaphysical account of God, then one must reduce God-talk entirely to a functionalist mode of discourse. The presupposition that talking about God as an independent reality demands an exhaustive conceptualization of the nature of God is unwarranted for an analysis of religious language. One may master a language and know what words mean without mastering linguistics or analytic philosophy. Similarly, one may learn to use religious language without becoming an expert in theology or metaphysics. The history of religion and the history of theology are logically distinct.

Jews rarely engaged in metaphysics. Instead, they related dramatic stories in which God appeared as one of the protagonists. What is the Bible if not a grand epic involving the relationship between a people and its God? Kaplan was not satisfied with this dramatic mode of discourse. Because of the purism of his approach to truth and theology, he had difficulty in affirming God's transcendence in the modern world. He may be described as "a lonely man of truth." He loved truth as a fundamentalist does, and he therefore rejected the use of any concept that defied rigorous intellectual formulation. Religious reductionism may often be described as an overcompensated reaction to a frustrated metaphysical passion.

Kaplan's theology is wholly determined by his humanism, which invariably reduces religion to a form of human projection. One may also argue that he was too much of a theologian.[35] His refusal to restrict his functionalism to the normative domain and his repeated attempts at formulating definitions of God along the lines of a functional immanentism led, ironically, to his emptying theology of religious content. His concern with truth led him to a reduction of theology to human, functional concepts rather than to a functional use of metaphysical concepts whose meaning was not exhausted by their functional import.

Although I have criticized Kaplan for not fully expressing Isaiah's sense of the awesome holiness of God, my major criticism is not of his failure to do this in theology, but rather of his failure to create an experiential framework that contains the elements of *yirah* (awe) and *kedushah* (holiness). Kaplan's religious anthropology is one-dimensional. It lacks the tension between human-serving functionalism and commitment beyond the self. His Halakhah fails to provide Jews with the experience of transcending the limits of their immediate world and needs. Kaplan's God and his Halakhah mirror the given reality of the practitioner. His religious man is totally immersed in the twentieth century, and in fact, within the immediate context of the here and now. As a result of his quest for contemporary relevance and his earnest struggle to incorporate the modern sensibility within Judaism, Kaplan crushed all forms of religious symbolism that express silence and awe.

A philosophy of Judaism becomes religiously exciting when it captures the tension between self-interest, immediacy, and the claims of transcendence beyond the immediate, self-serving present. Judaism always gave expression to the dialectic between "my God" and "the God of my fathers" (Ex. 15:2). The character of Jewish religious experience was complex and multidimensional; although Jews often shared a common universe of discourse, they did not speak with one voice. Jewish religious experience was shaped both by present needs and sensibilities and by symbols and memories of past generations. Religious thinkers interpreted the Torah from Sinai in terms of their contemporary concerns and values, but they always retained a profound loyalty to symbols and forms of behavior that could not be easily translated into the language of contemporary culture.

The rabbis liken *yirah* (awe) of parents with *yirah* of God. The experience of *yirah* with regard to parents is spelled out in Halakhah by the prohibitions against interrupting one's parents when they speak and against sitting in their designated place. *Yirah* involves the experience of distance. The parent must be accessible and caring for the child's needs, but the parent also represents memory, history, distance, and the mystery of that which cannot be wholly assimilated to the child's reality. One speaks with parents, yet one is also silent before parents.[36]

The experience of silence and distance is lacking in Kaplan's approach to Judaism. God is practically synonymous with optimism, activism, and moral goodness. Kaplan's religious attitude to life ignores the tragic, the absurd, and the incomprehensible. His religious humanism does not allow for experiences of surrender and submission to claims beyond one's self. Religion, according to Kaplan, fits smoothly into the context of the worshipper's mundane wants and desires. The overwhelming and demanding dimensions of religious experience are lacking. Kaplan's religious man never feels claimed by the "wholly other." He is comfortable, relaxed, and inspired to do a good job of improving the imperfect conditions of his given reality.

One ought not to disparage Kaplan's optimism and his desire to energize the human will to act productively to ameliorate the conditions of history. Halakhah relates to God as a model for human imitation: as He buried the dead, so shall you bury the dead; as He teaches Torah, so shall you teach Torah; as He pursues justice, so shall you pursue justice. Halakhah, however, also reveals the shaping influence of a God who is unapproachable and terrifyingly other—a "consuming fire."

My critique of Kaplan is less concerned with the absence of the notion of divine transcendence in his theology than with the absence of the doctrine of transcendence in his "Halakhah." Not only does his metaphysics of religion lack the element of *kedushah* (holiness), but his presentation of the dynamics of religious life lacks *kedushah*. Kaplan offers no Halakhah of *kedushah*. Although Kaplan does speak of holiness, his notion of holiness is exhausted by the ethical and rational affirmation that life is worth living. *Kedushah* was traditionally expressed in the rational categories of the ethical, yet it always contained nonrational elements that intimated otherness and transcendence.[37] His picture of the religious human being is one-dimensional insofar as his orientation to life is automatically naturalistic and humanistic. His religious man is predictable and lacking in complexity.

Soloveitchik, by contrast, retained the productive tension of Judaism in terms of the contrast between "Adam the First" and "Adam the Second": the majestic, function-oriented man of Genesis 1 and the lonely man of faith of Genesis 2. Although Soloveitchik encourages cultural translation and making Judaism intelligible to the world in which Jews participate as productive members, he is, nonetheless, fully cognizant of those moments when translation becomes impossible and the "man of faith" stands apart, alone, and incomprehensible to others.

204

If the job of translating faith mysteries into cultural aspects could be fully accomplished, then the contemporary man of faith could free himself, if not from the ontological awareness which is perennial, then, at least, from the peculiar feeling of psychological loneliness and anguish which is due to his historical confrontation with the man of culture. The man of faith would, if this illusion came true, be at peace with the man of culture so that the latter would fully understand the significance of human dialectics and a perfect harmonious relationship would prevail between both Adams. However, this harmony can never be attained since the man of faith is not the compromising type and his convenantal commitment eludes cognitive analysis by the *logos* and hence does not lend itself completely to the act of cultural translation. There are simply no cognitive categories in which the total commitment of the man of faith could be spelled out. This commitment is rooted not in one dimension, such as the rational one, but in the whole personality of the man of faith. The whole of the human being, the rational as well as the nonrational aspects, are committed to God. Hence the magnitude of the commitment is beyond the comprehension of the *logos* and the *ethos*.[38]

The ground of the loneliness of the man of faith in Judaism, according to Soloveitchik, stems from the fact that the faith posture and so much of halakhic practice cannot be translated into categories intelligible to man anchored exclusively in twentieth-century culture. Although Soloveitchik loved America, his profound commitment to traditional Halakhah prevented him from making Judaism totally translatable into contemporary categories of understanding. The isolation and separation engendered by halakhic practice act as a behavioral framework that mirrors the idea of transcendence.

Judaism cultivated a multifaceted, complex religious personality by never allowing Jews to abandon a behavioral framework that often demanded self-transcending commitment and loyalty. Halakhah, and not only theology, points to divine transcendence. Notwithstanding Maimonides' belief in the rationality of all the commandments, many halakhic norms defy strict utilitarian explanation. Many aspects of Halakhah appear to the modern Jew to be nonmoral and nonrational and, consequently, they point to the otherness of God. The notion of nonrational commandments which "the nations of the world mock" is the basis of the experience of being totally claimed by a spiritual system that transcends one's immediate reality insofar as it defies explanation in contemporary functionalist categories.[39]

The dramatic acting out of the nonrational symbolic norms of Judaism—in the absence of a fully explicated theology—distinguishes traditional Judaism from Kaplan's reconstructionism. When a mourner proclaims *"barukh dayan ha-emet"* ("Blessed be the True Judge"), he is

205

not necessarily expressing a justification of God's ways nor is he committing himself to a moral justification of the deceased person's death.[40] My own experience of mourning was that of standing silently before a universe which I failed to comprehend. In uttering *"barukh dayan ha-emet,"* I was affirming God's reality and expressing my commitment to remain loyal to Torah despite the impenetrable mystery of divine justice. The tragic is incorporated into one's religious consciousness through the normative act of reciting the prescribed *berakhah* (benediction). When one becomes involved with the innumerable details of the dietary laws or with the complex rules relating to leavened and unleavened bread on Passover, one enters the domain of nonfunctional transcendent otherness. One symbolically acts out one's acknowledgment of the otherness of God. Judaism does not only serve human needs. There are moments when Halakhah demands self-transcendence in order to worship God.

Judaism contains *mitzvot* that anchor Jews to their immediate social context as well as *mitzvot* that lift them out of their immediate reality and place them in the context of the dramatic history of the Jewish people, where the rational and the nonrational, the functional and the numinous, love and awe, justice and tragedy, are integral components of the religious life.

Kaplan's philosophy of Judaism suffers from its failure to intimate the ultimate mystery. What he considers the whole picture is but a part of it, albeit a significant part. Though Judaism shares the modern humanist ethos that affirms human adequacy, assertion, and the unfolding of human powers, it is not an idolization of humankind. Judaism, ultimately, is the worship of God.

An Open Letter to
a Reform Rabbi

Jerusalem, August 1989

Dear Sam,

Thank you for your comments on my talk to the Central Conference of Reform Rabbis. As you know, although I disagree with the Reform movement's approach to Halakhah, I am nevertheless deeply disturbed by the lack of tolerance and respect for Reform Judaism in Israel.

The Reform rabbinate has been exposed to a great deal of abuse here in Israel. Reform rabbis, who command the respect of their congregations and communities abroad, are either ignored or delegitimized by the Orthodox establishment in this country. Israel, which has opened its gates to Jews from all corners of the world, has not yet learned to appreciate the heterogeneous approaches to Jewish identity, history, and spirituality which have developed over the last two hundred years.

One ultra-Orthodox rabbi recently remarked that, just as the government of the state refuses to speak to the PLO, so should it refuse to speak to Reform rabbis. Any sitting together or mutual discussion implies recognition, and any recognition of the Reform or Conservative movements would endanger the security and well-being of Judaism.

It is outrageous that you should be compared to the PLO, which seeks the destruction of the Jewish State. The pain and humiliation that you are experiencing must be understood as part of the difficult process of rebuilding the Jewish nation in the midst of the enormous ideological diversity within the Jewish people.

I regard the Law of Return, which welcomes Jews from all over the world to make Israel their home, regardless of their ideological views, as the most profound expression of Zionism's Jewish soul. As a religious Zionist who is committed to the aspiration embodied in that law,

207

I cannot say to Reform Jews, "Your bodies are welcome, but not your value systems."

Israel must be a place where diverse Jewish groups, with their own perceptions and values, can engage in serious discussion with one another. Respect for religious pluralism is a vital necessity if Israel is to serve as the spiritual and physical home of the entire Jewish people. One cannot embrace Zionism and the Law of Return, yet delegitimize Reform and Conservative rabbis throughout the world. One cannot say, "All are welcome because we share a common destiny," yet deny them religious freedom and dignity because of their nontraditional belief systems.

In the Diaspora, Jews are not forced to live intimately together. The neutral public space of the non-Jewish world in Europe and North America allows for a psychological distancing of Jews from one another, which in turn diminishes their hostility and aggressiveness. Israel, by contrast, focuses the disagreements within the family and does not allow us to enjoy the type of space that the Diaspora gives to Jewish life. Politically, economically, and socially we are thrown together into a common life; we must face each other and learn what it means to be a family whose members disagree about the heritage of our parents and grandparents.

The violently aggressive language used by certain Israeli circles toward the Reform and Conservative movements, which offer different interpretations of our Jewish heritage, is a direct result of the fact that we have come home. When one comes home after a long absence, one expects that all the members of the family will fit one's own conception of what the family and the community should be. In coming home, one relaxes, but one also allows oneself to manifest the type of hostility found among members of a family. One can expect hostility of this kind when members of a family discover how different they are from each other, how deeply they disagree about the family's past, present, and future.

You may ask, Why should we expose ourselves to this type of humiliation? Why participate in a political environment that treats us with such animosity and abuse? Shouldn't we reformulate our vision in such a way that the State of Israel becomes less important? Why not divorce ourselves from Zionism and the State of Israel?

I believe that your refusal to divorce yourself from the State of Israel is based on a profound appreciation of the connection between peoplehood and convenant in Judaism. Judaism does not begin with an individual leap of faith, but with a leap of solidarity with the Jewish community. The Jewish child learns the essence of Jewish identity at the Passover Seder in saying, "We were slaves to Pharaoh in Egypt." The emphasis is on the "We"—that is, each generation must see itself as if it has come out of Egypt.

One cannot appropriate Judaism's language of faith without identifying with the Jewish people's struggle for political and social liberation. One cannot enter a covenantal relationship with God outside the collective framework of the Jewish people.

Regardless of how one interprets the notions of revelation and election, it is clear in Judaism that God elects a people, not single individuals. Peoplehood and nationhood are the central frameworks for building spiritual meaning in our daily life. Israel prevents us from identifying faith as "the leap of the alone to the Alone."

Israel is not just another Jewish community. To understand the concern for Israel among Jews in the Diaspora, we must appreciate how Israel has succeeded in mediating the Jewish nation's visibility in the world. A Jew's sense of connection with the people of Israel, his or her historical and collective identity, is shaped by the State of Israel.

The Jewish people is not just a faith community; it is not merely the longing of the individual to connect himself or herself spiritually with God; rather, Judaism is a way of life of a people chosen by God to be the medium of His vision of holiness and justice. In a religious sense, therefore, Jewish life in the Diaspora would be impoverished if your congregations were disconnected from the drama of Israeli society.

One of the great men of faith in the twentieth century, Rabbi Joseph Soloveitchik, taught me how to understand the deep connection between the renewal of convenantal Judaism and the commitment to the State of Israel. For Soloveitchik, the shared suffering and common historical fate of the Jewish people represent what he calls a *brit goral,* a "covenant of destiny," which is the foundation of the halakhic category of collective responsibility (*arevut*).

In contrast to Soloveitchik, a small minority of the Jewish people see no religious significance in the establishment of the State of Israel. They believe that the Jews were meant to live as a powerless people until the coming of the messianic age. For them, any assertion of political power, any manifestation of the will to national self-determination, distorts what was meant to be Israel's historical destiny. The very meaning of being a holy, covenantal nation is to submit to the rule of the Gentiles until God, through His gracious love, brings about the messianic redemption of Israel.

The majority of the Jewish people have repudiated this understanding of Jewish history; they see the effort of the Zionist revolutionaries to establish a national home for the Jewish people as a legitimate expression of our historical destiny. As you know, there are many different ways of interpreting the covenantal significance of Israel. The mystic Rabbi Kook, for example, believed that God's redemptive design for history was being enacted through the secular Zionist drama. Alternatively, for Soloveitchik, the religious significance of the state lies in the fact that Israel has galvanized the Jewish people's will to manifest their identity publicly in Western civilization. Israel has given Jews the courage to be an activist community rather than to live permanently as Marranos.

Although the Reform movement has interpreted the covenant of *mitzvah* very differently from Soloveitchik, you clearly share his appreciation of the "covenant of destiny" (*brit goral*). Because of your loyalty to the covenantal community of Israel, you are exposed to a humiliating and painful dilemma. On the one hand, you cannot build your spiritual self-understanding independently of Israel; on the other hand, by allowing Israel into your consciousness, you suffer the indignation of being delegitimized. Indeed, you are even told that you are enemies of that very covenantal faith experience which connects you with the people of Israel. How can you sustain your commitment to the covenant of destiny if Israeli law prevents you from being an active participant in the effort to renew the covenant of Sinai? This is the profound burden that the Reform movement, as well as the Conservative movement, is forced to bear today.

Paradoxically, if you were total secularists who had abandoned your covenantal loyalty to Torah, you would be welcome in Israel. The State of Israel knows how to welcome secular Jews but has not yet learned how to accept radically different orientations within the life of faith.

You are subjected to abuse because you are people of faith who proclaim that the Sinai covenant can be appropriated differently from the way it has been interpreted within traditional halakhic Judaism. Your determination to remain loyal to your understanding of Judaism should be understood by your own Reform movement as an act of spiritual heroism. The extent and duration of your humiliation will depend on how quickly Jews throughout the world come to understand the religious significance and far-reaching implications of the "Who is a Jew?" issue.

As you know, this issue does not merely concern a handful of Reform converts who wish to immigrate to Israel. The real question is how to build a people and a nation in the midst of radical ideological diversity.

We have built a country; we must now learn to build a nation. The pioneers who built this land endured malaria, abuse, and poverty. The soldiers who defended this country paid a high price for its security. Many died in order to make Israel a viable national home for the Jewish people. Nothing was ever achieved in this country without great pain. Your own suffering is the price you must pay in order to bring the Jewish people to a new level of spiritual dignity, which can embrace the value of religious pluralism. Your refusal to abandon Israel, despite your humiliation, is a testimony to your willingness to fight the war for the moral well-being of this nation.

The indignation that you are forced to undergo is the sacrifice you must make for loving a people that does not yet understand how its members can live together in radical spiritual disagreement. I believe that your profound spiritual mission is to continue to struggle until we have discovered new foundations of pluralism within our religious heritage.

Modern Israel has taught us that the Ingathering of the Exiles is not as uplifting and redeeming as we had thought. It is one thing to pray for the Ingathering of the Exiles. It is quite another challenge to live together afterwards amidst our differences. The liberal notion that religious faith should express the individual's free choice is not easily understood by Jews who have lived in totalitarian political environments or traditional ghettos.

In Israel, pluralists are often labeled as relativists lacking any serious convictions. It is feared that acknowledging the dignity of the "other," of the person who offers an alternative meaning structure, leads inevitably to anarchy or to the loss of society's central values. Many religious Jews therefore find it easier to deal with secularists than with Reform and Conservative Jews. No Judaism is preferable to a Judaism that is different from what one believes to be the essential will of God.

It is important that we learn that respect for other points of view does not imply relativism. One can simultaneously maintain that the way one lives reflects the truest interpretation of Judaism and yet respectfully recognize that this position is not held by all Jews.

The fight for pluralism in Israel does not require Orthodox, Reform, or Conservative Jews to compromise their appreciation of Halakhah and Torah. It *does* mean that no group may use the instruments of the state to impose its own interpretation of Judaism on the entire society.

Please appreciate how far we are from understanding that intense religious commitment is compatible with respect and appreciation for those who differ with us. Your suffering and constant exposure to abuse from religious circles in Israel indicate how far we are from appreciating the meaning of civilized disagreement. We have not yet learned how to build a society in which communities holding different religious convictions can flourish without asking the state to enforce their position.

So far I have tried to explain why it is important that you continue your struggle to validate your spiritual integrity within the public space of Israeli society. I would also like to share with you my perception of how your movement's convenantal commitment can enrich Israel's religious life. I referred earlier to two moments in the faith experience: solidarity with the people's struggle for national liberation, and commitment to the covenantal framework of *mitzvot*. The covenant of *mitzvah* presupposes empathy and solidarity with the whole community, irrespective of its moral and religious quality.

However, it is important to remember that solidarity does not imply agreement with whatever the community does; it does not mean that whatever policy the Israeli government pursues must be accepted unconditionally. Unconditional loyalty to a nation or a state is tantamount to idolatry. Many modern Jews mistakenly believe that peoplehood is the necessary and sufficient condition of Jewish identity. The Reform movement must help correct this one-sided view of Jewish identity. It must struggle against the tendency to make loyalty to the nation the exclusive framework for organizing Jewish life.

The Reform movement's covenantal perspective can serve as a prism through which one can properly define the value of solidarity with the community. In other words, you must remind the Jewish community that the covenantal moment is constitutive of Jewish identity.

The Reform movement was not quick to embrace Zionist nationalism. Initially it defined itself as a faith community, rather than a national and political movement. Although Reform leaders eventually recognized the importance of peoplehood and solidarity with the State of Israel, their initial reluctance can still be utilized to remind us that Jewish identity goes beyond empathy with the suffering condition of Jews. Solidarity with the suffering of the Jews in Egypt is only a preparation for the covenantal experience of Sinai.

It would be a tragic mistake for Reform Jews to identify themselves with secular Zionism in Israel. Your repudiation by the religious Zionist establishment in Israel must not lead you to choose the secular option. The Reform movement is a religious movement and its appreciation of Israel must be expressed in religious categories. You are a religious community, and in participating in Israeli society, you must be loyal to your religious perspective.

212

It is important that Jews rediscover the old talmudic principle, "He who rejects idolatry is as if he accepts the entire Torah." In order for faith in God to possess any vitality, we must understand what it negates. By clearly denouncing the new forms of idolatry, you will help Jews discover ways in which faith can be a vital option in the modern world.

You can contribute to the effort to free Jews from their embarrassment in talking about God and the passion of the faith experience. How often have I heard it said that Christians talk about God, while Jews talk about Halakhah. You can help to correct this distortion because of your ease in celebrating the covenantal moment of faith at Sinai.

In addition to your contribution to the battle against idolatry, and to the rehabilitation of covenantal faith, you can also help articulate the human values and characteristics implicit in the life of *mitzvot*. Even though you do not speak the language of Halakhah, you can contribute to the realm of Aggadah. For example, although you reject the halakhic interpretation of "You shall not work on the Sabbath," you can embrace the idea that the Sabbath celebrates God's Creation and human finitude. Articulate how the Sabbath develops the characteristic of gratitude, the sense that life is a gift, and the need to give up the longing for absolute power. By focusing on the human characteristics implicit in a life of *mitzvot*, you may clarify how Israel's calling to be a holy people should affect our perception of power.

By contrast, the Conservative movement, does understand itself as a halakhic movement. Therefore, its task in Israel is not only to rehabilitate covenantal consciousness but also to show the wide range of interpretative possibilities allowed for by Halakhah. To be true to its claim to be a halakhic movement, Conservative Judaism must show that its halakhic positions can be validated by the interpretative power of Halakhah. In this way, the Conservative movement can show the Jewish world that "the four cubits of Halakhah" are wider than we ever imagined, and that the Jewish tradition always contained the resources to meet new situations and appreciate new values. Conservative Judaism bears the burden of legitimizing its present actions in relation to the authority of the past. The Reform movement, however, is not burdened by a concern for halakhic continuity; it is burdened by the claim of God upon human life, by its receptiveness to the covenantal moment, and by its rejection of nationhood as the exclusive value defining Jewishness.

Your expansion of covenantal consciousness must be welcomed within the Israeli context. What a rich Jewish community we would

213

have, both in the Diaspora and in Israel, if members of different synagogues—those who build their lives around the covenantal focus and those who build their lives around Halakhah—were to gather in each other's homes to discuss Torah and the different ways that their respective rabbis are interpreting the tradition!

Such a dialogue would ensure that Jewish faith would be based on conviction rather than habit. Theological diversity within the Jewish community would encourage the development of communities founded upon conviction, knowledge, and choice.

Orthodoxy, both in Israel and abroad, would thrive on vibrant Conservative and Reform movements. The presence of alternative options would challenge its membership to build conviction out of understanding. Intense concern with the details of the Law would then grow from a perspective of joy and love, rather than from an authoritarian mode of being in which the Conservative and Reform movements are delegitimized. I have no objection to rabbis, whether Orthodox, Conservative, or Reform, who try to persuade through argumentation that their way is the correct expression of Judaism in the modern world; but nothing is more destructive of the religious life than enforcing one's point of view through violent demonstrations or coercive legislation.

America has founded a great civilization on the principle of Live and Let Live. Freedom actually facilitates conviction. Political coercion is ultimately self-defeating, because it prevents the individual from seeing his or her collective life as an expression of personal dignity. Living a Judaic way of life can become an expression of personal conviction when the Jewish people are given the opportunity to choose between alternative spiritual options.

The Talmud says that any argument for the sake of heaven must endure. I believe that our discussions and disagreements are for the sake of heaven. To be sure, I have tried in my writings to clarify why I cannot accept your celebration of autonomy at the expense of halakhic authority. Indeed, there are many issues that divide us. But I am grateful that you came to Israel and enabled me to witness your religious passion. Your presence contributed to my own quest to serve God with joy and love. In conclusion, I can only express my hope that the Reform movement will not understand the covenant of *mitzvah* in such a way that it burns the bridges to communal solidarity. It is important that you reconsider your approach to halakhic issues, such as your controversial claim that Jewish identity should be defined by both matrilinear and patrilinear descent, which threaten our shared covenant of destiny.

214

All the movements in Judaism must find the way in which our common covenant of destiny controls our interpretation of the covenant of *mitzvah* and Halakhah.

Sincerely,

David Hartman

Who Is a Jew?:
An Interview

T he following remarks are excerpted from an interview for the Israeli media after the 1988 elections and the subsequent attempts to introduce legislation on the "Who is a Jew?" issue.

Dr. Hartman: Jewish identity in the Diaspora is built on communal belonging in a synagogue. So what happens if we say that we do not accept the authority of Reform and Conservative rabbis, and their right to accept people into the Jewish fold? This, after all, is the question of conversion: who defines membership in this family? The question is not how many people come on *aliyah,* but that you declare that the synagogue of the American Jew is not authentic. It is very interesting that atheist heretics in Israel's parliament, who eat *treif* on Yom Kippur, are asked to determine which synagogue is authentic. This is the absolute lie in the whole matter. That is why the Jews in the Diaspora are screaming, "You have said that our synagogues are *treif,* that our rabbis are not authentic mediators of the Jewish tradition. If this is so, then I am not in your eyes a full-fledged member of the family." This cuts into their souls, like a child whose mother says that he or she does not belong to the family, that he or she is not wanted any longer.

Many Israelis do not understand the pain and humiliation that Diaspora Jews feel because for many Israelis the synagogues and their rabbis are completely marginal to their identity as Jews. Israelis have the army service and the Hebrew language. For Diaspora Jews, however, the synagogue is a major bearer of their connection with Israel and Jewish history. So, when you say that conversions have to be according to Halakhah, you in a sense declare that what binds them to Israel does not exist any longer. But what do Israeli newspapers write? "Jews will no longer contribute money; Diaspora Jews are making threats." I believe that if the Israelis were really aware of what a change in the law would do to these people, they would not allow the law to be amended.

216

This is the most cynical denial of the Diaspora I have ever witnessed. It is ugly for Israelis to say, "Do not butt in, just give us your checks and see to it that your senator takes care of our security and economic interests. Keep silent. Do not criticize." This is utterly vulgar.

Interviewer: Is this your personal interpretation or are these the things that American Jews are saying?

Dr. Hartman: I have just been there and this is what I heard. I am not talking as an ivory tower philosopher. It is very painful to listen to the outrage that Jews in the Diaspora feel.

I am an Orthodox rabbi and I am very attached to Halakhah. But I am also a Zionist, and this means that I am prepared to accept the Torah together with the whole Jewish people. Had I wanted to live only with an Orthodox community, I could have lived in Boro Park. But I decided that not only those who are committed to Halakhah are my people. Zionism changed my whole outlook on Judaism. I cannot live in Israel as I did in the Diaspora. There has to be a Torah, a spiritual way for the people living here who do not accept the authority of Halakhah. I therefore object to all forms of religious coercion. In their folly, the Zionists who built this country gave Judaism to the ultra-Orthodox. This is why I hope that the threat of the amendment to "Who is a Jew?" will forever hang over us. That way, people may understand that the custodians of Judaism should not only be the ultra-Orthodox.

Interviewer: How did this Israeli misunderstanding come about?

Dr. Hartman: The present situation is the direct result of many years of alienation and lack of interest on the part of the political leaders in Israel regarding the content and quality of Judaism. They were not interested in pluralistic religion because they were not interested in religion. Israelis thought that they had solved the problem of a Jewish identity through a new Israeli identity: army service, speaking Hebrew, even playing basketball. Anything you did in Israel was sufficient to define Jewish identity. However, none of these apply to people who do not live here. We did not grant any spiritual or cultural value to the Jewish people in the Diaspora. We negated the spiritual worth of Diaspora Jewry, yet nevertheless remained dependent on them economically and politically. We saw them in terms of our needs, either as a reservoir of future *aliyah* or as economic and political allies, without appreciating what they personally need as a Jewish community and how Israel could contribute to the quality of their Jewish identity and heritage.

Diaspora Jews acquired a new historical dimension to their identity

217

after the Six-Day War. As a result of the Six-Day War and the Yom Kippur War, a deep bond was created between Jews in the Diaspora and the State of Israel. The fear of the possible destruction of Israel and the profound sense of relief and joy at our victory created a deep sense that the key players who are defining the direction and moral agenda for the Jewish people are Israelis. Israelis were seen as those who returned our corporate national body and power to the Jewish people. Among the Jews of the Diaspora, there arose a new feeling of confidence and pride in Judaism and the future of Jewish history. As a result of the new spirit that Israel generated toward the Jewish people, Jews felt a new public pride, a new sense that one could appear visibly as a Jew in the public spheres of life. Jews no longer defined themselves as "Americans of the Mosaic persuasion." Their American and Jewish identities were merged into a unified sense of self-understanding. The link between the United States and Israel was important for Diaspora Jews because emotionally both countries were their homes. They expected Israelis to share similar values and expected from Israel the same pluralistic, egalitarian, and tolerant attitudes that they found in America.

I claim that we here have not understood our influence upon the organization of the Jewish community in the Diaspora, upon their collective sense of belonging to the Jewish people and history. The link with the State of Israel is essential to their identity as Jews. It is not only a religious question, because Judaism is not just a religion. In order to be a Jew, you have to be linked with the destiny of your people. Even in a conversion according to Halakhah, you do not only say "I believe in God." You have to identify with the Jewish people, with its suffering and its passion for redemption. Therefore, the Jewish spiritual calendar does not begin on Shavuot, with the giving of the Torah, but on Passover, when you identify with the suffering of those who were slaves to Pharaoh in Egypt. Without identifying with this suffering, you cannot accept the Torah.

Interviewer: How does all this relate to the "Who is a Jew?" issue?

Dr. Hartman: Zionism built the Land of Israel in a spirit of revolt against traditional Judaism. The revolt, however, took place in our biblical home. We built a new political framework in a place that always linked us to the past. This is very paradoxical. In Israeli society, there has not been a generation as alienated from the Judaic heritage as the present one, yet nonetheless so committed to historical continuity.

Interviewer: There are many Israelis who think that there is a sort of commercial link between us and the Jews in the Diaspora. We provide

218

them with a shelter for emergencies and they pay for this insurance policy with money and influence.

Dr. Hartman: It is not like that. They do not give money so that they have a place to run to. There is love. They feel a bond with the people living in Israel. They feel, "I belong there, I am interested in what happens there. This is my people." It is this feeling that inspires them to contribute. Money is just a symbol of this bond. They do not feel guilty for living in the Diaspora. They feel at home in their respective countries. They do not contribute in order to atone for their dwelling in the Diaspora; there is not even a question of refusing to come on *aliyah*. Israel is in many ways the "synagogue" of the Jewish people: it is the framework that organizes their bond with their historical tradition.

Interviewer: Perhaps this is the role they have assigned to us, against our wishes, and now we find it is too much for us?

Dr. Hartman: No. This is not a role that they have assigned to us. We chose it. We demand from them total commitment to us, interest in what happens here, contributions, care, involvement—we demand that.

Interviewer: What do we promise in exchange?

Dr. Hartman: No promises; there is no exchange. This is not a financial transaction, it is a love affair, a relationship! Israel caught the soul, the concern of the Jew in the Diaspora. We did not create an *aliyah* movement, but we created the feeling that Jerusalem is the center, that here is the real action. It is vulgar to think that we Israelis give Diaspora Jews pride and they give us money. The UJA is only a symbol. A Jew in the Diaspora gets up in the morning, reads the paper, and the first thing he looks for is whether there is any report on Israel.

Interviewer: And what does a Jew like that feel when he reads about the intention to amend the Law of Return?

Dr. Hartman: We in Israel think it is only a question of a few converts, or making some rabbi feel good. Israelis do not understand what the problem is all about.

What is the Law of Return? It is the soul of the State of Israel. People in revolt, revolutionaries, always want to break their bond with the past. Israeli revolutionaries, however, said, "We want every Jew, whoever he is, to feel that this is his home." There are no quotas. There were enough of those during World War II. The Law of Return says, "You are welcome to come by right, by virtue of your belonging to the

Jewish people." Zionist revolutionaries created a home which was not meant only for revolutionaries, not only for people who identify with their revolution. In building their new state in the land of Jewish historical memories, the early Zionists demonstrated their strong bond with all who belong to the history of the Jewish people. They fought and sacrificed and declared that their sacrifice is also for those who do not live here, in order, among other things, to preserve that sense of continuity. It is precisely because we also invite our grandfather that ultra-Orthodoxy can expand its influence. We invite people who do not identify with Zionism, without checking their Zionism. This is the home of Jewish history, not of Zionism, despite the fact that Zionists built it.

There is another important element. The Law of Return says, "You are welcome." Who are welcome? That was kept vague: any Jew. The law did not define the correct interpretation of Jewish history. It allowed several interpretations to flourish: "Let all who hunger come and eat." It would have been easier to build a Jewish home in the fifteenth century when there was a consensus, but we proclaimed a state at a time when there were deep ideological conflicts among the Jewish people. We knew there was an essential problem: there was a family, but it was not organized. The Law of Return took heed of Jewish pluralism because it was enacted when a normative consensus was lacking about how we should live. Now the implicit recognition of pluralism is being threatened by the suggested change in law.

Interviewer: What will the Jews in the United States do if this threat materializes?

Dr. Hartman: If the amendment indeed goes through, there will be an explosion. The conflict and anger will become very intense. Diaspora Jews are deeply insulted. As an Israeli, I personally feel defiled by the things that we are saying and doing. From the perspective of the lengthier drama of Jewish history, the political parties of Likud and Labor are as a passing wind, in comparison to the need to enrich our Jewish heritage and quality of life throughout the world.

The issue before us today is: how can we create a Jewish nation? How can we give significance to our history and yet retain a respectful appreciation for the radical diversity present in Jewish life throughout the world? Diaspora Jews have a vital role to play in creating new foundations of pluralism both in Israel and in the Diaspora. Jewish pluralism in the Diaspora will be weakened if Israel does not have a genuine religious, pluralistic society.

The concern of Diaspora Jewry should not only be about the amendment of the Law of Return but about the moral and spiritual quality of Israeli society. If in Israel we delegitimize the Reform and Conservative rabbinates, then Israel is not the spiritual home of world Jewry. Israel must radiate a message through the quality of the pluralism that it builds in its own society. This issue will define the future of Diaspora Jewry's connection with Israel. Israel cannot demand loyalty and commitment to its well-being if the social and moral and political life of the society violates and humiliates the integrity of Jewish identity throughout the world.

Unconditional loyalty to a state is idolatry. However, in spite of my deep commitment to Israel, I do not believe that we can weaken the bond with the Jewish people without paying a price for it. There must be consequences for the way we act. If we do not pay for our neglect, we will never become a mature, moral people. Diaspora Jews must be perceived as a serious community. We dare not turn them into puppets and objects to serve our own national interests. The Jewish people are not instruments to serve the state, but rather the state is an instrument for intensifying one's loyalty to Jewish history and Jewish continuity.

I believe this crisis will result in the maturation of the Jewish people, of the content of Jewish life. The responsibility of Jews in the Diaspora is not only to help in security needs but equally concerns the moral and spiritual quality of our society.

Interviewer: Have they a chance of succeeding?

Dr. Hartman: This is a beginning. It is the beginning of the battle, the beginning of maturation. I do not want this subject to disappear; that would be worse.

Interviewer: You do not think that the price may be too high—for instance, a breaking of the bond between us and them?

Dr. Hartman: No, I think that this will not happen. Conflict will bring forth serious and concerned leadership. Israelis will learn to understand the need for spiritual pluralism. Israelis will stop looking at Jews in the Diaspora as a checkbook. This struggle has a cleansing quality. As the Talmud teaches us, there is no purity without conflict and pain. I feel that we are on the threshold of building a healthy and respectful relationship with world Jewry, although I am not happy knowing the suffering that Jews in the Diaspora are going through now that the Law of Return could be amended. The real issue of "Who is a Jew?" must never leave the agenda of Jewish discussion. The elections brought home both to Israel and to world Jewry that we are living through a great *Kulturkampf*. What values do we believe are essential in defining ourselves as Jews? The issue of who joins the community is fundamentally related to what the community believes is essential for being a Jew in the modern world. There are many different approaches that people have to what they believe constitutes Jewish identity. In asking ourselves "Who is a Jew?" we are beginning a process in which Jewish identity is defined by choice and conviction rather than the accident of birth or the demonic intentions of the Hitlers of history.

I believe we must always keep on the agenda the "Who is a Jew?" issue, but we must never resolve that question with legislation in the Knesset. Israel has engendered this concern and conflict. In so doing, it has potentially done a great service to the Jewish people. It will fail in its role as a catalyst for new thinking if it thinks that the arena to resolve this issue is through the legislative wheeling and dealing of the Knesset. Israel must be the center that invites Jews to talk, to disagree, to argue passionately for their convictions but yet to realize deeply that Israel will say "Welcome" with love and respect for all Jews who want to participate in the genuine discussion of "Who is a Jew?"

PART FOUR

"And You Shall Love the Stranger"

THE DIGNITY OF THE OTHER

The Quest for Peace

The Past

Any discussion of the Israeli-Palestinian conflict must be sober and balanced and not divide all concerned into saints and devils. Overly moralistic criticism provokes self-righteous responses and fruitless arguments about who is the real victim. The concern must be, not to ease the critic's conscience, but to encourage Israelis and Palestinians to believe in the fruitful possibilities of negotiation.

For many Israelis, criticism will be listened to and have a healing effect only if it is appreciative of the pain and rage that result from having been delegitimized by modern Arab propaganda and by Christian and Islamic theological teachings over many centuries. We live in a geographic area which refuses to know anything of the creative spirit of our culture. The radios of even moderate Arab countries, like Saudi Arabia and Kuwait, habitually refer to Tel Aviv and Haifa as "occupied Palestine" and to Israel as "the enemy." Jordan Television switches off the live Eurovision Song Festival when the Israeli pop group appears; the joy of our songs must not be heard. Even a mere sports event in which Israel participates must not be seen on Arab television. Sermons heard in mosques, schoolbooks used in Arab countries, and a constant flow of anti-Jewish hate literature obstruct the search for a dignified solution to the Israeli-Palestinian struggle.

The distinctions which PLO spokesmen make between Jews who came to Israel from all corners of the globe and those born in Israel cut deeply into the soul of Israelis. These distinctions negate our history, our traditions, and the prayers which nurtured an unbreakable bond between the Jewish people and its land. Our unease is reinforced when even supposed "moderates," like King Hussein, join the Arab campaign to stop Soviet Jews from coming home to Israel.

As far as our neighbors are concerned, Israel is often perceived as a

225

post-Holocaust phenomenon created out of Western guilt for the destruction of European Jewry. We are described as an alien growth in the Middle East, not indigenous to its soil, history, and culture. The refusal of Arab regimes to cope with the tragic homelessness of Palestinian refugees epitomizes the perception of our return as only a temporary mistake, an aberration, which will in due time disappear.

For Jews, Israel's rebirth represents the fulfillment of our long historical commitment and connectedness to this land. When Jews walk in this land, they enter into a dialogue with thousands of years of Jewish history. Deeply engraved in our national consciousness is the knowledge that it is still only our military power and determined loyalty to our history that make Israel a viable political reality.

Our hope was that our presence would gradually seep into the consciousness of our Arab neighbors and evoke a significant degree of acceptance. Regarding most of them, this, tragically, has not been the case. Our isolation from our neighbors creates a paradoxical feeling: although we have come home and built a strong nation, we still share the painful alienation and loneliness experienced by Jews throughout their exilic history.

The Present

The recent Palestinian revolt in Gaza and the West Bank, together with the need for young Israeli soldiers to use brute force to quell the riots, has made Israelis more aware than ever before that Palestinians possess a national consciousness. Our future security and moral well-being as a nation will be jeopardized if we are indifferent to their desire for self-determination.

There are two options. We can recognize their fundamental human desire and seek to accommodate it, while at the same time building safeguards so as not to weaken our own national security, or we can create a society that rules by force and intimidation over a million and a half vehemently resentful people. Even if arguments could be found that this form of rule is militarily and politically feasible, it would inevitably undermine the moral and religious significance of our national renaissance. During two thousand years of wandering and waiting, we never imagined a Jewish nation that would find itself obliged to suppress and humiliate an entire people. Palestinians as homeless victims will make us constantly feel like strangers in our own home.

To reduce the Palestinians to a subject population who live in dread of Israeli power is to destroy any significant connection between the best of our traditional, spiritual teachings and contemporary Israel. Permanent control over the Palestinians will eventually destroy the centrality of Israel for world Jewry.

A Palestinian political reality, in which they will find it necessary to become responsible for the social, economic, and political well-being of their citizens, may begin the process of healing the present negative and destructive identity of many Palestinians. However, if we continue to control them, their identity will be fed by hatred and rejection of Israel.

There is a vicious dialectic that must be broken. In controlling them, we lose ourselves. When our youth act with brutal anger against women, children, and elderly people, we become alienated from everything normally identified as Jewish behavior. We will not heal our own rage and frustration through military control over the Palestinians but only through dealing constructively with their will for self-determination.

At the same time, we must emphasize to them and to the world that their national existence must not in any way jeopardize our security. One way to do this is to insist on total demilitarization of any Palestinian national entity. No military offensive equipment must exist on this side of the Jordan River.

In stating this, it is evident that we do not seek to subjugate a people, but equally we show a healthy awareness that the Messiah has not come. We must not confuse security needs with questions of political control or with grandiose visions of Jewish historical destiny. We must insist on very clear safeguards for our national security. We thereby manifest our clear will to live in peace with our neighbors, but also our sure knowledge that only a secure and strong Israel will enable the development of good will and understanding between the different nations in the Middle East.

Into the Future

The confrontation with Palestinian nationalism has become the most urgent issue facing the Jewish state and world Jewry today. The future identity of both national communities hangs on their finding the wisdom and good will to resolve this tragic condition.

The conflict has deep roots within our respective religious traditions. In contrast to America, whose founders consciously rejected much of their European past, in this land the power of tradition and historical memory is embedded in all that we do. The problem is how to live by the memories and aspirations of our past without creating a nightmare which destroys all innovative thinking in the present.

For centuries, Christianity, Islam, and Judaism each believed in its eventual triumph in history. Each sought to prove that it had the exclusive keys to God's kingdom, either through its political subjugation of other religious communities or through proving the falsity of the others' scriptures and religious traditions. Victory, whether military or intellectual, confirmed who was God's elect in history.

What we must now learn from history is that in the battle to demonstrate exclusive favor in the eyes of God, no single community was victorious. The crusades to liberate Jerusalem from the "infidels" failed, leaving bitter memories of suffering in all communities.

Jews were the most frequent victims of the belief that one community, and only one, is God's elect in history. Israel's suffering and exile were interpreted to confirm that God had rejected them and their way of life. The roots of the twentieth-century slaughter of European Jewry can be traced to that deep delegitimization of the Jews implied by an exclusivist, triumphalist view of God in history.

In the State of Israel, we find ourselves today locked in a great struggle with religious communities who share the biblical perception of history. We must all find a way to free ourselves from habits of thought which have brought so much suffering to all. The catastrophes of the past must teach us that no sacred text, historical memory, or tradition should be given greater weight than the sacredness of human life. What Jews, Christians, and Muslims need to learn afresh is that God's creation of all human beings in His image must have central importance in the interpretation of our religious traditions.

Within Judaism, giving primacy to the prevention of human suffering is implicit in the halakhic ruling that saving human life takes precedence over Sabbath observance. The Sabbath law is central to Judaism. Desecrating the Sabbath is considered equivalent to embracing idolatry. Our covenantal identity and entire belief system are irrevocably tied to observance of the Sabbath.

Nonetheless, rabbinic teaching ruled that when danger to human life comes into conflict with the observance of the Sabbath, the Sabbath must be put aside. Orthodox halakhic jurists have ruled that this principle applies to all human life, irrespective of race or creed. Maimonides treats the sacredness of human life as a guiding principle for understanding the whole Torah.

228

The commandment of the Sabbath, like all other commandments, may be set aside if human life is in danger. . . . Furthermore, it is forbidden to delay such violation of the Sabbath for the sake of a person who is dangerously ill, for Scripture says, "Which if a man do, he shall live by them" (Lev. 18:5), that is to say, he shall not die by them. Hence you learn that the ordinances of the Torah were meant to bring upon the world not vengeance, but mercy, loving-kindness, and peace. [*Hilkhot Shabbat* 2:1,3]

If, as Maimonides insists, the whole aim of the Torah is to bring about "mercy, loving-kindness, and peace," then holiness, be it of the Sabbath, land, or temple, must submit in situations of conflict to the sacredness of human life. The holiness of the Land of Israel does not hinge on whether we speak of "the occupied territories," "Judea and Samaria," or "the West Bank." If we are seriously concerned with the holiness of Israel and with God's indwelling in the land, then it is imperative that we ask what will happen to the moral character of the nation, what will become of our Judaic heritage if we dispossess or subjugate a vast population? How can we observe the Sabbath, whereby Jews bear witness to God as Creator of the universe, yet at the same time forget that Palestinians are human beings created in the image of God? How can we educate our children to imitate God's love for all His creatures and yet deny political freedom and national dignity to an entire people?

The Bible does not begin with the history of Abraham or with Israel's liberation struggle from Egypt, but with the story of God as the creator of all life. What Creation signifies for the understanding of our particular identity can be seen in the three benedictions recited at the Grace after Meals.

The first benediction addresses God as the creator and sustainer of all life. In the second, the Jew thanks God for the covenant, the Torah, and the land. The third expresses the yearning of the Jewish people for the rebuilding of Jerusalem and the reestablishment of the kingdom of David. In arranging the benedictions in this order, the Halakhah teaches us that only after we acknowledge our solidarity with all of humanity is it appropriate to give thanks for our particular spiritual identity. The renewal of Jerusalem, the strengthening of our commitment to Torah, must flow from our deep awareness that all human beings are sustained by God's gracious love.

If we build our national life while ignoring the moral demands that come from belief in Creation, we significantly undermine our belief in the unity of the God of Creation and the convenantal Lord of history. This belief will best be manifested if both national communities can so flourish in this land that the celebration by each of its particularity does not require the delegitimization of the presence of the other.

If we allow the God of Creation to channel our particular religious traditions, the future need not be buried by the past. We must never be discouraged by the obstacles encountered in our search for peace. The anger and bitterness of the past must not inhibit new thinking and bold initiatives. Our total commitment to resolve the tragic conflict with the Palestinians will be the finest expression of our loyalty to a tradition which seeks to unify solidarity with all of humanity and gratitude for the gift of Judaic particularity.

Living with
Conflicting Values

I n the past fifteen years, my thinking and teaching have focused almost exclusively on internal Jewish issues. It is easy to pray for the Ingathering of the Exiles, but can we live with that ingathering? Can we live with the fact that Jews today have no shared normative consensus about how we understand Jewish history and our own character as a nation? The very meaning of Zionism, of the establishment of the State of Israel, was the bold attempt to bring home a people whose members were in disagreement with each other. This was Zionism's fundamental courage—its belief that a national community could be forged although a national consensus was lacking.

The question central to my thinking, as a halakhic Jew in the Orthodox tradition, was how to appreciate Judaism in a way that allows for the flourishing of a variety of ideologies. Can I live as a Torah-observant Jew while knowing that there are many other Jews who have totally different views of what Jewish history could and should be?

There are, however, times when a new problem—or an old problem that has been lurking in the background—invades our consciousness in ways which do not allow us to return to everyday normalcy. For me as for many others in Israel, just that has now happened regarding our problem with the Palestinians.

This problem relates not only to the future physical existence of our society in Israel. Everything we value Jewishly, historically and spiritually, is at stake.

It is of such urgency, of such proportions, that it touches the very soul of the nation. Who we are as a people, what connection we have with our stories and our history—all will be decided by how we deal with the Palestinian question. What is at stake is the significance of our national renewal and our identity as Jews.

This is not only an Israeli issue; it is also world Jewry's concern. Therefore, it is not only people who vote in Israel who must be engaged

231

by it, but all who care about Jewish history, Jewish spirituality, and Israel's vision of the future.

There is a fundamental characteristic of a certain type of apologetic thinking that took place during our exile, in which Jewish theology or Jewish philosophy sought to find room for Jewish existence in non-Jewish environments. Traditionally, the way to find that room was to establish legitimization for Jews in the eyes of others. If Jews decided to be part of the surrounding world, they felt obliged to explain themselves in the other's categories. A German philosopher like Rosenzweig had to explain how Judaism fitted into Christianity. Hermann Cohen had to show that Judaism possesses a universalist ethic. If Jews preferred to live in the ghetto, on the other hand, then they did not have to speak a strange language and self-legitimization grew out of their own internal experience.

When Jews came home to their own land, one of the most refreshing things about Zionism and its quest for normalcy was that the need for self-justification ceased to be urgent. A Jew could say, "I do not have to justify my right to live and to be a people."

Coming home meant the end of apologetic thinking. It became enough to speak our own language, to have our own history, to read our own Bible. We could build our culture on our own story and allow our elemental passions to exist without justification.

We did not have to win the "Moral Man of the Year Award" by being a light unto the nations. Like any other nation, some of us were noble, some weak. It was so good just to be able to breathe free that in coming home we did not see that someone else was also there.

It is crucial to understand that in the Bible there is only one people's story. Where in the Book of Joshua do we find how the Canaanites or the Jebusites felt when the Children of Israel came into the land? Who ever spoke about what it meant to be a Canaanite? The only time we meet Ishmael or Esau is when they enter or leave the Jewish story. The Bible gives us a story of the world in which the history of the Jews is what excites God. He is like an enormously involved Jewish supreme being, even though in the beginning God was not Jewish. He began to be Jewish only when he met Abraham.

There are some brief passages in the Prophets on other people's history, but it is fundamentally a private story. Coming home to the biblical land, we inherited that biblical sensibility in which there is only one story. Unpreparedness to deal with the other is therefore deeply related to our elemental sense of coming home. It is easy for us to feel that the other is just invading our territory.

In Germany, Samson Raphael Hirsch interpreted "And you shall love

232

your neighbor as yourself" to include the non-Jew as well. In the Exile, neutral space, we could find room for the other without feeling that our own identity and integrity were being violated. The question is whether we can find room for the other within the context of our own intimate, passionate home. Does "my place" mean that he has no place? Does "his place" mean that I have no place? This is the true question, and the passions it unleashes are enormous.

The fact that the other, the Palestinian, also speaks as if there is only one story, and acts as if I am not here, makes it all the more complex and intense. We have a history of two peoples, each one living in its own story, unable to understand what it means for the other to be in this land. In the Bible, only one receives the paternal blessing. One is the blessed son; the other is the rejected son. There is no room for both Ishmael and Isaac. There is no room for both Esau and Jacob. There is only one blessing and only one son gets it.

Can there be any way to resolve this issue? Before we begin to deal with it, we have to appreciate the magnitude of the passions that this land unleashes, and reflect on how it feels for a people so long homeless to come home.

Nahmanides, Judah Halevi, and in our times Rabbi Joseph B. Soloveitchik in *Kol Dodi Dofek*, speak of the desolate land waiting for its lover to return. The land cannot be inhabited by anyone who is not part of Israel, part of the Sinai covenant.

Nahmanides, for instance, bases one of his central concepts on his reading of Leviticus 18:25: "the land vomits out its inhabitants." This land cannot tolerate sin because it is the land where the God of the covenant lives. It can only be inhabited by Israel, and only when Israel does not stray in the manner of other nations. It has been desolate for a thousand years, waiting for its lover to return.

These are the passions that this land awakens. Unless they are understood, we cannot deal with the basic problem that Jews in Israel face today. We cannot talk about justice or utter moralisms like "Love your neighbor as yourself" unless we first empathize with the passion of a people who believe they and only they have redeemed this land from its desolation and therefore it is theirs in the deepest elemental sense.

I would like to distinguish between two forms of moral conflict. One is a conflict between good and evil. The question here is, Do we give in to passion, or can we overcome it? In response to the question "Who is the mighty?" the Mishnah says, he who can control his impulse—his *yetzer*. There is *yetzer ha-ra*, the instinct that leads to evil, and *yetzer tov*, the one that leads you to good. Judaism believes that you can win this struggle through an act of will. *Yetzer tov* can conquer the *yetzer ha-ra* through a victory of will.

From a certain perspective, this is a simple conflict. It is a problem that requires determination and personal resources in order to be solved, but it is not confusing in terms of values. It does not touch the core of your value system. The question is merely, Are you weak or not? Can you overcome temptation or not?

However, there is another form of conflict in the Talmud, which is not one between evil and good, but between good and good. Examples of such conflicts are represented by various dilemmas. Does saving a life take precedence over keeping the Sabbath? If you, your father, and your teacher are captives, who has the right to be ransomed first? If you find objects lost by your father and your teacher, to whom do you return his lost object first? A more poignant variation asks, If you see that your father and your rabbi are poor, whom do you help first?

The issue here is not a firm will against eager passion but a conflict between two positive values, obliging us to evaluate the foundations of these values. Establishing priorities in this second kind of conflict requires analysis, reflection, and a sense of clarity, since this type of question touches upon the core of a whole value system.

Our conflict with the Palestinians is not an issue of good versus evil, where there is no uncertainty about the moral choice. The conflict involves two goods, two legitimate claims, which are mistaken in their narcissism but legitimate in their sense of justice and fairness. The first is justice, the dignity one accords to human beings and their collective history and culture. The second is survival, security, and self-preservation. The dilemma can be summarized as follows: How much can I risk survival for the sake of justice and how much am I allowed to give up for the sake of love?

I would like to offer the perspective of two teachers who might guide us in this conflict: Judah Halevi and Maimonides. For Halevi as for Nahmanides, the very meaning of the Jewish people is to bear witness to the concept of miracle in history. In Halevi's book *The Kuzari*, the rabbi is asked by the king, "Whom do you believe in?" The rabbi replies, "I believe in the God of Abraham, Isaac, and Jacob." The king continues, "Why not say, 'I believe in the God who created heaven and earth?'" Basically, the king is asking, "Why not say you believe in the God of nature?" Halevi's answer is that the God of nature is the God of the philosophers. The God of the Jews is the God of history.

In the God of history, Halevi sees a God who is not enchained by the principle of necessity. He is the God who announces revolutions, who can take a slave people and offer them a new future. He is the God who announces that through Israel He bears witness to the notion of radical surprise, radical innovation. Given that this is our God, the past does not restrict what we can expect from the future. Wisdom is not accustoming ourselves to necessity, as in the Greek stoic notion. Wisdom is living with the expectation of radical innovation.

Israel's future is open, an uncharted possibility. Who would have dreamed that a slave people would become the People of the Book? Israel is the bearer of that experience and therefore the major story for Jewish identity is Passover.

What do we love to do when we tell this story? As we dip our finger into the wine on Passover night, we count ten miracles. Then we begin to expand: "No, not ten. There were fifty. Not fifty, two hundred. Even two hundred and fifty." We are a people who love to tell stories like that of the rescue at Entebbe. Our need for miracle is in our very nature. Miracle embodies the notion of surprise, of hope.

In this context, what is God's name, for Halevi? God's name is *Ehyeh asher ehyeh*—"I will be what I will be." Israel's story is the source for revolutionary aspirations in history. Messianism is a Jewish innovation. It did not come from Plato and Aristotle. The Greeks gave us rigor and truth; they gave us the scientific understanding of nature. It was the prophets who gave us a dream which enabled us to believe that tomorrow could be radically different from yesterday.

For Halevi, this is the fundamental meaning of being a Jew, of Jewish nationhood, of "I am the Lord your God, who brought you out of the Land of Egypt." The Jews are the people that convey to the world the experience of miracle. That is their story and no other; not the story of truth, not the story of necessity. Their story is the parting of the sea—*the* miracle par excellence.

Therefore, the Jewish story requires a beginning. The Jews do not speak, as Aristotle does, of the world as a necessary reflection of the power of God. For Aristotle, the world is the necessary effect of God as the divine cause. The effect lives as long as the cause. Therefore, the world is eternal as the cause is eternal.

For Jews, the starting point is not eternal necessity but Creation. In the beginning was God's will, which produced the world out of chaos. If God's will is what drives the world, then history is an open drama. Herzl's Zionist vision had this attitude in common with the traditional Judaism that classical Zionism sought to supersede. His famous saying was "If you will it, it is no dream." Jews as a people believe in will. To want it all is a deep part of being Jewish.

The Creation story in the Bible is not told solely for its own sake. What is its point? According to Nahmanides, the point is that the cosmos is in order when Israel is in its land. The Creation story is a prolegomenon, a preamble, to the Jewish claim of will. It is the underpinning of the belief in miracle. The Creation story enables us to say that when we live in this land, we live under divine protection. Israel is a people defined by divine and not by human causality.

So also when we consider our coming home today, the category that we use to explain it is miracle. I would say that the interpretative category of Zionism is miracle, but the success of Zionism is reality. We interpret what we do in the category of surprise and wonderment. When we think of Auschwitz, and then think of that decimated people coming home, we think of Ezekiel and the resurrection of the dry bones.

Given that sense of history and national identity, it is understandable that many Israelis should reject realism as a value. They are impervious to the arguments of Abba Eban or Shimon Peres, who are worrying about the demographic time bomb on the West Bank and Gaza. They are likely to agree with Israel Eldad or Hanan Porat, that if we had been realistic we would not have come here in the first place. If we had been realistic, we would not even have built Degania Alef. Who could have thought that the *yeshivah* boy could turn into a pilot? That is what Zionism brought about.

So, in Israel they use the word "Zionism" to mean "to do the impossible, not the realistic." To be a Jew is to believe in miracles. Forget demography and other difficulties. With will power, all is in our hands. It means that there is no causal principle outside our own will, that Aristotle's principle of causality has no relationship to Jewish political self-understanding. This land breathes with the power of will. If we give up believing in will, we give up everything, because that is the Jewish story.

That is the legacy of Halevi and Nahmanides. Even Marxist visions of utopia come from this deep perception of will, of a God who says "I will be." That is the passion deep in the soul of the Zionist revolution, both religious and nonreligious.

If this were the only tradition that could unlock our memory, the only interpretative key for Jewish self-understanding, I would be deeply pessimistic. A theology of will creates political narcissism, a private story in which reality becomes the outgrowth of an internal decision. What is, is what I claim must be. Therefore, nature, the other, the external world, do not channel or bridle the inner passion of my own will.

However, there is another voice in our tradition, that of a great teacher who passionately hated dependency on miracles. Every time

236

he read about a miracle in the Bible, he sought a natural explanation. This is the voice of Maimonides. In contrast to Halevi, Maimonides believed that the story of Creation was not meant to teach the principle of will; rather, Creation was only a founding catalytic moment to be absorbed by the principle of necessity.

Maimonides said that Judaism requires only the belief that he world started, whereas we could believe in the eternity of the world after Creation. It may seem strange to discuss medieval metaphysics in the context of our problems in Israel today, but I hope Maimonides' relevance will soon be clear. In his eyes, the causal structure of the ordered patterns of reality does not vitiate, violate, or minimize the passion of his love for God. On the contrary, Maimonides saw the presence of God not in surprises but in principles of order and necessity. For Maimonides, if you lose nature, you lose God.

Maimonides does not teach about miracle, but about the importance of causal necessity, of the natural order, of respecting the given world. In other words, reality is not the product of our will. Reality imposes itself on our consciousness. Who, then, is God?

For Halevi, when God introduced Abraham into the covenant, it is as if He told him, "Forget all you learned about philosophy. Now you are meeting the God of the covenant." For Maimonides, Abraham found God through philosophical reflection on nature. At the age of forty, Abraham found God by understanding the mystery of the cosmos. Abraham is not the announcer of miracle; rather, he announces that God is the principle of order and wisdom and not the principle of will. It is not miracle that tells you that there is a God, but predictability, causal necessity, order. Therefore, the God of Maimonides is also *Ehyeh asher ehyeh*, but understood as "I am that I am: I am the principle of necessity."

The big question for Maimonides was, What are the limits of necessity? How much room is there for freedom in this world? What do the Jewish people bear witness to? What is their task? It is not to announce miracle in the world. Their central task, as Maimonides sees it, is to do battle against every form of idolatry. What infuses the passion of the *Guide of the Perplexed* is Moses announcing to a people, "Your task is to fight the false gods of the world. Your task is to fight against fantasy." The priests of idol worship, what were they? They played on human weakness. They exploited people who were frightened of their children dying. The priests told them, "Do this, and your children will live." All paganism thrives on human vulnerability and fear, on the manipulation of human weakness.

Therefore, Israel's task, for Maimonides, is not to allow human beings to fall prey to their fears, to their longing for cheap solutions. God is not a product to satisfy fantasy, to open up a world in which all is possible, but rather, God ensures that within the principle of necessity, there is room for freedom and creativity. Within the principle of limit, there is ample room for dignity and achievement.

Maimonides' messianism is not utopian but, rather, fundamentally rooted in an appreciation of reality. When asked why the Second Temple was destroyed, he answered in a letter: it was because Jews were reading astrology books and forgetting to learn the art of war. Fantasy is the source of idolatry because fantasy removes the principle of limit. Losing the principle of limit, we lose the principle of reality, and when we lose the principle of reality, God becomes a figment of our own imagination and our own needs.

Who is Israel? For Maimonides, Israel is the people that tells the world that dreams must be anchored in what is humanly feasible. For we can dream even though remaining tied to reality.

What does it mean to be a Jewish nation? It does not mean we announce utopia or we say that nothing in the past limits the future. The meaning of being a Jewish nation is to declare war against the distortion of the imagination, against fantasy, against idolatry. We must be the people that bears witness to the futility of the idolatrous quest.

For Maimonides, Creation is not the story of how God gave the Jews the land; Creation is what takes the Jews out of their own story and places them in a cosmic drama. The Bible begins with Creation in order to teach us that God is not Jewish, that there is a world which has a drama and a dignity not defined by the Jewish story. Halevi makes the creation narrative a Jewish historical story. Maimonides views it instead as a corrective, as a larger cosmic filter placing limits upon our private story.

What does this mean for today? I shall try to clarify how I believe we must approach the conflict between the Palestinians and the Israelis. The events of the last months have forced us to acknowledge a nation in revolt rather than individuals in revolt. Rabbi Druckman argues that the "disturbances" are the work of a few rabble-rousers. This view assumes that on the other side there is not an organized national will because in the Jewish story the land has one nation. People who share Druckman's views can allow individual Palestinians to be here but not a Palestinian nation. The first question for us to face is, Whom do we see facing us—individual Palestinians or a people with a national will seeking political freedom and political sovereignty?

Our first step toward recovering our sense of reality is to recognize that what we see is a nation. The second question is then, Can this home to which we have returned contain another nation? In terms of our own history, the land has one nation, the God of history elects one people. If there is no corrective to this vision of history, then the ultimate resolution is total war. If there is only one way or people that mediates the God of history, then Jerusalem will be a city in flames.

What is the thrust of the idea of Creation, how does it filter our historical memories? Does the God of Creation enable us to understand ours as one possible story, but not the only one? Does the God of revelation announce an exclusive truth or one particular way? Is Israel the bearer of Halevi's principle of miracle, or is it the bearer of the rejection of idolatry and of the claim to the *only* story?

For Maimonides, the details of history are not important. What counts is the integrity of a people who are committed to the principle of reality, committed to wage war on fantasy and on the rejection of the principle of limit. Can this understanding of Creation enter into our story, so that room can be made for the Palestinians to be here as a nation? Can we feel the joy of our story, the joy of being home, knowing that another nation also feels that this is its home?

We have to deal with this problem in the manner of Hillel. Why, according to the rabbis, is the Halakhah according to Hillel? Because whenever he taught, he brought the words of Shammai, his rival, first. Accordingly, those of us who seek to find a way with the Palestinians have first to understand the passion of Gush Emunim and not call them Fascists or Nazis. We must not be seduced by integrity as a validation of a principle. The great mistake of existentialism was to think that if something is sincere, it is right. Sincerity is not a criterion for content.

We shall not attain reconciliation unless we can explain the position of those who disagree with us. We have to understand the elemental passions that feed their love for this land, and only then argue with their position and offer an alternative. We cannot ignore that they are speaking out of a definite strand in the Jewish tradition. We have to understand the passion of those who think that there is only one people in this land. By admitting their passions, we can argue constructively with them. By denying them, we risk being haunted by them. We stop listening to each other and substitute name-calling for dialogue. If we continue to do this, total chaos will ensue.

When there is a conflict of values between a positive and a negative commandment, the Talmud teaches that the positive commandment takes precedence over the negative. Nahmanides explains that a positive commandment is grounded in love, while a negative commandment is ground in fear. Abstention from wrongdoing derives from fear of punishment, fear of God. Doing something good grows out of love.

A positive commandment takes precedence over a negative one because love is mightier than fear.

In the conflict with the Palestinians, there is a conflict of two values. Although it may sound romantic, I believe that love can make room for the other in a way that allows us to retain our own identity without feeling threatened by the other.

The meaning of Israel, of Zionism, is the affirmation of Jewish identity. When Jews sought justice in exile, they felt they had to deny their Jewishness. When admitting the other's moral claim, they felt they had to give up their identity.

Given this situation, it is understandable that people in Israel often say, "Liberalism, caring constantly about others, is a *galut* (exile) mentality. If I allow concern for the other too much weight, I commit suicide as a Jew. When Jews become overly moral, they lose their healthy instinct for survival. This was true for German Jews, Russian Jews, and it is true for North American Jews."

The beauty of being in Jerusalem is that we do not have to make this choice. Being at home, we allow elemental passions to surface. That is why we sometimes see violent behavior by people who feel threatened and think they are losing their home. When they think they are losing their home, they act in ways which are often alien to our most cherished values. But must they behave thus, or is there an alternative?

I believe and hope deeply that the instinct of our people in this land can be guided by the spirit of Maimonides. I believe that we neither seek nor require the degradation of a whole nation. We can live as lovers of God and Torah, which means making room for the other without negating our own dignity. In embracing the Palestinians, we show the power of love to allow another story into our reality. It is to show that our story has room for them because it is defined not by fear but by love. It shows that we have not come home because we are frightened by the world, that it is not fear that keeps us here, but the love of our own story, the love of our own history, the joy of recreating our own culture.

It is then not the fear of Hitler that nurtures us. During the war in Lebanon, Prime Minister Begin said, "Nine hundred thousand troops in twenty-four hours. A ghetto people! Look what we have become." We do not need to mass nine hundred thousand troops in order to compensate for the Warsaw ghetto. We do not need to work through the horrors of the Holocaust to find meaning here. If fear and terror control our reality, then ultimately there is no room for the other.

Of course, I do not call for a love that leads to national suicide, as was the case in Russia and Germany, where we did not see the reality of evil. Therefore, we have to make room for the Palestinians on the clear condition that they understand that we will not allow them to jeopardize our security. We will not interpret Arafat sophistically or mystically. We need straight answers when we ask, Do you see me or do you hope I disappear? Not only do you see me, but do you recognize that I never left here?

The nightmare can only be healed by Palestinian voices that will say, with pristine clarity, that they are willing to give up military power for political dignity. If they are prepared to do that, then we can say that there can be room in this land for both our story and theirs. We can make room for the Palestinians when they give up all thoughts of our disappearance. That is the condition, the sine qua non, of our ability to be open to a Palestinian national entity. Security, however, must not be confused with political control.

What if the Palestinians do not say that they are willing to give up military power for political dignity? Then, I am afraid, the viewpoint of our hawks will win. The Palestinians have to understand that if they themselves cannot change, Israel cannot heal its own trauma. We will only be able to find room for love in our story if they, too, make a major change. Monologues among ourselves only create fears.

Therefore, the time has come for another voice, the Palestinian voice, to speak with great clarity and strength. If it does not, then I fear greatly what will be in this society. It will tax all the strength of what is, I believe, the most passionate and vigorous democracy in the world. It is amazing that in our country, which has always been under constant threat of war, there is such public debate and discussion and arguments and disagreements.

There will be no future in the Middle East if we do not have new interpretative keys to help make sense of our past. The past will come back to haunt us and may possibly fall into the hands of a Kahane or a Levinger. There will be no future in our homecoming unless we unlock our memories in a new way.

Gush Emunim echoes a voice in the tradition, but it is not the only voice. I have presented a perspective showing that there is room within Jewish theological thinking for multiple voices to be drawn from the tradition. Halevi and Maimonides give us different approaches to Jewish memory. Our past has to be rethought, reevaluated, and not given over to one group.

The keys we use to open up our past and the way in which we make sense of our stories are today life and death matters. Unless we reinterpret the Torah, we will choke with each other's dogmatism. Torah is open to creative possibilities and the last chapter has not yet been written. That is the meaning of oral tradition in Judaism. We never live by the literal word alone. We live by a word that is open and reinterpreted and recreated.

As we face the Palestinians, everything that we were in Jewish history calls for reinterpretation. We cannot yield up our past to those who see no way to find room for another people. We must go back into our memory, open up our source books. Only then can we find our way.

Pluralism and
Biblical Theology

Chosenness and Religious Pluralism

I t has often been felt that scriptural revelation and divine election are incompatible with religious pluralism. Belief in the biblical Lord of history, Who reveals Himself to His chosen people, seems to reduce the faith commitment to one central question, Which faith community mediates the true way to God? From such a viewpoint, religious tolerance and openness to other faith communities are symptoms of modernity and secularization which weaken the uncompromising spirit of true faith.

The revelatory tradition of the Bible, which in the broader sense includes Islam as well as Judaism and Christianity, is often noted for its zeal and passionate commitment, but not always for its liberalism and tolerance. It has been said that if one is seeking the spiritual person who lives easily with his god and lets others live with theirs, one must look to Greece or Rome. Jerusalem, in contrast to Athens, symbolizes the religious wars of zealots claiming to have an exclusive possession of the keys to the Kingdom.

The Locus of the Problem:
Revelation and Chosenness

Traditionally, Christian theology regarded the Jews as those who blindly persisted in living according to a superseded divine dispensation. Islam treated the Jewish and Christian scriptural tradition as willful distortions of the truth proclaimed in the eternal Koran. Responding on behalf of Judaism, Maimonides portrayed Christianity and Islam as aberrations, and argued that their adherents would repent of their folly when the Messiah came to reconstitute the Jewish polity and establish respect for the Torah among the Gentiles.[1] But are divine love and election subject to a scarcity principle that limits the authenticity of the faith experience to one and only one religious tradition? Must believing Jews view Christian pilgrims coming to Israel as earnest devotees who are ultimately misguided in their spiritual quest? Need their persistent advocacy of Christianity be an embarrassment and a threat to a Jew's faith commitment?

It should be understood that the locus of the problem is not the acknowledged uniqueness of God, the commitment to monotheism, but the claimed uniqueness of divine revelation and election. Theologies in the spirit of Aristotle and Plotinus, which recognize a monotheistic principle without incorporating election and divine intervention in history, are readily compatible with tolerance for religious pluralism. Divine worship in which God is the principle of perfection eliciting adoration and religious fervor can make room for multiple faith communities.[2]

The God who is above history is also above any community. Similarly, eighteenth-century deism was a philosophically attractive alternative to biblical religion because it neutralized Revelation and history and therefore allowed for the inclusion of toleration and pluralism in a monotheistic framework.

Those committed to the biblical tradition, however, cannot follow the deistic route to accommodate religious pluralism. They do not worship the "ground of being," but a God who is very much involved in human history.[3] The biblical drama is concerned essentially with history and not with nature. As Leo Strauss correctly emphasized, it is man and not nature that is fashioned in God's image.[4]

History and Revelation mediate the divine reality that seeks to be embodied in the structures of the faith community. This raises the inevitable question, To whom is the word of God addressed? Even if world history as a whole is the framework within which the Divine Presence operates, the principle of election implies an exclusive providential relationship to the history of a single community.[5]

Biblical revelation asserted God's involvement in human history. Because God has a stake in history, the divine-human encounter answers both divine and human interests. However scandalous it may sound to the metaphysician, the biblical tradition maintains that God cannot execute His designs for history without the cooperation of at least some part of humankind. Revelation to a particular person or people thus becomes essential to the aims of the biblical Lord of history.

The notion of Revelation implies that the human way to God is confined to the revealed word of God. Were the faith experience a matter of human beings' seeking to express their feelings of awe and love for divinity, that is, were it a one-directional expression of man toward God, then the criterion of legitimate expression of faith would be subjective, allowing for a variety of religious attitudes and approaches. The existentialist dictum "truth is subjectivity" could be used to justify a plurality of faith postures channeling the worshipper's feelings toward God. But in a revelatory system where there is reciprocity between the human being and God, the will of God plays an essential role in determining the nature of religious life. It is not sufficient to express my own will and feelings. I must also ask, What does God want of me? Revelation draws us into a dialogic relationship with God; natural theology, deism, and the worship involved in "ground of being" religions are ultimately monologic. Unlike the latter, revelatory systems require some source of knowledge of what God wants and how He responds to our religious life. The individual's sincerity alone is not religiously self-validating—he or she must await God's response in order to determine the validity of his or her religious way of life.

Since God has such a stake in the divine-human relationship, the content of Revelation is a vital component of biblical religion. A spouse may choose a gift for his or her beloved with infinite passion, yet the beloved may derive no pleasure from the gift per se. Or a gesture may be noble and expressive of deep emotion, yet its content may be unappealing. A wife may spend hours devotedly preparing a meal for her husband, yet what she cooked may simply not be to his taste. Revelation entails the issue of whether God is prepared to sit down together with us at the table we prepared with infinite passion. Questions of cultic practice and ritual are thus vital in a revelatory framework.[6]

Herein lies the importance for biblical religion of who has access to the revealed Word. The Torah and the New Testament disagree about the suitable forms of worship.[7] Why did God like Abel's food and reject that of Cain? Whose food will God accept and whose will He reject? Here is the obstacle to pluralism for all those who claim to worship the same God but rely on differing revelations. Centuries of rivalry and conflict—during which those who thought their offering was preferred by God treated their brothers as Cain did Abel—bear witness to the importance of confronting this issue.[8]

An Alternative Approach to Biblical Theology

It is possible, however, to outline an *alternative* approach to biblical theology which would show that biblical faith need not be antithetical to religious pluralism. This approach claims only to be exegetically compatible with the central themes of the Bible; not that the Bible may not consistently be interpreted otherwise. I offer this alternative outlook for the consideration of those struggling to combine biblical faith commitments with a pluralistic religious outlook.

The biblical drama is marked by a dialectical interaction between the themes of Creation and Revelation. The Torah begins with God acting in freedom and love to create the universe. One's very existence thus implies a relationship to God.[9] But this elemental relationship does not involve any notion of election or history. All things created, animate as well as inanimate, are products of divine abundance and joy: "And God saw that it was good." The relational experience that grows from human awareness of Creation may be termed the "ontological relationship" to God. In the context of this relationship, divine consciousness embraces all of being inasmuch as all beings are equally creations of one God. By becoming conscious of one's own situation, the human being becomes aware of the connectedness of all being, bound together by virtue of the divine love expressed in creation.

The Jewish prayer book speaks of God "who in His goodness renews the act of Creation continually each and every day," thereby implying that divine creation is an abiding feature of reality and not merely something that happened once. All things share an enduring ontological relationship with God. The joy of hearing a bird sing, of viewing a sunset, of feeling the wind—all can make one conscious of the sacred dimensions of existence. All of life is sacred, because it mirrors the loving God's power to generate being out of nothing.

Creation, however, also contains the seeds of the dialectical movement to history, since, when the first man was created, he was uniquely endowed with freedom. Human freedom gives rise to human rebellion and sin, thus initiating a process leading to divine revelation and election. Freedom allows humankind to become separated and estranged from God. Sin and estrangement introduce the principles of divine judgment and divine responsiveness. The God of Creation can remain nondiscriminating: the whole of existence equally reflects the overflowing energy of God. When the unity of existence is ruptured by human estrangement, however, God repairs the rupture by regaining human loyalty. The early chapters of Genesis relate God's various attempts to accomplish this goal. But these efforts are frustrated by humankind's repeated opposition to God's will. A lasting solution does not begin to emerge before the story of Abraham, which introduces the principle of *election*. Through election, God seeks to create a community that will restore the primal relationship of being, not through existence as such, but through commitment and choice.

The relationship between human beings and God is now mediated by human freedom. God no longer simply speaks and produces results automatically as in the Creation ("And God said . . . and there was . . ."). He addresses human beings without being sure of their response. With revelation and election, the arena of the God-human encounter shifts from nature to history[10]. Because of the unpredictability of human history, the biblical story now becomes truly dramatic. God agrees, as it were, to share the stage with humanity, to limit His own freedom and power so as to sustain human freedom, and to accept the risks of relating to human beings from within the context of history.

In contrast to Buber, who understands Revelation and election in terms of radical spontaneity,[11] classical Halakhah interpreted Sinai in terms of the revelation of law to a *community*. Pure spontaneity is feasible for human beings who live in a world of single individuals. If, however, the aim of Revelation is to build a community, then spontaneity must be superseded or at least balanced by categories of structure and order. Revelation for the sake of establishing a holy community restores continuity and order to the dynamics of the divine-human encounter in history. Divine involvement in history must therefore transcend radical spontaneity and singular moments of surprise. The classical Jewish view stressed that the Sinai Revelation established a community through Halakhah, a system which expresses the structure of a permanent relationship with God.

Revelation in history is always fragmentary and incomplete. Divine-human encounters cannot exhaust the divine plenitude.[12] Revelation expresses God's willingness to meet human beings in their finitude, in their particular historical and social situation, and to speak to them in their own language.[13] All of these constraints prevent one from universalizing the significance of the revelation. One cannot easily apply the revelation to later developments in the life of the community that received it: new human situations demand reinterpretation of the content of revelation. That is why commentary on the revelation becomes a continuing activity in the community.[14] While the commentator does not create an original, independent work, he plays a creative role in determining the content of Revelation. If the divine speech were not aimed at the varying and changing capacities of human beings, there would be no need for commentary; one would simply listen and act.[15]

The Greek Neoplatonic tradition created the illusion that human reason could ascend to the level of divine thought and thereby liberate the individual from the limits of human finitude. When Christian, Islamic, and Jewish theologians adopted this Greek notion of participation in the divine, they abandoned an essential feature of biblical religion, namely, *creature consciousness*. Medieval philosophers consequently had to make great efforts to justify the very need for Revelation. What need is there for it if the human can participate in the divine through reason?

Revelation, as I understand it, was not meant to be a source of absolute, eternal, and transcendent truth. Rather, it is God's speaking to human beings within the limited framework of human language and history. Reason and Revelation are not competing sources of knowledge; it is not by virtue of its cognitive content that Revelation is unique. Revelation is an expression of God's love and confirmation of human beings in terms of their finitude and creature consciousness. God does not compete intellectually with Plato or Aristotle. Revelation is God's speaking to human beings for their own sake and not for the sake of uncovering the mysteries of the divine mind.

Human beings become idolators when they believe that they can transcend the limited framework of the human condition. Hegelian philosophy of mind, for instance, smacks of paganism insofar as it blurs the distinction between the finite and the infinite, between creature and creator.[16] Mysticism can lead to an idolatrous equation of the finite human being with the Infinite God. If people are preoccupied by God alone, they are liable to lose sight of the gap separating them from God because of their feeling of oneness with divinity.

The modern individual can be saved from such hubris, because today it is much easier to encounter other persons of faith who disagree with us and thereby mirror our own limitations. There is nothing more efficacious for restoring humility to the human spirit than confronting people of dignity and conviction who disagree with you. Because Buddhism, Hinduism, Christianity, Islam, and Judaism are distinct spiritual paths, they bear witness to the complexity and fullness of the infinite. The lack of unity within Christianity and Judaism testifies to the radical diversity within human consciousness and to the rich mosaic of views and practices inspired by divinity in human history. Being conscious of the existence of multiple faith commitments is spiritually redemptive. It helps one realize that one's own faith commitment does not exhaust the full range of spiritual options, and that no human being can transcend the limitations of human finitude and comprehend the infinite reality of God.

When the particularity of Revelation is recognized, biblical faith does not have to seek to universalize itself. We may be living in a redemptive period of history precisely because religious pluralism has acquired legitimacy in the eyes of so many people. Even though ecumenism is often based on political motives, the very fact that people feel the need to appear tolerant and committed to pluralism, whatever their inner convictions, indicates how deeply pluralism has become ingrained in the spirit of the age. In modern societies, people have little patience with exclusivist, doctrinaire religious attitudes. The secular, democratic world and secular, liberal society, despite their problems, have created conditions for the emergence of religious humility and the restraint of the human propensity to universalize the particular.

A Pluralistic Understanding of Messianism

Although biblical revelation is given to a particular community and election is a divine commitment to a particular community's history, Revelation and election carry important implications for all humankind. This is only too evident in the case of ancient Israel, which was faced with the threat of conquest or even obliteration by surrounding empires. In those conditions, there arose the messianic vision: the idea of a time when Israel would again have a king as mighty as David, and when the Gentiles would make pilgrimages to Jerusalem to offer homage to the God of Israel. This vision accompanied the Jews during the centuries of exile after the fall of the Second Temple.

While the messianic vision starts from the universal conditions necessary for the survival of the particular community, it can obviously turn into a vision of the universal triumph of that community's faith above all others. It would be "bad faith" to advocate tolerance and pluralism in unredeemed history, yet maintain a triumphant monolithic universalism with regard to the End of Days. It must be shown, therefore, that Jewish messianism need not have this consequence if the above-mentioned distinction between history and Creation is maintained.

Creation can be viewed as a metahistorical category. The creation story in Genesis is not a prolegomenon to history. It is not primeval history, but rather serves as a corrective to possible distortions of history. In particular, it implies that humankind should recognize the universal sanctity of life, since all life was given through the creative power of God. This follows a long tradition of Jewish understandings of Genesis. Nahmanides and many other Jewish commentators claim that initially humankind was forbidden to take the life of any animals. Only after animal life had been preserved from extinction by Noah's ark was humankind permitted to eat "every moving thing . . . as I gave you the green plants," and even then only without "its life, that is, its blood" (Gen. 9:3–4). Concerning humankind itself, the Mishnah asks; "Why was man created as a single person? To teach us that he who destroys one life is to be regarded as if he destroyed an entire world, and he who saves one life as if he saved an entire world."[17] Commenting on this statement, the Babylonian Talmud adds a midrash: God collected elements from the four corners of the earth in order to form the first man.[18] The implications of these two statements is that the principle of the sanctity of life must not be limited by considerations of race, color, nationality, or creed. The principle of Creation universalizes the sanctity of life and thereby goes beyond any historical particularization.

Creation may thus serve as a ground of ethics. An ethic based on the sanctity of life would satisfy Kant's condition of universalizability, since Creation stands beyond history and is prior to both Revelation and election. The ethical demands stemming from Revelation transcend those implied by Creation and cannot contradict them. Conversely, as the talmudic sages were aware, norms that are exclusively derived from Revelation ("Had they not been written, we *would not* have known them") need not be automatically universalized, whereas norms derived from Creation ("Had they not been written, we *would* have known them") apply universally to all human beings. The philosophical task of distinguishing between the two kinds of "oughts" is beyond the scope of this article; the point is mentioned to indicate the further development of an ethical theory based on the distinction between metahistorical Creation and historical Revelation.

The present task is to characterize messianism in terms of the universal ethical conception derived from Creation. Faith commitments based on Revelation require the universal, *not* in order to universalize a particular revelation, *but in order to universalize the ethical consciousness demanded by Creation.* No particular community can fully realize itself if the ethical fails to become embedded in human consciousness throughout the world. So long as violence or brutality are dominant anywhere in the world, no particular community can fully realize its unique spiritual way of life, since it has to adopt measures to counter the threat posed by such violence or brutality. Historical redemption is impossible so long as Eichmanns and Himmlers walk the earth.

Herein lies the proper universal dimension of messianic aspirations. The messianic dream must be of a world in which all human beings realize that they were created in the image of God, that they all owe their existence to God, and that, therefore, all of life is sacred. Only then can the God of Creation reign in history.

The different ethical dimensions of Creation and history may be further characterized in terms of justice and love respectively. Justice is universal, love is particular. I can respect the rights of all people everywhere, but I cannot love them all. Love is always of one's neighbor. We love those who are close to us; we are attached to the memories and customs of our own particular people. Love presupposes knowledge ("And Adam knew Eve"), whereas justice must in many respects be blind. Those whom I do not love claim me ethically simply by virtue of their humanity.[19]

Love is always particularized; those who seek to universalize it make it empty and meaningless. Contrary to what Erich Fromm claimed,[20] one never loves "universal man." One loves a particular friend, not friendship. The passion of love is confined to the particular. Those who fail to recognize this feature of the human condition may become not only incapable of love but blind to their capacity to hate.

Revelation implies that God accepts the limitations of human love and recognizes that human beings realize their human potential only within particular communities. For the committed Jew, loving Judaism means loving one's people's memories and one's parents' songs, loving Rabbi Akiva and Maimonides, living in a particular city and being a citizen of a particular country. The belief that space can become holy to God means that God allows the finite and particular to contain Him symbolically. This was God's message to Solomon at the dedication of the Temple. And this is the meaning of the promised land: God allowed Himself to be mirrored for a particular people in a particular land.

Nevertheless, the Jew lives out Judaism with great anticipation that one day all human beings will give up war and acknowledge the sacredness of life. Until there is the universal triumph of the ethical, history will remain a fragile and inhospitable home for every human being. Does this mean that all humankind must embrace the Jew's history or recognize its superiority? No. Messianism may instead aspire to see universal redemption through universal acknowledgement of the Creator God, that is, the principle of the sacredness of all life. The knowledge of God that will fill the earth on "that day" will be knowledge derived from Creation over and above Revelation.

Conclusion

The understanding of Revelation and election just outlined can make room for religious pluralism. The key concept is the particularity of revelation. Revelation is not made to universal man, but to a particular individual or a particular community. Just because of this particularity, it need not invalidate the faith experience of other religious communities.

Election represents a particularization of God's relationship to humankind by way of divine involvement in history, but *without* implying that there can be only one exclusive mediator of the divine message. Consequently, theologians who claim that worship of the universal God is incompatible with election are making a "category mistake." The universal God is the God of Creation. It is God as the Lord of history Who enters into specific relationships with human beings and Who may be perceived in a particularistic manner.

The distinction between Creation and history enables biblical faith to admit the possibility of religious pluralism without neutralizing the passionate commitment to the biblical Lord of history. Revelation and election belong to the domain of history, wherein the individual community serves God in the manner mediated by its particular memories. The radical particularization of history eliminates the need for faith communities to regard one another as rivals. Competition between faith traditions arises when universal dimensions are ascribed to historical revelation. When Revelation is understood as the concretization of the universal, Whose truth is *the* truth? becomes the paramount religious question and pluralism becomes a groundless religious ideal. But if Revelation can be separated from the claim of universality and if a people of biblical faith can regain an appreciation of the particular that characterizes the divine-human encounter, then pluralism can become an integral part of biblical faith experiences.

The dream of a *universal community* under the Kingdom of God should be divorced from history: it becomes terribly dangerous when it is made the historical goal of a particular faith. The significant differences between particular communities means that those who aspire to a universal community of the faithful are driven toward a universalism of the sword. The dream of a universal, ethical awakening of human consciousness emerges, not from the concepts of community and history, but from the concept of Creation. The Jew, the Christian, and the Muslim are all one insofar as they are all creatures of God. One responds to the sacredness of life common to all human beings irrespective of their way of life. Anyone who takes the life of any human being mars the image of God in the world.

The Jewish people suffered for centuries from the misplaced emphasis on history as the domain in which to establish universal religious truth. The Jewish people had the opportunity to learn this lesson long before the twentieth century. Time and again it suffered for its stubbornness in resisting visions of universalization. As a representative of particularity in history, its very existence was often treated as a scandal. Thus, although a tendency toward universalization may have existed in Judaism itself during the late biblical and early rabbinic periods, the lived history of the Jewish people in later times became a testimony to the evil that results from universalizing the particular.

Jews can express loyalty to their tradition not only through allegiance to the Bible and the rabbinic literature but also by recognizing the implications of the lived experience of their people: "And I shall be sanctified in the midst of the children of Israel" (Lev. 22:32). We can respond "halakhically" to our past suffering by striving in the contemporary world to discover how the presence of the other can be spiritually redemptive. Thus the attempt to establish a secure framework for religious pluralism and tolerance in the State of Israel is not spiritually tangential to our national rebirth. Our return to independent political existence affords us the opportunity, as the earliest bearers of biblical faith, of becoming the first religion to acknowledge that Revelation never exhausts the plenitude of Creation. One bears witness to the God of Creation by rejoicing within the limits of one's own finitude.

Our return to normalcy is a reassertion of the religious significance of particularity. We have returned, not to a universal, heavenly Jerusalem, but to a particular, earthly Jerusalem, where we walked before the God of old and walk before Him anew. The dream of history should not be the victory of one community over others, but that each should walk before God in the way that He taught it, while remembering that no community can claim to exhaust the will of the universal God of Creation.

253

Pluralism and Revelation

I n his article "Confrontation," Rabbi Joseph B. Soloveitchik asserts that it is of the essence of a faith community's commitment to God to believe that history will ultimately justify its own exclusive way and demonstrate the error of all others.

> The axiological awareness of each faith community is an exclusive one, for it believes—and this belief is indispensable to the survival of the community—that its system of dogmas, doctrines and values is best fitted for the attainment of the ultimate good. . . . each faith community is unyielding in its eschatological expectations. It perceives the events at the end of time with exultant certainty, and expects man, by surrender of selfish pettiness and by consecration to the great destiny of life, to embrace the faith that this community has been preaching throughout the millennia.[1]

The approach to religious pluralism that I shall adopt in this discussion does not presuppose this belief. I shall argue, further, that acknowledging the existence of other faiths in their own right need not be a violation of our convenantal faith commitment. The very presence of a dignified other enhances our covenantal creature consciousness.

My exposition will be divided into three parts. The first will deal with the theological tensions between tradition and modernity. In the second, I will explain how the State of Israel is a catalyst for a new covenantal self-understanding. The third part will offer an understanding of the way the tradition affirms the dignity of the other in our midst.

I

There is an inner tension within the spiritual life of those who are nurtured by a living tradition like Judaism. The tradition provides a total framework for our spiritual self-understanding. It provides the cultural ambience, the language, the theological categories, the way in which we begin the spiritual life. In contrast to Descartes, we do not find our identity through a retreat to the isolated self of *cogito ergo sum.* One who lives within the Judaic tradition begins, together with other members of the community, by being claimed by God. Fundamentally, the point of departure for Jewish religious consciousness is communal and historical. We begin by being situated in the framework of a community of listeners.

> You stand this day, all of you, before the Lord your God—your tribal heads, your elders and your officials, all the men of Israel, your children, your wives, even the stranger within your camp, from woodchopper to water-drawer—to enter into the covenant of the Lord your God, which the Lord your God is concluding with you this day, with its sanctions, to the end that He may establish you this day as His people and be your God, as He promised you and as He swore to your fathers, Abraham, Isaac, and Jacob. I make this covenant, with its sanctions, not with you alone, but with those who are standing here with us this day before the Lord our God and with those who are not with us here this day. (Deut. 29:9–14)

Only within the community do we hear the commanding word of the living God of Israel. The sin of the wicked son in the Passover Haggadah is his separation from community. Heresy in Judaism is imagining that the self alone is addressed by God. Maimonides has taught:

> One who separates himself from the community, even if he does not commit a transgression but only holds aloof from the congregation of Israel, does not fulfill religious precepts in common with his people, shows himself indifferent when they are in distress, does not observe their fast, but goes his own way, as if he were one of the Gentiles and did not belong to the Jewish people—such a person has no portion in the world to come.[2]

The community so invades one's identity that it would be correct to claim that one's primary consciousness is of a "we." I am a "we" before I become an "I," and the "I" surfaces only after it has appropriated fully the sense of "we." The "I" in Judaism is often so difficult to discover that Spinoza believed that there was no "I" at all. For Spinoza Judaism must be understood in political-legal categories. Conformism and obedience are the central virtues needed to make the Halakhah a workable system, as Spinoza sees it. The modern critique of Judaism has often focused on the way Halakhah collectivizes the religious consciousness. In terms of the Kantian contrast between heteronomy and autonomy, it is claimed, there is no autonomous moral personality within the Jewish framework. Buber, who sought religious immediacy and spontaneity, could not find his way to God through the elaborate framework of the halakhic tradition.

Can you be rooted totally in a community on one level, yet on another level find your own identity as an individual? Or is rebellion essential for a person's sense of self, because as long as that person is in the context of a traditional community, the self is crushed? Do you need to distance yourself through total rejection in order to begin to surface as a self? These are some of the questions that individuals shaped by modernity pose to the Judaic tradition. How can the tradition respond to these concerns?

The traditional Jew does not begin with immediacy, but by listening to a story from his or her parents, by first participating in the drama of the collective standing before God at Sinai. On the other hand, the Midrash says that each Jew standing at Sinai hears the word of God in terms of his or her own individual sensibility. The Word of Revelation is similar to the manna in the desert: just as each person tasted the manna in accordance with his or her own fantasy, so each heard God saying, "I am the Lord *thy* God" (Ex. 20:1)—not *your* God in the plural. The Ten Commandments go on to say, "Thou shalt . . . Thou shalt . . ." The appropriation of the hearing is individualistic even though the context is totally collective.

> The divine word spoke to each and every person according to his particular capacity. And do not wonder at this. For when manna came down for Israel, each and every person tasted it in keeping with his own capacity—infants in keeping with their capacity, young men in keeping with their capacity, and old men in keeping with their capacity. . . . Now if each and every person was enabled to taste the manna according to his particular capacity, how much more and more was each and every person enabled according to his particular capacity to hear the divine word. Thus David said: "The voice of the Lord is in its strength" (Ps. 29:4)—not "The voice of the Lord in His strength" but "The voice of the Lord in its strength"—that is, in its strength to make itself heard and understood according to the capacity of each and every person who listens to the divine word.[3]

The two aspects of immediacy and of tradition appear also when the election and the covenant are recalled in Deuteronomy.

> The Lord did not set his love upon you or choose you because you were more in number than any people; for you were the fewest of all peoples. But because the Lord loved you, and because He would keep the oath that He swore to your ancestors, the Lord has brought you out with a mighty hand. . . . (Deut. 7:7–8)

To be sure, God had said to Israel, "I chose your ancestors and this is why I am connected with you." It is because of His love for Abraham, Isaac, and Jacob that He feels bound to Israel. On the other hand, the text recalls God saying, "not because you were many, not because you were powerful, but because I loved you." He begins with His love of Israel and then adds, "and because of My oath to your ancestors." There is a personal immediacy to God's love: He loves us not just because Jews are the children of Abraham, Isaac, and Jacob.

The covenant of the ancestors—*brit avot*—has played an essential role in supporting the belief in the eternity of the covenant. The covenant is unconditional because of God's promise to Abraham. One is confident that one is accepted by God because of the memory of Abraham's covenant. Because a traditional Jewish thinker begins with Abraham's covenant, he must bring hundreds of generations into his discussion. My grandfather must understand what I am speaking about. In other words, a Jew's self-assertion has to be within the family. This is why much of Jewish philosophy takes the form of midrashic exegesis. The self does not emerge only in rebellion, but in intellectual struggle to unfold and clarify in a new way what one's grandfather possibly intended. Even if he did not say it, at least he should be made to feel that you are speaking his language and using his authority to validate your insights. A classic example of this attitude is found in the following talmudic story:

> Rav Judah said in the name of Rav: "When Moses ascended on high, he found the Holy One, blessed be He, engaged in affixing coronets to the letters of the Torah. Said Moses, 'Lord of the Universe, who compels Thee to do that?' He answered, 'There will arise a man, at the end of many generations, Akiva ben Joseph by name, who will spin out of each tittle heaps and heaps of laws.' 'Lord of the Universe,' said Moses, 'permit me to see him.' He replied 'Turn you round.' Moses went and sat down at the end of the eighth row and listened to the discourses upon the Law. Not being able to follow their arguments, he was ill at ease, but when they came to a certain subject and the disciples said to the master, 'Whence do you know it?' and the latter replied, 'It is a law given to Moses at Sinai,' he was comforted."[4]

Accordingly, the individual "I" surfaces in the collective halakhic framework in two ways. One is in the experiential appropriation of the *mitzvah* (the way each individual "tastes" it); the other is in the intellectual reinterpretation of the tradition.

II

The Judaic tradition's openness to novelty finds expression in the moment of God's encounter with Moses at the burning bush. God gives Moses two messages for the children of Israel.

Moses said to God, "When I come to the Israelites and say to them, 'The God of your fathers has sent me to you,' and they ask me, 'What is His name?' what shall I say to them?" And God said to Moses, "'*Ehyeh-Asher-Ehyeh* sent me to you.'" And God said further to Moses, "Thus shall you speak to the Israelites: 'The Lord, the God of your fathers, the God of Abraham, the God of Isaac, and the God of Jacob, has sent me to you.'

This shall be My name forever, This My appellation for all eternity. (Ex. 3:13–16)

He is the God of history and community, the God of the covenant of the ancestors, but also a God who says that radical novelty and surprise are possible in a spiritual life in which the covenantal ancestors follow you constantly. I take *Ehyeh-Asher-Ehyeh* to mean "I will be—I will come in new ways."

There are new possibilities in a living tradition. Therefore, Jews live the spiritual life from two perspectives: on the one hand feeling surprise, wonderment, and openness to what new possibilities will arise, and at the same time feeling totally claimed by the vision of Abraham, Isaac, and Jacob.

Nowhere is the tension between tradition and modernity felt more strongly today than in the State of Israel, and above all in its capital, Jerusalem. One senses in the tradition-bound eternal city of Jerusalem that something radically new is being demanded of the Judaic spirit. It is hard to articulate it clearly, but a Jew living there can feel that something explosive is beginning in the new reality of the Ingathering of the Exiles.

On one level, Jews from everywhere have come home. No longer does one meet one's people in history through praying for the Ingathering of the Exiles. Yet only in the home to which we have returned do we find that we are actually so divided. Here we may even wonder, have we really been a family? The slogan We Are One sounds questionable when Jew meets Jew and each of us wonders if we can understand each other. The most serious question in Israel is, Could the chronic dissension turn into civil war? The polarization between religious and secular is increasing. In the newspapers, the big issues are often not security, but whether the cable car will run on the Sabbath in Haifa or whether a Petah Tikvah cinema will show a film this Friday night. The chief rabbi of the town, locked in jail for leading a violent illegal demonstration against the opening of that cinema, claims to be above the law of the state because he is speaking in the name of God. Four hundred policemen could not spend the Sabbath with their children because they were trying to prevent Jews from fighting with one another. Anger, cynicism, and intense polarization are created over religious issues between brothers who have come home after praying so long for the Ingathering of the Exiles.

Not only do brothers of the same faith meet as strangers, but to an even greater extent do we meet the other, the different one, the stranger, in our encounter and struggle with the Palestinians. We thought that in coming home we had finally fulfilled our long-held dreams of returning to our covenantal biblical land, only to discover that there are Arabs who also feel a deep affection for that land. We have come home to be forced immediately to face an other who feels rooted in that land.

In this land, we are confronted with so many others who have different experiences connecting them with it. The Mormons start to build a university in Jerusalem and many Jews try to stop them, claiming it to be a missionary plot. The *muazzin* calls thousands of Muslims to their mosques as thousands of hasidim go to the Western Wall. Believers of different faiths rub shoulders in the alleys of the Old City, the music of different religions rings out simultaneously.

We have come home, yet to a home which does not offer us security and serenity but forces us to meet the other. The other invades our self-definition. Usually, when you come home, you free yourself of having to integrate all the dissonant sounds that you hear outside. The paradox is that it was easier to do that when we lived in the Diaspora because there we could build a ghetto. The ghetto is not defined just by a physical area. The ghetto allowed Jews to define themselves in their own language without having to meet otherness. The ghetto is an opportunity to build a cultural self-definition in which all that surrounds you confirms your own internal communal language, in which cultural monism is possible. In coming home to Jerusalem, however, we are invaded by multiple experiences of radical diversity.

As I look at the teeming diversity of faith experiences in Jerusalem, I believe that the God Who in the Exodus drama answers, "I will be" is calling us to respond in some new way. Something new is going on when the other, the stranger, the different one, thus impinges on our self-definition. The return of the Jewish people to Israel is a challenge to rethink the long tradition of messianic triumphalism in monotheistic traditions. Our return was not only meant to provide a haven against antisemitism but a new way in which the other, the different one, might enter into our consciousness. Can the committed believer build an identity in which the other, as stranger, as different, is present in his or her own dignity? Or must the religious self, in order for it to experience any dignity, claim absolute, universal truth? In the full flowering of Jewish particularity in the city of Jerusalem, the people who taught the world to strive for the unity of mankind through the fatherhood of

God are now called upon to offer a different understanding of the universal vision of God's kingdom in history. In Jerusalem, the city of holy wars, we bear witness to the dignity of particularity and the redemptive significance of celebrating the partial and the incomplete.

What new religious sensibility is now required in order to meet this challenge? We must overcome the longing to be saved from history. We must develop an appreciation of the world and humanity as God's creations. Creation is the affirmation not of the exclusive worth of eternity but of the value of temporality.

The Gnostics could not understand the world as the expression of a loving God. Human suffering, death, tragedy, evil, pain, loving a child and watching him or her die—these could not be expressions of a loving God. The very experience of the world, they thought, defies the notion of God as love, and therefore God as love has in some way to be anchored in the drama of eternity. One must get away from the world to discover the true God.

Judaism, however, has affirmed that the creature is good in the eyes of God, as it is said repeatedly in the first chapter of Genesis. God affirms our humanity in its otherness, in its difference, in its finitude. Although we are fragile, corporeal creatures, who are here today and gone tomorrow, who experience pain, tragedy, and loss, this reality is not sin, for "God saw all that He had made, and behold it was very good" (Gen. 1:31). Creation, therefore, introduces a new value in the mind of divinity: finitude. The human being as a creature has ontological worth. As the Midrash says, "'God saw that all he had made was very good'—He has seen death and proclaims that also death is good." Accordingly, we do not have to go beyond our human finitude in order to feel dignified. We do not have to go beyond the concrete and the temporal in order to feel that we are living an authentic life.

The affirmation of human beings, with all their human limitations, is the soul of the covenantal message. The covenant is not God's desire for humanity to escape from history, but God's gracious love, which accepts humanity in its finite, temporal condition. In the covenant, God seeks to enter the temporal; He does not ask the temporal to become absorbed in His eternity. It is in this sense that the covenant—as Buber and Soloveitchik sensed—is contrary to the mystical, to the absorption into the One, to the quest to lose individual consciousness. But whereas Buber loved the passage in Exodus 19 which states, "I carry you on eagle's wings," I love the story of the manna. God gives manna and asks Israel, "Please, just take enough for one day and trust that tomorrow I will bring you more. But on Friday, take double the amount, and trust that it will last over the Sabbath. So do not go out on the Sabbath to gather manna." It would have been a nice story had Israel gathered just enough for one day and said, "God, we trust you." But if we look at the story, it goes on: "And Israel nonetheless gathered more than enough manna and tried to set some aside, but it rotted. . . . Then the Sabbath came and nonetheless they went out." God asks them, so to speak, "Can't you spend one night sleeping with uncertainty?" And their response is "No. Not that we don't trust you, but . . ." The amazing thing about the manna story is that it was to these people who could not sleep with uncertainty that God gave the covenant.

It is so different from the Creation story. In the beginning, God creates human beings in His image, but He has a great dream for what He thinks they will be. When they do not turn out the way He thought, His love turns into rage and He destroys the world, because great love can turn into tremendous hate if it is not grounded in an appreciation of the limitations of the beloved. If you love your dream too much, you destroy reality on its account. This is what happens in the Flood story. Great revolutionaries, in the name of their love of humanity, turn into haters of humanity because what they love is an abstract dream of humanity rather than an appreciation of what humanity is in the concrete.

The covenant was made in the desert to tell us that God gave up His fantasies about humanity. Israel in its limitations is accepted by God, as is Israel who builds a golden calf, Israel who wants to go back to Egypt every time water or food is in short supply. Israel in rebellion is still loved, because God's covenant is based on what human beings really are, not on His expectations. If it were based on God's fantasy, I would be frightened of accepting the covenant of Sinai. But because of the description of Israel's failures, I know that His love is based upon reality. Weak and fragile human beings are given the Commandments. So when I put on my *tefillin* to pray in the morning, it is not human grandeur which is confirmed but human vulnerability, my weakness in which I can nonetheless love God and sense God's acceptance. I am a "commanded one" within the context of human limitations.

The covenant, therefore, signifies the reestablishment of the dignity of the concrete. It is the celebration of human finitude. It is the ability to love in spite of human limitations, to build meaning in the face of death, to affirm today without any certainty about tomorrow. George Steiner is mistaken when he claims that "tragedy is alien to the Judaic sense of the world."[5] One has only to read the Book of Job to understand that Job's problem was never resolved. At the end of the story, God does not answer Job's questions, but, as Maimonides understood, Job gains a new perception of history and God.[6] People may think it is

261

a happy ending, but anyone who has experienced the death of a child knows how painful it is to love after seeing that death has become a permanent reality. Yet Job had the courage to raise a new family in spite of that uncertainty.

God does not offer us a framework of meaning that is completely worked out. The longing for certainty, for a world filled with bliss and beauty, is not satisfied; only the longing to say that there is meaning in a world full of violence and persecution is satisfied. The rabbis in the Talmud rightly understood this when they related how the angels asked God, "Why do you show favoritism to Israel?" God answers, "Shall I not show favoritism to Israel? For I wrote in the Torah: 'And you shall eat and be satisfied and bless the Lord your God' (Deut. 8:10). But they are able to say grace after eating merely an olive or an egg." I understand this to mean that in the Bible, God promised them a full meal, and only after a full meal did He require them to say Grace, but Israel has learned in history to say Grace even though they remain hungry.

Can the spiritual life be based upon the fact that I do not have the full meal? I claim that it can, although I understand people who cannot bear the fact that human suffering is not ultimately intelligible as part of some larger scheme. When I was a synagogue rabbi, I could never say to congregants who had suffered some tragedy, "Oh, God just called your child back." I could only weep with my congregants; I could never offer them the type of comfort that suggests "your child was so loved by God that He wanted it back in heaven."

The existentialists expressed deep insight when they said that we must live with the understanding of death. However, they mistakenly made it the exclusive category of authenticity. Death invades our efforts. It often makes our efforts appear to be some sort of metaphysical joke. Yet, knowing that we are ants, we still love. We know all our weaknesses and yet take our lives very seriously. Can we live with that tension? For many people, it is impossible. Therefore, they have to believe that in some way there will be a total resolution of the world's madness. There is eternity; there is Redemption; there is the ultimate liberation from death. It is difficult to argue with people who have that need. But I am convinced that this longing for eternity and redemption also creates the dogmatic need for certainty. The yearning to be saved can become so profound that you doubt whether your way is truly valid if you see another person enjoying his or her different way. The result is that people have to be deaf to each other's music in order to feel sure that they are on the side of the redeemed.

Yet there is another spiritual sensitivity in the Judaic tradition, one which suggests that limited humanity can love God even in an imperfect world. We can experience joy in the spiritual life that we have, while knowing that it is only a fragment, that God's infinite richness cannot be exhausted by any community in history. From Maimonides we learn that history is not the revelation of eternal truth, but God's ability to love us in our imperfection.[7] "The Torah speaks in the language of human beings," as the Talmud repeatedly says. The Torah teaches us to celebrate our finitude, knowing that we remain permanently human, that we never transcend the human in our spiritual life. God in His love for us does not ask us to become divine, but to accept ourselves with our own limitations.

III

I believe that the fear of death is in some important sense similar to the fear many people have of religious pluralism. The consciousness of death arouses fear, uncertainty, loss of control. Similar reactions can arise in a pluralistic society when you meet the other who cannot be absorbed by your own categories. Meeting radical difference shakes your sense of certainty. Can you live with the principle of uncertainty, or must you long for absolute, ironclad truth according to which God says, "Here is My way; if you follow it, you are saved; deviate for a moment, and you are lost." Do we need that in order to build the spiritual life? Must I believe that ultimately the other is merely an instrument for my own redemption, and that the end of history will show who was right?

That there may be an alternative religious sensibility which is not fed by the need for cognitive certainty, I find in a famous passage in the Babylonian Talmud (Eruvin 13b). The rival schools of Hillel and Shammai were in such disagreement that the Torah threatened to become two Torahs, with the community divided totally. The dispute ended only when a heavenly voice was heard, saying, "These and these are the words of the living God, but the Halakhah is according to Hillel." Either would be acceptable, so why did God prefer Hillel? The Talmud answers: Because when he used to speak in the house of learning, he would always begin by mentioning Shammai's position. He was so "kindly and modest" that when he spoke to his students, he told them first the contrary view and argued for its plausibility, and only afterwards did he present his own opinion. He never taught Torah while pretending to possess the sole truth; he admitted that two opinions might both have plausibility and meaning. So let us also count ourselves among those teachers who taught a way of commitment to Judaism and the love of God, while maintaining the unsettling idea that "these and these are the words of the living God."

Although the Law is in accordance with the majority, the minority point of view was never regarded as devoid of cognitive or religious significance. The potential for the return of the minority opinion was held as a permanent possibility in one's spiritual life.

> And why do they record the opinion of the individual against that of the majority, whereas the Halakhah may be only according to the opinion of the majority? That if a court approves the opinion of the individual it may rely upon him, since a court cannot annul the opinion of another court unless it exceeds it both in wisdom and in number; if it exceeded it in wisdom but not in number, or in number but not in wisdom, it cannot annul its opinion; but only if it exceeds it both in wisdom and in number.[8]

Therefore, in living in accordance with the majority opinion, one could never believe that one was building one's spiritual life on the only authoritative option for the person of faith. The haunting uncertainty that an alternative way is religiously viable and authentic cannot be avoided if one builds one's spiritual tradition on the basis of learning, discussion, and agreements between scholars and not only on the absolute word of prophetic Revelation.

Judaism was able to accomplish the transition from the biblical tradition, based upon Revelation, to the talmudic tradition, based on reasoned argumentation. Despite this radical difference between the prophet and the rabbinic sage, Judaic teachers were able to convince the community that the oral and the written tradition together form a religious unity. This achievement may shed light on the way we ourselves can structure a spiritual communal life which does not require absolute, dogmatic certainty.

In the rabbinic tradition, no particular school of thought exhausts and captures the wisdom and intention of God. For rabbinic Jews do not leave their human skin when they mediate and reflect on the word of God. From Maimonides' perspective, even Revelation cannot transcend the limited context of a particular historical frame of reference.

The rabbinic and Maimonidean tradition leads us to understand how one can be claimed by the revealed word of God, while allowing this word to be filtered through finite human beings whose arguments and decisions give substance to the application of Torah in our daily life.

The rabbinic tradition does not provide the immediate certainty of the word of God, which is not shaped by a human hand. Human argumentation, based upon plausibility rather than absolute certainty,

264

mediates the covenantal word at Sinai. For the contemporary Jew, God's word at Sinai is filtered through two thousand years of human discussion. If one cannot build one's spiritual life on the limited framework which human beings can construct, then in some important way one cannot live within an Orthodox halakhic tradition.

Israel's election at Sinai and the renaissance of the third Jewish commonwealth sustain our appreciation and celebration of human finitude and particularity. In the spirit of Maimonides, the longing for the messianic kingdom must sustain the sensibility that we learned to appreciate through the founding moment of Sinai.

The experience of diversity in Israel, the presence of the dignified other, be it a Christian, a Muslim, or a Palestinian, brings home to Jewish spiritual consciousness the important empirical fact that no one person or community exhausts all spiritual possibilities. The Bible emphasizes two important notions of love, one related to the love of the neighbor and the other to the love of the stranger. In neighborly love, we meet one with whom we share common values, familial and communal solidarity. The neighbor who is like oneself gives expression to a love which extends the self and expands one's communal solidarity.

In the love of the stranger, we meet the other, the different one, the one who cannot be defined exclusively by our own categories. In this context, the Bible frequently recalls our own historical experience of suffering under a totalitarian system, within which we had no dignity because we did not fit into the ruler's framework of values. Ours was an abused life in which differences were not respected, but rather became a source of fear and intolerance. It is this experience of Egypt, says the Bible, that must teach us how to empathize with and not feel threatened by those who are other. "And you shall love the stranger because strangers you were in the land of Egypt."

The Jewish community, because of its loyalty to its own particular way of life, suffered in different Egypts of history at the hands of those who sought to impose one way, one truth, on all of humanity. Jews have always embodied the scandal of particularity. We were the permanent strangers in history. We were the stumbling blocks to all who sought to impose a monolithic framework on the social and political order. We challenged all national groups to find security in living with that which is proudly other, which sings a different tune, and gives a different flavor to life.

We who have now returned to build the third Jewish commonwealth, in which we are the majority culture, in which the national, social, and political frame of reference supports our own national dignity—must also recognize that our Egypts of history should teach us how to appreciate and celebrate the dignity of the stranger in our own midst. Loyalty to our historical roots demands that we learn from history not to enact the trauma of the victim, who builds exclusively out of fear and suspicion. Rather, our memory of suffering must transform the profound sense of isolation we have felt in history into new energies to celebrate the dignified flourishing of strangers within our own national community.

Reflections on
Rosh Hashanah and
Yom Kippur

A s I look about me in Israel and in the Jewish world today, I cannot help but notice the deep concern and anxiety that Jews feel about the future of Israel. They are asking, Is the situation insoluble? Is the threat of war a permanent feature of Jewish life in Israel? Must we gird ourselves to live in perennial conflict with the Palestinians? How long will the tragic suffering of both peoples continue?

In the season of the High Holy Days, when Jews rediscover their roots in their own spiritual tradition, it is, I believe, appropriate for us to ask whether the tradition can offer some guidance to our agonizing concern about the future of the Jewish people. In the following pages, I will try to reflect on the way Rosh Hashanah, Yom Kippur, and the Jewish festival year as a whole can serve as wellsprings of renewal for dealing with these concerns.

The Jewish festival year is divided between two fundamental motifs. On the one hand, most of the holidays are related to specific events in history, which shaped the collective identity of the Jewish people. There is Passover, the struggle for freedom; Shavuot, the commitment to the covenant and to the Ten Commandments; Sukkot, the festival of trust and joy; Hanukkah, the struggle for religious freedom; Purim, liberation from the threat of Haman's scheme of genocide; Tisha be-Av, the destruction of Jerusalem and the Temple; Yom ha-Atzmaut, Independence Day, the freedom and dignity that come with political independence. All these festivals have one fundamental thing in common: they bind Jews to each other by reminding them of their common destiny. They enrich our communal memories and solidarity.

Rosh Hashanah and Yom Kippur, however, have no connection to any particular event in Jewish history. According to Jewish teaching, Rosh Hashanah celebrates the creation of the world. The central motif that repeats itself again and again in the liturgy of Rosh Hashanah is the proclamation of God as king. The shofar is sounded on Rosh Hashanah to announce the divine coronation. We all gather and proclaim with awe and trepidation God's kingship over all of humanity. How is this proclamation channeled into the way we live our daily life? How do we show allegiance to the God we proclaim as king on Rosh Hashanah?

The prophets taught us that God's kingdom in history must be built upon ethical foundations. For them, God's majestic power in history must be visible in the way society is structured around principles of social justice, in the way we respond to the needs of the poor and the stranger. The belief in God as universal king prevents Jewish spirituality from being identified with ghettoization or with feelings of alienation from and disillusionment with humanity.

On Rosh Hashanah we proclaim the universal kingdom of God throughout the world. Judaism teaches that all of humanity is morally accountable to God; all creatures must recognize that life is a gift and that there is a divine purpose for all of human life. Rosh Hashanah proclaims the centrality of the idea of Creation, of a universal brotherhood of humankind, of a universal ethic which declares the dignity of the single human life. "Beloved is man, for he is created in the divine image." "He who saves one life is as if he saves an entire world." This profound principle of the singular dignity of every individual grows from the Rosh Hashanah festival.

Rosh Hashanah, therefore, gives the Jewish people a universal framework grounded in Creation and not a family framework grounded in their particular history. Jews were not meant to live in isolation from the world, to build a sense of internal life which lives in conflict with the world. Ultimately, Jewish particularity must be integrated into the notion of God as the universal king of all humanity.

Rosh Hashanah is a permanent challenge to build bridges of understanding with all human beings created in the image of God who is king over all of humanity. Rosh Hashanah calls on Jews to act in such a huway that the world senses that there is one God for all of humankind. Rosh Hashanah shows Jews and the world that Jewish particularity and Jewish family connections are not antithetical to a universal ethic.

How does Yom Kippur complement the experience of God's coronation ceremony on Rosh Hashanah? In placing these two festivals next to each other, I believe that the tradition sought to remind us that God's commanding moral presence, the seriousness with which we are to take His moral imperatives, must never evoke paralyzing feelings of sin, guilt, and moral inadequacy. The God who is proclaimed king on Rosh Hashanah is felt on Yom Kippur to be a loving father who constantly accepts the human frailties of his children and keeps open the doors of moral renewal.

Yom Kippur breathes the spirit of *teshuvah,* of repentance and reconciliation, of freeing oneself from the prejudices and moral failures of the past. Yom Kippur announces a vision of hope, of rebirth, of discovering new potentialities for human love within society. The phrase that clings to us throughout Yom Kippur is "Remember us for life." The word *hayyim* (life) is repeated countless times throughout the liturgy. Contrary to what most people believe, there is no sadness or mourning on Yom Kippur. Yom Kippur celebrates the passion and vitality of life. According to many halakhic authorities, it is a day of joyous reflection, nurtured by a deep conviction that human moral potential has not yet been fully realized. Yom Kippur gives us the courage to dream and to work for a new future.

Rosh Hashanah and Yom Kippur are therefore a corrective to the despair that pervades so many Jewish hearts today. The spirit of Rosh Hashanah and Yom Kippur should inspire Jews to proclaim clearly to the Palestinians that they are our brothers in creation, that we share a deep moral reverence for the sacredness of human life. Jews have come home to Israel because of their deep historical sense of community. However, in coming home, we do not seek to weaken or destroy our profound sense of brotherhood with the Palestinian people. It is imperative that our respective histories and traditions not destroy our common humanity born of our shared belief in God as the Lord of Creation and majestic moral king over all of humanity.

Those Jews who are embarrassed by the Israeli-Palestinian conflict and who emphasize the Jewish people's ethical universalist mission, those whose solidarity with Israel has weakened, have not sufficiently appreciated and understood the message of the historical festivals. One who has celebrated Passover or Shavuot can never abandon Jewish particularity. Equally, those Jews who believe that our sense of isolation and loneliness are permanent conditions of history, and who seek to bring us back to the terrifying feelings of a ghettoized mind or of a Massadah complex, have also not learned the message of Rosh Hashanah and Yom Kippur.

Neither the move toward isolation nor the move toward the universal reflects the full experience of the Jewish tradition. To live as a full Jew is to live intensely and with total commitment to Jewish particularity, and equally to share in the universal framework of Creation celebrated in the holiday of Rosh Hashanah.

Rosh Hashanah and Yom Kippur are catalytic spiritual forces bringing us into deep moral dialogue with the world. We live in the intense polar rhythm of family intimacy and universal solidarity. Those in the Jewish world who seek to bring us back to a mentality of Jewish isolation and suffering have not learned the message of Rosh Hashanah and Yom Kippur. Those who abandon the depth of commitment to the family and to Jewish historical intimacy in the name of universalism have not learned the lesson of the total Jewish festival year. To live as a full Jew is to live in both rhythms, in the framework of Jewish history and in the framework of Creation.

Notes

INTRODUCTION

1. See David Hartman, *Joy and Responsibility: Israel, Modernity, and the Renewal of Judaism* (Jerusalem: Posner, 1978).
2. Maimonides, *Mishneh Torah, Hilkhot Mamrim* 3:3.
3. See Pirkei Avot 5:21.
4. See Pirkei Avot 3:18.
5. Talmud Eruvin 13b.

THE CHALLENGE OF MODERN ISRAEL TO TRADITIONAL JUDAISM

1. See Arthur Hertzberg, ed., *The Zionist Idea* (New York: Harper Torchbooks, 1965), chs. 7 and 8. Also Shlomo Avineri, *The Making of Modern Zionism* (New York: Basic Books, 1981).
2. See Abraham Isaac Kook, "Essays," *The Lights of Penitence* (New York: Paulist Press, 1978). Also ch. 7 (on Kook) in Nathan Rotenstreich, *Jewish Philosophy in Modern Times* (New York: Holt, 1968); ch. 4 (on Kook) and ch. 7 (on A.D. Gordon) in Eliezer Schweid, *Ha-Yahadut ve-ha-Tarbut ha-Hilonit* (Tel Aviv: Ha-Kibbutz ha-Me'uchad, 1981); and Schweid, *The Land of Israel* (Madison, N.J.: Fairleigh Dickinson University Press, 1985).
3. Yochanan Muffs, "God and the World: A Jewish View," in Seymour Siegel and Elliot Gertel, eds., *God in the Teachings of Conservative Judaism* (New York: Ktav, 1985), pp. 170–88.
4. See David Hartman, *A Living Covenant: The Innovative Spirit in Traditional Judaism* (New York: Free Press, 1985), pp. 27–32.
5. See David Hartman, "The Joy of Torah," *Joy and Responsibility*, pp. 15–37. Also J. D. Levenson, *Sinai and Zion* (New York: Harper & Row, 1985).
6. According to Rabbi Johanan in Berakhot 4b, those inherit the world to come who, in reciting the evening prayers, pass immediately from the *geulah* (redemption) benediction to the *tefillah* (Eighteen Benedictions). See Rashi and Rabbenu Jonah ad loc. on the significance of joining the two prayers without interruption.
7. Abraham J. Heschel, "The Sabbath," *The Earth Is the Lord's* (New York: Harper Torchbooks, 1966).
8. See David Hartman, "Torah and Secularism," *Joy and Responsibility*, pp. 54–72.
9. See Moshe Weinfeld, *Deuteronomy and the Deuteronomic School* (New York: Ox-

ford University Press, 1972), ch. 3, "Purity and Impurity in the Deuteronomic Concept of Holiness." Further, Moshe Greenberg, "Biblical Attitudes Toward Power: Ideal and Reality in Law and Prophets," *Law in the Near East and the West* (Winona Lake, Ind.: Eisenbrauns, 1990). Also Daniel J. Elazar, ed., *Kinship and Consent* (Washington, D.C.: University Press of America, 1983).

10. See the discussion of *kavvanah* (the intentional attitude with which one fulfills a commandment) in Hartman, *A Living Covenant*, pp. 165–68.

11. *A Living Covenant*, pp. 213–20. See also Martin Noth, *The Laws in the Pentateuch* (Philadelphia: Fortress Press, 1966), pp. 60–85; P. R. Ackroyd, *Exile and Restoration* (Philadelphia: Westminster John Knox Press, 1968).

12. See Yoma 86a. Further, my discussion of how Maimonides' *Epistle on Martyrdom* deals with heroism under persecution, in the volume by A. S. Halkin and me, *Crisis and Leadership: Epistles of Maimonides* (Philadelphia: Jewish Publication Society, 1985), pp. 67–83; also the discussion in *A Living Covenant*, pp. 84–88, of Soloveitchik's contrast between Greek and Jewish ideals of heroism and catharsis.

13. See Salo W. Baron, *A Social and Religious History of the Jews*, 2nd ed. (New York: Columbia University Press, 1952), vol. 1, pp. 16–25.

14. This spirit is expressed in the sixth, seventh, and eleventh of the Eighteen Benedictions, in the special benedictions of the Sabbath and festival prayers, in the grace after meals, and the benedictions said at weddings, etc.

15. Avot 3:7, among many examples.

16. Anti-Zionist traditional Jewish circles find a classic statement of their position in Ketubbot 110b–111a. Rabbi Jose son of Rabbi Hanina, commenting on Song of Songs 2:7, 3:5, and 5:8, here asks: "What was the purpose of those three adjurations?" His answer: that Israel shall not return as one mass, that Israel "shall not rebel against the nations of the world," and that "the idolaters shall not oppress Israel too much."

17. The fifth book of Maimonides' *Mishneh Torah* is entitled *The Book of Holiness*—and is entirely devoted to laws concerning food and sexuality. See also how Nachmanides discusses "holiness" in commenting on Leviticus 19:2.

18. See Avineri, *Making of Modern Zionism*, p. 217 in the chapter "Zionism as a Permanent Revolution."

19. See Gershom Scholem, "Towards an Understanding of the Messianic Idea in Judaism," *The Messianic Idea in Judaism* (New York: Schocken, 1971), pp. 1–36; further, David Hartman, "Sinai and Messianism," *Joy and Responsibility*, pp. 232–58.

20. This is pervasive in Maimonides' *Mishneh Torah* (e.g., *Hilkhot Deot* 6:3–5, *Hilkhot Teshuvah* 3:11) and Nachmanides, as well as in modern Jewish thinkers such as Kook and Soloveitchik.

21. The "Prayer for the Well-being of the State of Israel" (used for some years now especially in the Sabbath morning prayers) describes Israel as, among other things, "the beginning of the sprouting of our redemption."

22. See Hartman, *A Living Covenant*, ch. 12.

23. The very existence of Israel is a refutation of the exclusively messianic and eschatological perceptions of Hermann Cohen and Franz Rosenzweig. The Jewish people has found itself a fitting place in the modern world, not as the

carrier of messianic aspirations (Cohen), nor as the witness to the end of history (Rosenzweig), but because of its courageous ability to reenter an imperfect world and assume the responsibility of building a social polity that struggles to embody the covenantal demand to become a holy people.

24. See Avot de Rabbi Nathan 4 (version A), in Judah Goldin's translation (New Haven, Conn.: Yale University Press, 1955), pp. 34–38; Gittin 55a–b. For how a Zionist historian of the rabbinic period perceived ben Zakkai, see Gedaliah Alon, *The Jews in Their Land in the Talmudic Age*, vol. 1 (Jerusalem: Magnes Press, 1980), ch. 5. Further, J. Neusner, *A Life of Rabbi Yohanan ben Zakkai* (Leiden, 1962).

25. E.g. Leviticus 24:10–18 and Numbers 27:1–12, where Moses goes back to God and asks Him how they should interpret some commandments already given.

26. See my discussion of how Maimonides reacted to popular expectations of the "end of days," in Hartman and Halkin, *Crisis and Leadership*, pp. 190–99.

27. Other ways of responding to divine silence and of appreciating the rebirth of Israel are familiar in the writings of Eliezer Berkovits, Emil Fackenheim, Irving Greenberg, and Richard Rubenstein.

28. See Eliezer Berkovits, *Not in Heaven: The Nature and Function of Halakha* (New York: Ktav, 1983), p. 1 and ch. 3 ("What is Halakha?"). Also Yeshayahu Leibowitz, *Yahadut, Am Yehudi u-Medinat Yisrael* (Tel Aviv: Schocken, 1976), pp. 13–36.

29. Compare Makkot 23b–24a; Shabbat 31a; Nachmanides, *Commentary on Exodus* 21:1–2.

30. Maimonides, *Introduction to the Mishneh Torah, Hikhot Mamrim* 2. Also Hartman, *A Living Covenant*, pp. 8–12, on "my God and the God of my father" (Ex. 15:2).

31. See Leibowitz, *Yahadut*, pp. 99–208.

32. Maimonides, *Hilkhot Melakhim* 2:6, 3:1–6. Also G. J. Blidstein, "The Monarchic Imperative in Rabbinic Perspective," *Association for Jewish Studies Review*, no. 7–8 (1982–83), pp. 15–39; and *Ekronot Mediniyyim be-Mishnat ha-Rambam* (Bar Ilan: Bar Ilan University, 1983), ch. 7.

THE RELIGIOUS STRUGGLE OF YESHAYAHU LEIBOWITZ

1. See Talmud Avodah Zarah 54b.

A CRITIQUE BY YESHAYAHU LEIBOWITZ

This review of *Joy and Responsibility*, by David Hartman, appeared originally in *Petahim*, (April 1979), pp. 82–88. It was translated from the Hebrew by David Weiner.

1. See the conclusion of David Hartman, "Israel and the Rebirth of Judaism," *Joy and Responsibility*, p. 286.

WILL AND SIGNIFICANCE: A RESPONSE TO LEIBOWITZ'S CRITIQUE

1. See Yeshayahu Leibowitz's collection of essays *Yahadut, Am Yehudi, u-Medinat Yisrael*.

2. See Leibowitz's essay "Mitzvot Ma'asiyot," ibid., pp. 13–36. Compare Maimonides, *The Guide of the Perplexed* 3:31.
3. This issue is discussed in David Hartman, *Maimonides: Torah and Philosophic Quest* (Philadelphia: Jewish Publication Society, 1976).
4. See "A Critique by Yeshayahu Leibowitz," pp. 84–85, in this volume.
5. Sotah 4b–5a; Shabbat 105b.
6. See Maimonides, *Guide* 2:25.

THE RESURGENCE OF ORTHODOXY

1. Yoma 69b.
2. From the High Holy Day Liturgy.
3. Ibid.
4. Ibid.
5. Maimonides, *Mishneh Torah, Hilkhot Teshuvah* 84b.
6. Tosefta Avodah Zarah 1:1.
7. Shabbat 33b.
8. Pirkei Avot 5:28.
9. Shlomo Pines, "The Philosophic Sources of *The Guide of the Perplexed*," in Maimonides, *The Guide of the Perplexed*, trans. Shlomo Pines (Chicago: University of Chicago Press, 1979), pp. cxxxii–cxxxiv.
10. For an elaboration of this point, see the essay "Maimonides' Response to the Challenge of Philosophy," in this volume, pp. 121–41.

MAIMONIDES' RESPONSE TO THE CHALLENGE OF PHILOSOPHY

1. Maimonides, *Mishneh Torah, Hilkhot Yesodei ha-Torah* 4:13.
2. Ibid., 3:27; *Hilkhot Teshuvah*, 9.
3. Maimonides, *Guide of the Perplexed* 3:52.
4. See the passionate yearning for *ha-olam ha-ba* (an ahistorical relationship to God) in Maimonides' introduction to *Helek*, in *Hilkhot Teshuvah* 8, and in the *Guide* 3:51.
5. See Rashi's commentary to Genesis 1:1 and *Midrash Tanhuma, Bereshit* 2; Leo Strauss, "Jerusalem and Athens," *The City College Papers*, no. 6 (New York, 1967), pp. 8–10, 20, for an analysis of the differences between the place of man in the hierarchy of being in Greek and in biblical thought; Maimonides, *Guide* 3:13–14; *Hilkhot Yesodei ha-Torah* 2:2; 4:12.
6. See *Midrash Rabbah*, Exodus 3:6.
7. Berakhot 9b.
8. Martin Buber, *Israel and the World: Essays in a Time of Crisis* (New York: Schocken, 1948), p. 23; see Buber, *Moses: The Revelation and the Covenant* (New York: Harper, 1958), pp. 39–55; Buber, *The Kingship of God*, trans. R. Scheimann (New York: Harper & Row, 1967), pp. 103–6; Emil L. Fackenheim, *God's Presence in History* (New York: NYU Press, 1970), pp. 3–34, for a serious attempt at making sense of God's presence in history in the modern world.
9. *Guide* 1:63.

10. See Judah Halevi, *Kuzari* 1:11, 25, 83–89; and *Mekhilta, de-Rabbi Yishma'el*, trans. J. Z. Lauterbach (Philadelphia: Jewish Publication Society, 1933), vol. 2, tractate *Bahodesh* 5, pp. 231 ff.

11. *Hilkhot Yesodei ha-Torah* 1:1.

12. *Guide* 1:54.

13. Ibid., 1:64; 2:5; 3:32, 51. See F. Heiler, *Prayer: A Study in the History and Psychology of Religion*, trans. S. McComb (New York: Oxford University Press, 1932), ch. 4.

14. *Guide* 1:59.

15. See Julius Guttmann, *Philosophies of Judaism*, trans. David Silverman (New York: Schocken, 1973), pp. 30–43; Isaac Husik, "Hellenism and Judaism," *Philosophical Essays*, ed. M. C. Nahm and L. Strauss (Oxford: Blackwell, 1952), pp. 3–14.

16. Shlomo Pines, "The Philosophic Sources of *The Guide of the Perplexed*," in *Guide of the Perplexed*, trans. Pines, pp. cxxxiii–cxxxiv.

17. *Guide* 3:29.

18. Maimonides, *Hilkhot Avodah Zarah* 2:4.

19. *Hilkhot Yesodei ha-Torah* 9:3, 5.

20. *Hilkhot Teshuvah* 3:15.

21. Isadore Twersky, *Rabad of Posquières* (Cambridge, Mass.: Harvard University Press, 1962), pp. 282–86.

22. *Guide* 1:35.

23. See Leo Strauss, "How to Begin to Study *The Guide of the Perplexed*," in *Guide of the Perplexed*, trans. Pines, pp. xx, xxiv. Harry A. Wolfson claims that openly declaring belief in divine corporeality, as opposed to simply accepting it "in one's heart," constitutes idolatry. See his interesting discussion in "Maimonides on the Unity and Incorporeality of God," *Jewish Quarterly Review* 56 (1965): 112–36.

24. *Hilkhot Avodah Zarah* deal with practices that were prohibited in order to protect the community from pagan and idolatrous influences. The laws of idolatry, therefore, begin with an account of how mistaken forms of worship were responsible for the growth of idolatry and the disappearance of monotheism. In ch. 1, of *Hilkhot Yesodei ha-Torah*, Maimonides deals with heresy based upon a false understanding of the notion of the unity of God.

25. *Hilkhot Avodah Zarah* 2:1.

26. *Guide* 1:55.

27. Ibid., 1:36.

28. Wolfson, "Maimonides on the Unity and Incorporeality of God," and *Philo: Foundations of Religious Philosophy in Judaism, Christianity, and Islam* (Cambridge, Mass: Harvard University Press, 1962), vol. 2, pp. 94–101.

29. See Hartman, *Maimonides*, p. 294, n. 92.

30. See Guttmann, *Philosophies of Judaism*, p. 159.

31. See Pines, "Philosophic Sources," pp. xcv–xcviii, cvi, cvx; Pines, "Spinoza's Tractatus Theologico-Politicus, Maimonides and Kant," *Scripta Hierosylmitana* 20 (1968): 26; and his foreword to Hartman, *Maimonides*, for the changes in Pines's approach to Maimonides' understanding of knowledge of God. Pines's present position is that Maimonides seriously doubted the possibility of metaphysical knowledge of God.

32. *Hilkhot Yesodei ha-Torah* 2:1–2.
33. See *Hilkhot Yesodei ha-Torah* 4:12.
34. *Guide* 3:24.
35. Ibid.
36. The description of Abraham in the *akedah* story should be balanced by other texts describing his efforts to establish a historical community dedicated to the belief in the unity of God: *Sefer ha-Mitzvot,* positive commandment 3; *Hilkhot Avodah Zarah* 1; and *Guide* 3:51, p. 624.
37. See *Guide* 3:51, pp. 620–23; 1:59, p. 139.
38. Ibid., 3:32.
39. See ibid., 3:26, 28, 31.
40. See Gershom Scholem, *Major Trends in Jewish Mysticism* (New York: Schocken, 1941), pp. 25–37; Scholem, *On the Kabbalah and Its Symbolism,* trans. Ralph Manheim (New York: Schocken, 1965), pp. 95, 127, 130.
41. Ephraim E. Urbach, *The Sages: Their Concepts and Beliefs,* trans. I. Abrahams (Jerusalem: Magnes Press, 1975).
42. Avodah Zarah 54b.
43. Deuteronomy 11:13–17.
44. Leo Strauss, "Notes on Maimonides' Book of Knowledge," in *Studies in Mysticism and Religion Presented to Gershom G. Scholem* (Jerusalem: Magnes Press, 1967), p. 273; Strauss, *Natural Right and History* (Chicago and London: University of Chicago Press, 1965), pp. 81–83. See Maimonides, *Eight Chapters,* ch. 8; notes by Prof. Louis Ginzberg to I. Efros, *Philosophical Terms in the Moreh Nebukim* (New York: Columbia University Press, 1924), pp. 134–35.
45. Gittin 56b.
46. See Scholem, *On the Kabbalah and Its Symbolism,* pp. 95, 120–21, 132–33, 130–35.
47. Midrash Rabbah, Song of Songs 1:2.
48. See Hartman, *Maimonides,* pp. 102–26.
49. Judah Halevi, *Kuzari* 1:1–13, 98, 99.
50. Ephraim E. Urbach, "Halakhah u-Nevuah," *Tarbiz* 18 (1946):1–27. See Hartman, *Maimonides,* pp. 116–22. In contrast to Maimonides' approach, see Judah Halevi, *Kuzari* 3:41. This difference is not unrelated to differences of their overall philosophical world views.
51. See Maimonides, *Treatise on Resurrection* and *Eight Chapters,* ch. 8; Hartman, *Maimonides,* ch. 4.
52. *Hilkhot Teshuvah* 9 and *Hilkhot Melakhim* 12.
53. *Guide* 2:27.
54. Maimonides, *Hilkhot Talmud Torah* 1:11–12. See Isadore Twersky, "Some Non-Halakhic Aspects of the *Mishneh Torah,*" in A. Altmann, ed., *Jewish Medieval and Renaissance Studies* (Cambridge, Mass.: Harvard University Press, 1967), pp. 111–18.
55. Gittin 60b. See Urbach, *The Sages,* ch. 12; *Guide* 1:71, pp. 175–76; 2:11, p. 276.

SOLOVEITCHIK'S RESPONSE TO MODERNITY

1. See Maimonides, *Guide of the Perplexed* 2:2.
2. See Simon Rawidowicz, "On Interpretation," *Studies in Jewish Thought*, ed. Nahum H. Glatzer (Philadelphia: Jewish Publication Society, 1974), pp. 45–80, and Scholem, "Revelation and Tradition as Religious Categories in Judaism," *The Messianic Idea in Judaism*, pp. 282–303.
3. See Strauss, "How to Begin to Study *The Guide of the Perplexed*," *Guide of the Perplexed*, trans. Pines, pp. xi–lvi.
4. See Maimonides, *Guide* 3:51, 52 for a medieval transformation of the halakhic notions of love and fear of God, and *Hilkhot Talmud Torah* 1:11, 12, where Maimonides includes the study of philosophy in the commandment of study of Torah; Guttmann, *Philosophies of Judaism*, pp. 176–79; Hartman, *Maimonides*, ch. 1.
5. See Pines, "Philosophic Sources of *The Guide of the Perplexed*," *Guide of the Perplexed*, trans. Pines, pp. cxxxiii–cxxxiv; Maimonides' introduction to *Shemonah Perakhim*; Abraham Maimonides, *Milhamot ha-Shem* (Jerusalem: Mossad Harav Kook, 1953), p. 59.
6. See Pines, "Philosophic Sources."
7. Maimonides, *Shemonah Perakhim* 4; *Hilkhot Deot* 1.
8. Joseph B. Soloveitchik, "The Lonely Man of Faith," *Tradition* 7, no. 2 (Summer 1965): 10.
9. Ibid., p. 9.
10. See Hartman, "The Joy of Torah," *Joy and Responsibility*, pp. 15–37.
11. See Hartman, "Torah and Secularism," *Joy and Responsibility*, pp. 54–73.
12. Soloveitchik, "The Lonely Man of Faith," p. 8.
13. Ibid., p. 16.
14. Ibid., pp. 11–12.
15. See Erich Fromm, *Man for Himself* (New York: Rinehart, 1947), pp. 143 ff. According to Fromm, the liberation of human creative powers is antithetical to submission to God's authority; Soloveitchik, however, sees descriptions of God as Creator and Lord of Creation as providing a model for human imitation.
16. Soloveitchik, "The Lonely Man of Faith," pp. 13–14.
17. Ibid., p. 14.
18. Bava Mezia 59b.
19. See Joseph B. Soloveitchik, *Halakhic Man*, trans. Lawrence Kaplan (Philadelphia: Jewish Publication Society, 1983; originally published in Hebrew in 1944); Simon, "Law and Observance in Jewish Experience," in Ernst Alfred Jospe, ed., *Tradition and Contemporary Experience: Essays on Jewish Thought and Life* (New York: Schocken, 1970), pp. 221–38, for an analysis of characteristic features of a way of life organized by Halakhah.
20. Soloveitchik, "The Lonely Man of Faith," pp. 27–28.
21. Ibid., p. 22.
22. Ibid., p. 27.
23. Ibid., p. 26.
24. Ibid., p. 45.
25. Ibid., p. 37.

26. Ibid., pp. 33–36.

27. Martin Buber, "Religion and Reality," *The Eclipse of God* (New York: Harper Torchbook, 1957), pp. 11–24. See M. S. Friedman, *Martin Buber: The Life of Dialogue* (New York: Harper Torchbook, 1960), pp. 113–32.

28. Soloveitchik, "The Lonely Man of Faith," p. 36.

29. See Fackenheim, *God's Presence in History;* Fackenheim, *Encounters Between Judaism and Modern Philosophy* (New York: Schocken, 1980), pp. 199–229.

30. See Nathan Rotenstreich, *Reflections on Contemporary Jewish Thought* (in Hebrew) (Tel Aviv: Am Oved–Tarbut Vechinuch, 1978), pp. 68–84; David Hartman, "The Renewal of Judaism in the Land of Israel" (in Hebrew), *Petahim*, November 1976, pp. 13–27.

SOLOVEITCHIK'S RELIGIOUS HERO

1. Berakhot 89.

2. See Maimonides, *Guide of the Perplexed* 3:34.

3. Deuteronomy Rabbah 2:14.

4. Exodus Rabbah 15:30.

5. Soloveitchik, *Halakhic Man*, p. 81.

6. Ibid., p. 45.

7. Ibid., p. 49.

8. Ibid., p. 39.

9. Ibid., pp. 37–38.

10. Ibid., p. 41.

11. Ibid.

12. Ibid., p. 94.

13. Soloveitchik, "The Lonely Man of Faith," pp. 61–62.

14. Ibid., pp. 35–36.

15. Ibid., p. 40.

HESCHEL'S RELIGIOUS PASSION

1. Abraham J. Heschel, *The Insecurity of Freedom: Essays on Human Existence* (New York: Schocken, 1972), p. 76.

2. Heschel, *The Earth Is the Lord's*, p. 107.

3. Heschel, *Israel: An Echo of Eternity* (New York: Farrar, Straus & Giroux, 1969), p. 225.

4. Ibid., p. 101.

5. Ibid., pp. 118–22.

6. Ibid., pp. 121–22.

7. *The Insecurity of Freedom*, pp. 191, 215.

8. *The Earth Is the Lord's*, p. 83.

9. Heschel, *Man's Quest for God: Studies in Prayer and Symbolism* (New York: Charles Scribner's Sons, 1954), pp. 102–3.

10. Heschel, *God in Search of Man: A Philosophy of Judaism* (New York: Farrar, Straus & Giroux, 1955), p. 8.

11. *Man's Quest for God*, p. 103.
12. Ibid., p. 68.
13. Ibid., p. 69.
14. Ibid.

KAPLAN'S CRITIQUE OF HALAKHAH

1. See Mordecai M. Kaplan, *The Meaning of God in Modern Jewish Religion* (New York: Jewish Reconstructionist Foundation, 1947), pp. 98–111, 330–68; Kaplan, *Judaism as a Civilization* (New York: Schocken, 1967), pp. 80–87; Kaplan, "The Way I Have Come," in I. Eisenstein and E. Sohn, eds., *Mordecai M. Kaplan: An Evaluation* (New York: Jewish Reconstructionist Foundation, 1952), pp. 308–10.
2. See Kaplan, "The Functional Method of Interpretation," *Judaism as a Civilization*, pp. 385–405; *The Meaning of God*, p. 25. Kaplan's entire book *The Meaning of God* is an example of his functional approach to Judaism.
3. See Mordecai M. Kaplan, "Jewish Religion in a New Key," *The Religion of Ethical Nationhood* (New York: Macmillan, 1970), pp. 1–18.
4. See Hartman, "Torah and Secularism," *Joy and Responsibility*, pp. 54–73.
5. Compare Maimonides, *Guide of the Perplexed* 2:31, and Nachmanides, *Commentary on Exodus* 20:8.
6. See *The Meaning of God*, pp. 61–81.
7. See ibid., pp. 20–29; *Judaism as a Civilization*, pp. 396–402.
8. *Midrash Rabbah Lamentations*, trans. A. Cohen (London: Soncino, 1939), pp. 2–3.
9. See Urbach, *The Sages*, pp. 21–36, 315–17; Adolph Buchler, *Studies in Sin and Atonement*, rev. ed. (New York: Ktav, 1967), pp. 52–68.
10. See *Judaism as a Civilization*, pp. 391, 394–97; Yeshayahu Leibowitz, *Yahadut, Am Yehudi u-Medinat Yisrael*, pp. 13–21.
11. Sotah 14a. See Maimonides, *Guide* 1:54.
12. See Bereshit Rabbah, Vayetzeh 68.
13. See Rashi's commentary to "And God said: Let us make man in our image . . ." (Gen. 1:26):

    Although they did not assist Him in forming him (man) and although this use of the plural may give the heretics an occasion to rebel (i.e., to argue in favor of their own views), yet the verse does not refrain from teaching proper conduct and the virtue of humbleness, namely, that the greater should consult and take permission from the smaller, for had it been written, "I shall make man," we could not, then, have learned that He spoke to His judicial council but to Himself. As a refutation of the heretics, it is written immediately after this verse, *And God created the man* and it is not written: *and they created . . .*

    Pentateuch with Rashi's Commentary, trans. A. M. Silberman and M. Rosenbaum (New York: Hebrew Publishing Co., 1972).

    See Mekhilta de Rabbi Yishmael on Exodus 20:11 regarding God's resting on the seventh day. See Max Kadushin, *The Rabbinic Mind* (New York: Bloch, 1971), pp. 273–87; R. T. Herford, "A Unitarian Minister's View of the Talmudic Doctrine of God," in Allan Corre, ed., *Understanding the Talmud* (New York: Ktav, 1975), pp. 149–59; A. Marmorstein, *Studies in Jewish Theology*, ed. J. Rabbinowitz and M. S. Lew (London: Oxford University Press, 1950), pp. 106–21.

14. See *Pesikta de-Rab Kahana*, trans. W. C. Braude and I. J. Kapstein (Philadelphia: Jewish Publication Society, 1975), piska 12, pp. 248–49; *Mekhilta de-Rabbi Yishma'el*, trans. J. Z. Lauterbach (Philadelphia: Jewish Publication Society, 1933), vol. 2, tractate *Bahodesh* 5, pp. 231 ff.

15. See T. J. *Nedarim* 4:3 and T. B. *Nedarim* 37a.

16. See R. C. Pollack, "Process and Experience: Dewey and American Philosophy," *Cross Currents* 9, no. 4 (Fall 1959): 341–66.

17. See *Judaism as a Civilization*, pp. 481–89, and *The Religion of Ethical Nationhood*, pp. 163 ff.

18. See Soloveitchik, "The Lonely Man of Faith," p. 11.

19. See Alasdair MacIntyre, "God and the Theologians," *Against the Self-Images of the Age: Essays on Ideology and Philosophy* (New York: Schocken, 1971), pp. 12–26; Peter L. Berger, *The Heretical Imperative: Contemporary Possibilities of Religious Affirmation* (New York: Doubleday Anchor, 1979), pp. 117–24. Berger's critique of the reductive option in Christian thought is similar in many respects to my critique of Kaplan.

20. See J. Abelson, *The Immanence of God in Rabbinical Literature* (1912; reprint ed., New York: Hermon Press, 1969), pp. 46–73; Urbach, *The Sages*, pp. 64–65.

21. *The Sages*, pp. 284–85.

22. Maimonides, *Guide of the Perplexed*, trans. Pines, 3:27, p. 510.

23. Ibid., 3:26.

24. See Hartman, *Maimonides*, pp. 188–200.

25. See Maimonides, *Guide* 3:22–24.

26. Maimonides, *Mishneh Torah: The Book of Knowledge*, trans. M. Hyamson (Jerusalem: Boys Town, 1965), *Hilkhot Yesodei ha-Torah* 2:2, p. 35.

27. See Hartman, "The Joy of Torah," *Joy and Responsibility*, pp. 15–37.

28. See Scholem, "Religious Authority and Mysticism," *On the Kabbalah and Its Symbolism*, pp. 29–31; Scholem, "The Meaning of the Torah in Jewish Mysticism," ibid., pp. 32–86; Scholem, "Revelation and Tradition as Religious Categories in Judaism," *The Messianic Idea in Judaism*, pp. 292–303.

29. See my "Soloveitchik's Response to Modernity," in this volume, pp. 142–59.

30. See Scholem, "Revelation and Tradition as Religious Categories in Judaism" and "Religious Authority and Mysticism"; Rawidowicz, "On Interpretation," *Studies in Jewish Thought*, pp. 45–80.

31. Avodah Zarah, 54b.

32. See *Judaism as a Civilization*, pp. 385–405, esp. p. 404, and *The Meaning of God*, pp. 2–6.

33. See E. Simon, "Are We Israelis Still Jews? The Search for Judaism in the New Society," in Arthur A. Cohen, ed., *Arguments and Doctrines: A Reader of Jewish Thinking in the Aftermath of the Holocaust* (New York: Harper & Row, 1970), pp. 388–401; compare Kaplan, *The Religion of Ethical Nationhood*, pp. 128–30.

34. *The Religion of Ethical Nationhood*, p. 16.

35. See William E. Kaufman, *Contemporary Jewish Philosophies* (New York: Reconstructionist & Behrman, 1976), pp. 202 ff.

36. See *Kiddushin* 31 and *Mishneh Torah, Hilkhot* 6:7.
37. Kaplan, *The Meaning of God*, p. 37. Compare Walther Eichrodt, *Theology of the Old Testament*, vol. 1, trans. John A. Baker (Philadelphia: Westminster, 1961), pp. 270–82; Max Kadushin, *Worship and Ethics: A Study in Rabbinic Judaism* (Chicago: Northwestern University Press, 1963), pp. 216–34.
38. Soloveitchik, "The Lonely Man of Faith," p. 60.
39. See Yoma 67b; Urbach, *The Sages*, pp. 320–21. Urbach's chapter "The Commandments" shows how the quest for reasons for the commandments in the rabbinic tradition did not undermine belief in the unconditional claim of Halakhah.
40. See Maimonides, *Commentary to the Mishnah, Berakhot* 9:5, 7.

PLURALISM AND BIBLICAL THEOLOGY

1. Maimonides, *Mishneh Torah, Laws of Kings* 11:4 (in the uncensored text). See also Judah Halevi, *Kuzari* 4:23.
2. See Judah Halevi, *Kuzari* 1:1–3, 2:49.
3. For a different view of the relation between biblical religion and history, see Paul Tillich, *Biblical Religion and the Search for Ultimate Reality* (Chicago: University of Chicago Press, 1955).
4. See Leo Strauss's lecture "Interpretation of Genesis," published by the Center for Jewish Community Studies and originally delivered in the series Works of the Mind at University College, University of Chicago, on January 25, 1957. Also his "Jerusalem and Athens," *City College Papers*, pp. 3–28.
5. Compare Yehezkel Kaufmann, *The Religion of Israel* (New York: Schocken, 1972), pp. 358–59, 447–51. Also Nachmanides on Leviticus 18:25 and Deuteronomy 4:15, and the end of Maimonides' *Essay on Resurrection*.
6. Compare Judah Halevi, *Kuzari*, esp. 1:79, 97–99, 2:49, 3:23, 37, 50–60.
7. Ibid., 1:2.
8. Among serious Christian attempts to deal with this issue, see A. Roy Eckardt, *Elder and Younger Brothers: The Encounter of Jews and Christians* (New York: Schocken, 1973); Paul van Buren, *Discerning the Way: A Theology of the Jewish-Christian Reality* (New York: Seabury, 1980).
9. See Maimonides, *Guide of the Perplexed* 3:53.
10. According to the Midrash, until the election of Abraham, "God, as it were, was king of heaven alone" and not yet "king of heaven *and* earth." See Sifre, *Ha'azinu*, piska 313.
11. Buber, *Moses*, pp. 101–40. Also his letter published in Franz Rosenzweig, *On Jewish Learning*, ed. Nathan N. Glatzer (New York: Schocken, 1955), pp. 111–12.
12. "No word is God's last word." Heschel, "The Ecumenical Movement," *The Insecurity of Freedom*, p. 182.
13. Maimonides claims that God commanded the Israelites to make sacrifices to Him, not because He was in need of them, but because sacrifices were customary in other religious communities of that time and the Israelites were not then capable of believing in a revelation that involved the abolition of sacrifices. He

therefore told them to offer sacrifice only to Himself, with the intention of gradually educating them in higher forms of worship later in their history. See *Guide* 3:22.

14. Commentary is not only understood as an unfolding of the infinite original content of the revelation, but rather as the transition from one finite understanding in one situation to another finite understanding in another. Commentary, of course, may also correct, enhance, or enlarge an existing understanding. The factor necessitating commentary is, therefore, not the infinite perfection of the revelation, as Scholem would have it, but the innate incompleteness of a revelation made in a finite human situation. Compare Scholem, "Revelation and Tradition as Religious Categories," *The Messianic Idea in Judaism*.

15. The rabbinic dictum that "the Torah speaks in the language of human beings" is used by Maimonides to argue that one often has to understand biblical statements figuratively. In particular, anyone who takes literally biblical statements implying that God has a body is guilty of heresy. See *Guide*, esp. 1:26 and 1:36. Also Hartman, *Maimonides*, ch. 4.

16. On this point, see Robert Tucker, *Philosophy and Myth in Karl Marx* (London and New York: Cambridge University Press, 1961), pp. 31–44.

17. Sanhedrin 4:5; see also Maimonides, *Mishneh Torah, Laws of Sanhedrin* 12:3.

18. Sanhedrin 38a; see further Sanhedrin Tosefta 8.

19. See Genesis Rabbah for the discussion between Rabbi Akiva and ben Azzai over which is the central principle: "Love thy neighbor as thyself" (Lev. 19:18) or "In the day that God created man, in the likeness of God made He him" (Gen. 5:1).

20. Erich Fromm, *The Art of Loving* (New York: Harper, 1956).

PLURALISM AND REVELATION

1. Joseph B. Soloveitchik, "Confrontation," *Tradition* 6, no. 2 (Spring 1969): 19.

2. Maimonides, *Book of Knowledge*, p. 85a.

3. Pesikta de Rav Kahana, paragraph 12.

4. Talmud Menahot 29b.

5. George Steiner, *The Death of Tragedy* (New York: Oxford University Press, 1980), p. 4.

6. See Maimonides, *Guide of the Perplexed* 3:23.

7. See ibid., 3:32.

8. Mishnah Eduyyot 1:5.

INDEX